Inside LotusScript

Inside LotusScript

Joe McGinn

 MANNING

Greenwich
(74° w. long.)

For electronic browsing and ordering of this book, see http://www.browsebooks.com

The publisher offers discounts on this book when ordered in quantity. For more information, please contact:

    Special Sales Department
    Manning Publications Co.
    3 Lewis Street
    Greenwich, CT 06830

    Fax: (203) 661-9018
    email: orders@manning.com

Library of Congress Cataloging-in-Publication Data
McGinn, Joe
    Inside LotusScript / Joe McGinn
        p.   cm.
    Includes index.
    ISBN 1-884777-48-1
    1. LotusScript (Computer program language)I. Title.
QA76.73.L66M34 1997
005.36--dc21   97-40461
                                        CIP

    Manning Publications Co.
    3 Lewis Street
    Greenwich, CT 06830

    Copyeditor: Margaret Marynowski
    Typesetter: Dorothy Marsico
    Cover designer: Leslie Haimes

Printed in the United States of America
1 2 3 4 5 6 7 8 9 10 – CR – 00 99 98

This book is dedicated to Natasha Leigh Lennam.

contents

about the author

Joe McGinn is a writer and computer programmer who lives in Victoria, BC, Canada. He's written a leading edge emergency management application in Lotus Notes 4 that is widely used, and he has over thirteen years of professional software development experience. Mr. McGinn has a B.Sc. in Computer Science from the University of Calgary.

preface

The purpose of *Inside LotusScript* is to make it easy to learn how to develop Notes and Domino applications, and to provide you with a practical, useful code base that you can use in your programs. This book is designed for novice and experienced Notes programmers. There is a strong emphasis on providing practical, usable code and solutions to common Notes programming requirements.

Lotus Notes 4.x is an extremely powerful software development tool. Using Notes, I can develop databases and groupware applications in one-tenth the time it used to take me using relational databases. This is partly because of the completeness of the Notes tool set. Notes 3 was already a powerful wide area network groupware database. Notes 4 added the LotusScript programming language, navigators, powerful agents, action bars, layout regions, subforms, new formula commands, new view features, and more. Notes 4.5 has added even more programming features: calendar views, LotusScript Libraries, new user friendly date and time popup fields, and, of course, Domino, the Internet programming tools covered in part 3 of this book.

Together these tools are a powerful combination. But it can be difficult, even intimidating, to learn such a large tool set. *Inside LotusScript* solves this problem by providing step by step tutorials for whatever you need to do, whether it's learning how to develop a Notes application from scratch, or adding a powerful feature like sequential number generation to an existing program. As you read this book, you will learn by doing, and, when you've finished it, you will have proficiency with all of the Notes tools.

acknowledgments

I would like to thank the colleagues who have provided me with friendship and support over the years: Ann-Marie Tilk, Lynda Bennett, and, last but not least, Janet Waterman.

I'd also like to thank Marcus Goncalves for believing in me, Chris Fales for his valuable feedback, and Sean O. Brady for his continuous support and encouragement.

about this book

The book consists of four distinct parts. Part 1 presents an introduction to Lotus Notes programming, and introduces the various components and tools available to Notes developers. You also will be taught how to set up subdirectories and filenames to physically organize your Notes applications.

Part 2 is a tutorial which takes you step by step through the process of building a professional quality multidatabase Notes application, including coverage of the key areas of graphical design and distributing your finished applications. Part 3 shows you how to use Domino to create corporate Web sites and Notes applications that run on the Internet's World Wide Web (WWW). Part 4 is a library of useful LotusScript and formula code needed to build powerful, robust, flexible, and low-maintenance Notes applications.

author online

Purchase of the *Inside LotusScript* book includes free access to a private Internet forum where you can make comments about the book, ask technical questions, and receive help from the author and from other LotusScript Notes users. To access the LotusScript Notes forum, point your Web browser to `http://www.manning.com/McGinn/forum/`. There you will be able to subscribe to the forum. This site also provides information on how to access the forum once you are registered, what kind of help is available, and the rules of conduct on the forum.

contents overview

Here is a brief overview of each chapter in the book.

Part 1: Introduction to Notes programming

Chapter 1 introduces you to the programming and development tools included in Notes 4.x.

Chapter 2 explains why Lotus added the LotusScript programming language to Notes, and then presents an overview of LotusScript for programmers new to Notes. You will learn when it's appropriate to use LotusScript, formulas, or a combination of both.

Chapter 3 focuses on how to create references between databases that are safe and reliable, and that work on both connected and remote clients (e.g., laptops). You also will learn how to create fully functional testing and backup versions of a Notes application and how to avoid potential filename conflicts with other Notes applications.

Part 2: Tutorial—building a Notes 4 application

Chapter 4 walks you through building the basic components of a customer support and call tracking Notes 4 application, one menu at a time. The application consists of three related databases.

Chapter 5 teaches you how to make your application more user friendly by streamlining the user interface.

Chapter 6, shows you how to put the finishing touches on your applications to give them a professional look and feel.

Chapter 7 shows you how to distribute your Notes applications once they are finished, how to set up a simple quality assurance program, and how to distribute application updates electronically through Notes replication.

Part 3: Internet programming

Chapter 8 presents an introduction to Notes Internet programming and Web site creation, and discusses the differences between programming for the Notes native client and programming for a Web browser. You'll also be introduced to the Domino templates, a group of Internet application templates that you will use as the starting point for creating a Web site with Notes.

Chapter 9 covers all the basics of creating a Web site using Notes. You'll learn how to create the Web home page, site database, discussion databases and other site areas, and hypertext links.

Chapter 10 teaches you how to implement Notes security for Internet applications, including coverage of user registration, Access Control Lists, how to secure individual forms and views, and other aspects of Domino security.

Chapter 11 shows you how to create interactive Web applications that allow you to get input from an Internet user. You also will learn how to change the appearance of a Web application based on user roles, how to use HTML formatting, and how to set up advanced Domino user interface techniques like view and navigator templates.

Chapter 12 shows you how to create intelligent Internet applications using Lotus-Script and agents. Several example agents are provided, including an agent to search for documents authored by the current Internet user and an agent to generate sequential document numbers over the World Wide Web.

Part 4: A programmer's toolbox

Chapter 13 shows you how to access the Notes user interface functions from Lotus-Script. You also will learn how to combine formula and LotusScript code using Notes agents, and how to create reports by combining forms and LotusScript.

Chapter 14 teaches you how to use all the new programming features of Notes 4.5, including calendar views, LotusScript libraries, date and time popup fields, and more.

Chapter 15 presents a LotusScript code library that interfaces to the formula language list processing functions.

Chapter 16, designed for programmers who have worked with relational databases, shows you how to simulate some common relations (i.e., one-to-many and many-to-many) in Notes, and how to implement some of the basic features of referential integrity.

Chapter 17 shows how to create a server-based document number system that generates sequential numbers for each new document. Record locking is explored and used to guarantee that each generated number is unique, and a number of different solutions for generating numbers over a wide area network are covered.

Chapter 18 contains tips on debugging server-based agents and some useful Notes agents to help make your applications more intelligent. The agents presented include one that searches a database for multiple documents and presents the results to the user, and another that searches all Notes databases within a subdirectory.

Chapter 19 demonstrates various tips and techniques that are useful in building Notes applications, including manipulating rich text fonts and colors using LotusScript, and implementing dynamic checkboxes and radio buttons.

Chapter 20 explores where Notes is going and what you can expect in future releases of Notes, such as full Java language support.

how to use this book

As you read *Inside LotusScript*, you may want to refer to the *Application Developer's Guide* that's included with Notes 4.x for more detailed information about specific features in some of the Notes development tools (i.e., the form designer, view designer, navigator editor, etc.). The LotusScript class reference is in the *Programmer's Guide Part 1*, and the formula language reference is in the *Programmer's Guide Part 2*. This book is designed for use with Notes 4.0, Notes 4.1, and the latest release, Notes 4.5. I will let you know when any feature I'm discussing is only available in a particular version of Notes.

If you want to learn how to design Notes applications, begin with part 1 *Inside LotusScript* and read it through, then proceed to the tutorial in part 2. If you are an experienced Notes programmer, feel free to skip chapters 1 and 2. All readers should at least glance through chapter 3, Directory and filename management, as it lays the foundations for safe, generic interaction between databases that are used in all the code throughout this book.

If you have bought this book for a specific function in the code library (part 4, A programmer's toolbox), you can go directly to it; you do not have to go through the tutorial. The code in part 4 includes complete descriptions and documentation that explain how to adapt it for use in your applications. Similarly, if you want to learn about Domino and Internet programming, you can start with part 3, Internet programming.

When you have finished this book, you will know everything you need to build professional quality Notes 4 applications. You will also have a completed customer support application and the code library in this book to use as a source code base for future projects.

I have tried not to use any platform-specific functions, so all code presented should run on any Notes 4.x client or server platform. It has been tested running on Windows95, both as a connected network client and as a remote client.

Using the Inside LotusScript CD

Inside LotusScript includes a CDROM having many valuable utilities for the Notes programmer:

- All formula and LotusScript code listings in the CodeList.NSF database.

- All the book's agents in Notes agent format, ready to be copied-and-pasted into your applications, in the Agents.NSF database.

- Full color versions of all screen captures and images in Figures.NSF.

- LNSpade, a new shareware utility that helps you debug and maintain Notes applications and databases. It allows you to list all fields that don't contain a help entry, find all references to fields, search all LotusScript code within a database and so on. LNSpade is currently only available for Windows platforms (Windows 3.1, Windows95, and Windows NT). You can use the trial version of LNSpade included on the CD for thirty days. Readers of *Inside LotusScript* can purchase LNSpade for the special price of $125 US, 50% off the regular price.

You can access these files directly from the CD, or you can install them onto your hard drive. See Appendix C, The *Inside LotusScript* CDROM, for instructions on installing the CDROM.

Introduction to
Notes programming

Part 1 of this book introduces you to all the components, development tools, and programming languages of Lotus Notes 4.x. If you are new to Notes programming, chapter 1 will explain each of the tools, what they are for, and why and when you need to use each one.

Chapter 2 presents a more detailed overview of LotusScript, and explains why Notes has two programming languages. The basics of using LotusScript are also covered.

Chapter 3 focuses on learning how to create safe and reliable references and relationships between multiple Notes databases. You will also learn how to set up multiple copies of an application on one computer, which will allow you to create test versions and fully functional backup copies of your programs. The techniques in this chapter are used in many code examples throughout this book, so you should take the time to go through chapter 3 before proceeding to the Tutorial or the Programmer's Toolbox.

C H A P T E R 1

Notes programming basics

1.1 What is Notes?

Lotus Notes is an extremely powerful software development tool. It includes all the tools needed to build complete database and groupware applications. Unlike other programming tools you may have used, such as Visual Basic (VB) or C, Notes does not need any external tools, libraries, or databases. From user interface implementation to email to macros and intelligent agents, Notes includes all the pieces you need to build complete groupware applications.

The components you will use to build your Notes applications are:

- The Notes database
- Database templates
- Documents
- Views
- Folders
- Navigators
- Forms
- Subforms
- Action Bars
- The formula language
- LotusScript
- Agents
- Security
- Domino

If it looks like a long list, don't let that intimidate you. I'll present an introduction to each of these tools in this chapter, and you'll quickly become comfortable with them by working through the Tutorial in part 2 of this book.

1.2 The Notes database

The Notes database format is an extremely flexible object-oriented data store. It does all the things that traditional databases do. You can store records (called documents in Notes), access information in tables and forms, and create reports. You can recognize Notes database files on your computer by their NSF extension. There are also several significant differences between Notes and regular databases.

The most basic difference between Notes and traditional databases is replication, with which you are probably already familiar. Replication allows Notes databases to be shared across wide area networks (WAN). This means that the users of a database can be spread across a city, a country, or even around the world. Yet through replication all users will be working with a consistent set of data, even if they are remote users who are connected to a network or Notes server only intermittently. Users can connect to a Notes server using virtually any networking technology—over a local area network (LAN) connection, over a modem with ordinary phone lines, or even over the Internet. Replication can be done on demand or on a schedule. For example, if you are connecting over a long distance phone line you can schedule the replication to occur in the middle of the night, when phone charges are lowest.

Another important difference is that all the components of a Notes application are stored in a Notes database along with user data. Forms, navigators, and even code you write using formulas or LotusScript are all stored in the Notes database. This design confers two major benefits upon the Notes developer. First, it makes it extremely easy to distribute your Notes applications to other Notes users, because all you need to ship is the database application file you have developed. There are no additional components or Dynamic Link Libraries (DLLs) that you have to distribute with your application. Second, it means that you and your users can take advantage of Notes replication technology to electronically distribute any future programming changes you make to the application. I'll discuss this in more detail in the next section.

As I mentioned, the Notes database format is object-oriented. This means that you can store virtually any kind of information in a Notes database. Text fields are all variable length, which makes things much easier on developers and end users. Rich text fields allow complex formatting similar to what you can do in a modern word processor, and also allow you to store pictures, sound, Object Linking and Embedding (OLE) objects, and any other kind of data.

Notes databases are email enabled, to allow for effective groupware applications. As you'll see in the tutorial in part 2, it's very easy to add email integration to a Notes database. Even if you don't do any specific email programming at all, any Notes form or document can be forwarded via email by selecting the Actions|Forward menu.

Last, but not least, Notes databases and applications can run on almost any computer. Windows 3.x, Windows 95 and NT, MacOS, OS/2, and most versions of UNIX can all run Notes and the applications you develop in Notes. And with Notes 4.5, Lotus has used its multiplatform expertise to make Notes one of the most powerful Internet development tools available by allowing Notes applications to be run on the Web. This subject will be explored in detail in part 3 of this book, on Internet programming. In future versions of Notes the platform support will be extended even further, allowing you to run the Notes server on powerful computers like the IBM AS/400 minicomputer and the System/390 mainframe.

1.3 Database templates

Notes templates provide the Notes developer with an easy method of distributing source code and application design changes to a Notes application. Identified as an NTF file on your disk, a Notes template is functionally almost identical to an NSF file. In fact, you can easily convert a template to a database (or vice versa) by simply renaming the file and changing a couple of the database properties. (This procedure is covered in detail in chapter 7.)

What is the difference between databases and templates? As the name implies, a template is like a "cookie cutter" that can be used to create new copies of a database design. When a Notes user tells Notes to create a new database, he or she has the option of basing that database on a template. Several templates are included with Notes.

For example, let's say you want to create a discussion database for your software development team to keep up to date on marketing issues. This is very easy to do: you just create a new database with `File|Database|New` and select the Discussion template that is included with Notes, as shown in figure 1.1. You might name the database Marketing Issues. The design of the database—forms, views, agents, and so forth—are all inherited from the Discussion template.

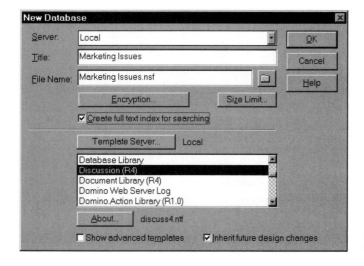

Figure 1.1   The new database dialog

Other groups in your company may want to create their own discussion databases for marketing issues, management, human resources, and so on. You now have four separate discussion database applications, which could quickly become problematic from a maintenance point of view. What if you wanted to customize these databases, say, to add an agent that regularly searches each database and emails reports to the company president?

That's where templates come in. Because all the databases came from one template, you don't have to make the change in each of the four databases. You make the change just once in the discussion database template, and the changes will automatically be rolled out to all databases that were created from it. As I mentioned earlier, Notes replication works not just on end user data but also on the programmed components of your application, like agents and forms. This means that template changes will get rolled out to all copies of the databases, even if they're on different servers spread around the country or the world. This makes Notes an extremely powerful and flexible tool for distributing application changes, with capabilities not yet available for traditional programming languages like C and Visual Basic. All Notes application changes can be distributed electronically and automatically through the use of templates and replication.

You will probably distribute your completed Notes applications as templates. But you don't have to worry about that during the development process. Because it's so easy to convert a database file to a template file, you can do this later, just before you distribute your application for testing.

1.4 Documents

In Notes, an entry in a database is called a document. This is the rough equivalent of a record in a relational database. Like a record, documents are made up of fields of various types. Notes features a full complement of field types: text, numeric, date/time, keywords (i.e., pick lists or radio buttons), and rich text fields that can contain virtually any kind of data. The rich text field provides advanced features usually found only in word processors: formatted and colored text, bulleted lists, sound, graphics, file attachments, OLE links and objects, and even a spell checker. There are also some special field types—authors, names, and readers—designed to interface with Notes user names.

You can have several different types of documents in a database, just as you can have several different tables in one relational database. It's a good idea not to have too many different types in one database, though, so that it does not become too complex. Your Notes applications will often consist of more than one database. You will learn how to set up a multidatabase application in the Tutorial, and in chapter 3.

1.5 Views

Views are what Notes uses to present a tabular display of data, a list of documents. For example, the view in figure 1.2 shows a view in a discussion database listing the topics that have been entered. This is similar to the way data might be displayed in a table in a relational database.

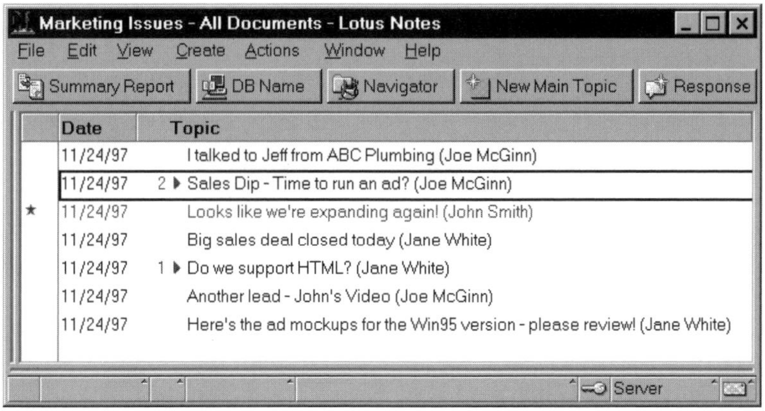

Figure 1.2   A simple view

Notes views are more flexible than simple tables, and have several features to help you manage information. Notice in figure 1.2 the line that has a star next to it. This tells you that you have not yet viewed or read this document. Notes keeps track of which documents have been read for each user, so that you can quickly and easily see what's new in any database.

Views also present relationships between documents. In figure 1.2 you can see that one of the documents in the view has a triangle pointing towards it. This means that there are child documents (normally called *responses* in Notes) available for this document. The parent/child document relationship in Notes is similar to a one-to-many relation in a relational database. By clicking on the triangle you can expand the view to show the child documents, as seen in figure 1.3. You can also expand all documents in a view by selecting the View|Expand All menu, or by clicking on the Expand All SmartIcon.

Notice how child documents are indented under the parent so that you can visually see the relationship between them. On the fourth line of the view in figure 1.3 you see a document that is indented again, because it is a response to a response—a child document of the original response, which is itself a child to the main parent document. This

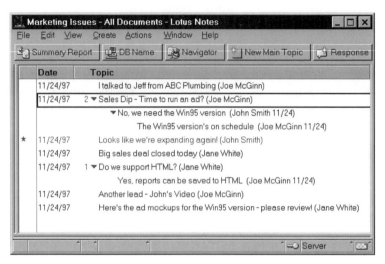

Figure 1.3   A view expanded

hierarchical relationship makes Notes applications very easy to use for discussions and other collaborative databases.

Views are also used as the means for accessing a complete Notes document. By double clicking on any line in a view, you can bring up the full document in form view. In figure 1.4 we see a document in form view. Notice that the title bar shows how many responses this document has. The title bar is actually set programmatically using a formula. I will discuss forms in more detail later in this chapter.

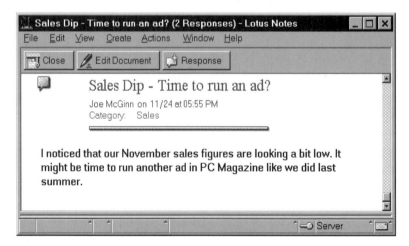

Figure 1.4   A document in a form

Views can also be used to search for and filter information. You can turn on the Notes search bar with View|Search Bar, and then search the view to show only documents that contain a specific keyword, or documents that were created on a certain date. By clicking on the Add Condition button, on the search bar, you can do more complex searches, such as searching for a set of words. (If you don't see the Add Condition button click on the Create Index button—a database must be indexed before you can do complex querying using Add Condition.) You can also set search criteria for a view programmatically at design time. For example, you could have a view that only shows discussion items that were added during the last seven days.

There is another kind of view, called a categorized view. This very useful feature allows you to organize and access your view by categories, where a category can be defined as any field in the database. For example, you could have a view that displays documents by author. Or, as in figure 1.5, you can have a view based on the category field. As you can see, the information is much better organized than in the All Documents view shown in figure 1.3.

Tip for Notes 4.5 Users

Notes 4.5 added a brand new kind of view called a calendar view. Using calendar views you can display any timestamped data in a calendar format, as in figure 1.6. As you can see by the action bar items, this kind of view can be displayed in a number of different formats: two days, one week, two weeks, one month, etc. I'll present full details on creating calendar views in chapter 14.

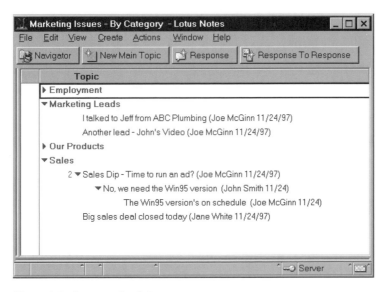

Figure 1.5   A categorized view

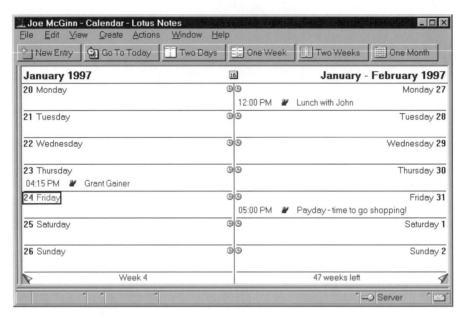

Figure 1.6   A calendar view

As a developer you will create a view any time you want to show a group of one or more Notes documents. You will learn how to create many different kinds of views in the Tutorial.

1.6 Folders

A folder is a special kind of view. The only difference is that a folder contains an arbitrary collection of documents, as opposed to documents that meet a search criteria. A user can put specific documents in a folder using drag and drop. Or you could write an agent that deposits certain documents in a folder programmatically.

1.7 Navigators

Navigators are a high level user interface development tool. As the name suggests, they make it easier for users to find their way around your application. The default Notes user interface sports a paned design that shows data on the right side of the screen and a list of views, folders, and design elements (i.e., forms, navigators, views, agents, etc.) on

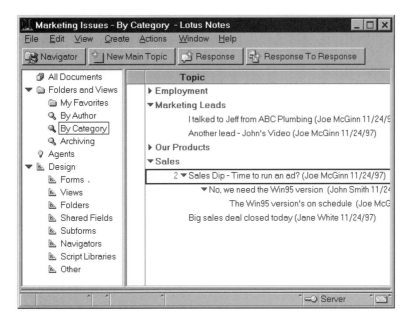

Figure 1.7   The standard Notes user interface

the left, as seen in figure 1.7. You can select a view or other element by clicking on it, and you can drag and drop documents into folders.

The standard Notes user interface is both powerful and flexible, but it can be a little intimidating for nontechnical users. Navigators provide the developer with a tool for constructing a simpler user interface that is easier to learn and use. When turned on, a navigator will replace the lefthand pane that normally shows the list of views and other components. For example, the navigator in figure 1.8 provides simple icons that allow the user to display the most commonly used views. Note that drag and drop still works—the user can drag documents to the My Favorites folder just as in the standard interface.

If you have users who don't like a lot of icons, you can present a more standard, simplified Windows look and feel by using simple buttons to access views, as shown in figure 1.9.

While navigators are the simplest way for the user to access information, they are quite sophisticated as a development tool. In the navigator in figure 1.10, a map of the USA has hot zones the user can click on that follow the outlines of the states. Notice that a hot zone does not have to be rectangular. I've defined a hot zone around the state of California that gets highlighted whenever the user's mouse moves over any part of that state.

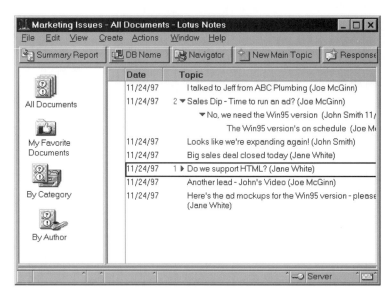

Figure 1.8   A simple navigator

In addition to selecting views and folders, navigators can trigger formula or Lotus-Script agents to carry out more complex actions that you have programmed. For example, in the graphical navigator in figure 1.10, clicking on a state could trigger a LotusScript agent that gathered a report on that state. (That is, the data might be in another Notes database, or even in some external data source that you import using a LotusScript function.)

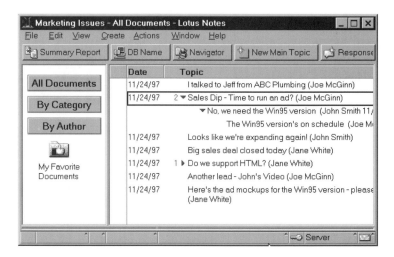

Figure 1.9   A navigator having buttons

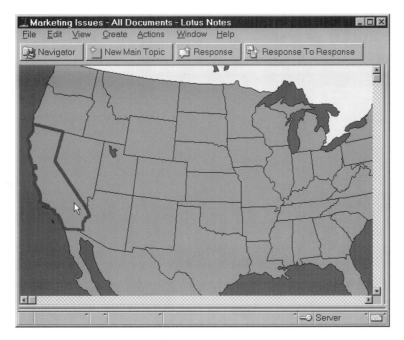

Figure 1.10 A graphical navigator

You should use a navigator to provide a high level, easy to use interface in all your Notes applications. Users who need access to the full standard interface can easily switch to it at any time using the View|Show|Folders menu (or by pressing the Navigator action bar button, as in the Discussion template).

1.8 Forms

As in most databases, forms in Notes are used to display detailed information about a document. When a user double clicks on a document in a view, the document is displayed in a form. As a developer you will spend a lot of time in the form designer. You can do all the things you would expect in a form designer—display fields from the document, add text, graphics, tables, and so on.

The form designer in Notes also adds some unique and extremely powerful capabilities you probably haven't seen in other form's tools. In most databases, relational databases, for example, the form designer is a graphical user interface (GUI) design tool and no more. You usually have to go through a complex and highly detailed process for building tables, fields, and relations before you even begin creating forms. Not so in Notes, where the creation of fields is integrated right into the form designer. This is an

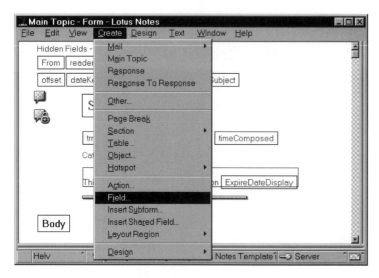

Figure 1.11   The Notes form designer

important difference that makes it possible to create complete database applications extremely quickly in Notes.

For example, let's say you want to add a new field to your discussion database to keep track of the department of the person who entered the note. You simply open up the Main Topic form and select the Create|Field menu, as shown in figure 1.11.

A dialog box pops up and asks you for a few details, such as the field name and type, and that's it (see figure 1.12). You haven't just added a graphical representation of a field (as in most other databases), you've created the new field in the database and it can now be added to views, used for searching and categorizing documents, and so on.

Note that documents and forms are two distinct entities. When you make a change to a form it doesn't affect old documents created with the old form until you reopen and save the old documents. The following form changes do not get updated on old documents until resaved:

- Adding a field
- Deleting a field
- Changing the type of a field
- Changing the form name (unless you keep the old name as a synonym)
- Changing the form type (i.e., from main/parent form to a response type form)

You usually create a new form when you want to store another type of document in a database. This is the equivalent of creating a new table in a relational database.

If you don't want to reopen and save old documents manually you can set up code that will make the changes for you. Just create an action button on a view with the following line of code:

```
@Command([ToolsRefreshAllDocs])
```

1.9 Subforms

Subforms are a special type of form that are extremely powerful and useful. It is common in database applications to have certain sets of common fields across many different forms. For example, a set of address fields that includes phone numbers, street, city, state/province, country, and ZIP code are often found on many forms. Without subforms you would have to add these fields to each form. This is a lot of work at design time, and can be even more problematic during maintenance if they need to be changed; you would have to somehow keep track of which forms have addresses so that you don't miss any when doing changes.

Subforms eliminate this problem in Notes application development. You simply put the address fields on a subform and add the subform to any form where you need to store an address. The form designer has a Create|Subform menu that makes it as easy to add a subform to a form as it is to add a field. When it comes time to update the address format you only need to do it once on the subform. The changes will be automatically

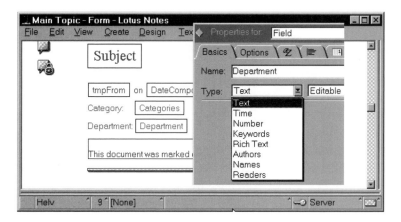

Figure 1.12 Adding a new field

reflected on any form that contains the subform. This is all completely transparent to the end-users. To them, subforms appear exactly as regular fields; they won't even know when a subform is being used.

You should use a subform any time you have a group of fields that is common to more than one form.

1.10 Action bars

Action bars are a very powerful and flexible tool for making your Notes application more user friendly. You can think of an action bar as a toolbar that is customized by the context of the user's action. Each view, folder, and form can have its own action bar that presents the user with a few simple context-sensitive buttons. For example, in figure 1.13 you can see the action bar for the All Documents view in the discussion database. It contains the basic functions a user might want to accomplish when in this view—toggle the navigator on or off, add a new main topic for discussion, or add a response to an existing topic.

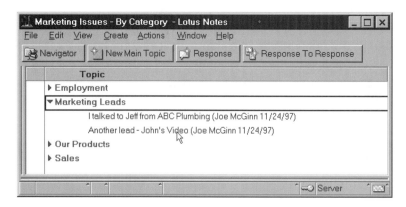

Figure 1.13   A simple action bar

Action bars can also be customized for more subtle context switches. The Main Topic form, for example, has a slightly different action bar depending on whether the user is viewing or editing the document. When in view mode the user has access to the four actions seen in figure 1.14—Close, Edit Document, and Response (i.e., add a response to the current topic), and Parent Preview.

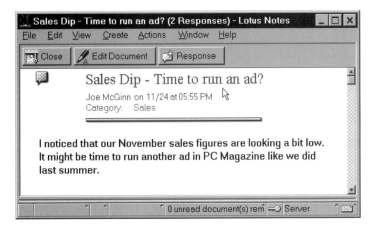

Figure 1.14   Main Topic form in view mode

When the user clicks on Edit Document, the action bar changes to represent the new context. As seen in figure 1.15, the Edit Document button disappears and is replaced by a Save and Mark Private button.

By making context-sensitive action buttons you can make your applications very user friendly. Users will never be confused by extra buttons and functions that aren't needed in the current context, and they will always have easy access to the functions that they do need (e.g., a Save button when editing a document).

1.11   The formula language

Notes has two complete programming languages Notes formulas and LotusScript. The formula language is simple, easy to use, and quite powerful. You can attach formula code to buttons, action bar items, and events. Events are code items that get triggered by certain user actions. For example, by using event-driven programming you can write code that gets executed when a user enters a particular field, when a certain form is closed or saved, and so on. In the form editor, a programming pane appears in the bottom half of the screen, as seen in figure 1.16.

You use the Event menu to specify which event you want to trigger your code (e.g., select the PostOpen event to add code that gets run whenever the user opens this form).

Tip

If you have a set of action bar items that are common to several different forms in a database, you do not have to enter the action bar items on each form. You can instead put the action items on a subform and include the subform in the main forms where you want those actions available. Just as with fields in subforms, you can then automatically change the action bar in all forms just by editing the action bar items in the subform.

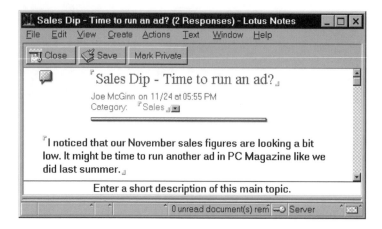

Figure 1.15   Main Topic form in edit mode

Under the Run radio button selection you choose what type of code you want to run formula or Script (LotusScript). In the example in figure 1.16, you can see how a formula is used in the Main Topic form's Window Title event to set the text that appears on the title bar when a user opens a document in this form.

You should use formulas if the function you need to implement is fairly simple, does not require complex looping structures like `While` and `For/Next` loops, or if you

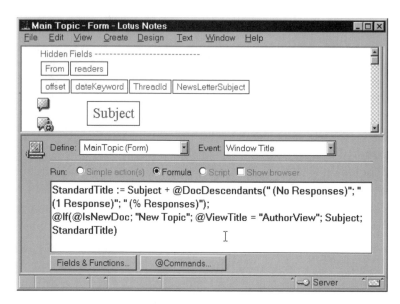

Figure 1.16   The programming pane

need to access Notes user interface functions (displaying menus, opening other documents or views, opening a form to create a new document, etc.).

You will also use the formula language to construct *hide/when* formulas. This is what Notes uses to create context-sensitive action bars and other context-sensitive changes, such as fields or buttons on a form that change under certain circumstances. For example, in a human resources database you might have a salary field that only certain users are authorized to see. Using a hide/when formula you can easily set up the field to be displayed only for users having a certain access level.

1.12 LotusScript

LotusScript is a more fully featured programming language than formulas. If you are familiar with Visual Basic then LotusScript will be easy to learn because the syntax is almost identical. You have most of the features you would expect in a programming language: variables of many different types, looping constructs (if/then/else, while, for/next loops, etc.), subroutines, and functions. You can even define new classes and methods to program in an object-oriented style. LotusScript also comes with a wide variety of built-in classes for accessing and manipulating Notes databases and documents.

You should use LotusScript when your function is too complex for the formula language. For example, if you want to loop through a number of Notes documents, collect some information from them, and put the results in a report, you would use Lotus-Script. LotusScript is generally more powerful and flexible than formulas when you want to manipulate back end documents (i.e., when manipulating Notes data programmatically, not through the user interface).

One big difference and apparent limitation in LotusScript as compared to VB is that LotusScript is really intended for manipulation of back end documents, and thus does not have many commands or classes for manipulating the user interface. Yet there are definitely times when you want to do just that. For example, many Notes programmers want to create a search function that is customized for an application, view, or form. You can attach LotusScript code to an action button to do this, and LotusScript certainly has very powerful searching capabilities. But it's not of much use if you can't display a menu asking the users what they want to search for or if you can't display the search results in the Notes user interface. Fortunately there is a workaround—using agents—for this problem. You'll learn how to do it in chapter 13.

1.13 Agents

Agents are a very powerful facility for adding intelligence to your Notes applications. Agents allow you to attach formula or LotusScript code to certain events. You can have an agent that runs whenever new documents are added to a database, or you can schedule an agent to run every day or every week. For example, you could create an agent that runs once a month, analyzes a sales database and collates a report, and then emails the report to the company president.

Agents can run on a particular workstation, or they can even run in the background on the server (as long as the agent doesn't access any user interface functions, of course). Server-based agents are especially powerful and useful, since they allow you to add intelligence to applications that are running over the Internet. For example, you might have a customer support application that runs on the Web. You could use an agent to forward customer entered requests and problems to your service representatives, and to maintain tracking information so that you can make sure that all customer problems are resolved successfully.

Agents are also useful when you want to manipulate a set of records that a user has selected. For example, in a customer support application, you might have an agent that allows the user to select several documents and then press a button to mark them all as high priority. Or you might want to create a report from a number of records a user has selected.

As a developer you will normally create shared agents that are part of your application. Your end users can also create their own personal agents to help automate their work.

1.14 Security

Notes includes a sophisticated and flexible security system. Each Notes user has a password to verify his or her identity. You can easily customize the behavior of your application based on security levels and roles, or based on specific user names. Security can be customized at the database, document, or field level.

There is also a powerful encryption system that allows you to encrypt whole documents or just certain fields in documents. This means, for example, that Notes can be used to securely send information and email over the Internet or other public networks.

1.15 Domino

Domino is the Notes Internet server. It is the piece of software that converts Notes applications to Internet formats like HTML so that they can be run on a Web browser (e.g., Netscape Navigator or Microsoft Internet Explorer). Unlike some Internet tools you may have used, Domino converts the Notes program and data in real time. This means that Internet users really are running a Notes application, as opposed to accessing a static Web site. Domino is included with Notes 4.5 as part of the Notes server. If you don't yet have Domino or Notes 4.5, you can download a ninety-day trial version of these programs from the following Lotus Web site:

```
http://www.notes.net/welcome.nsf
```

It's a file of about 35MB, so it may take several hours to download. It's probably a good idea to start the download late at night when Internet connection charges are usually lower, and then it will be downloaded by the next morning. I will cover Domino in detail in part 3.

1.16 Software design: waterfall or whirlpool?

Before proceeding to the practical elements of Notes programming, I want to make a comment on software development methodologies. There are many different ways of specifying a software application's design, from ad hoc to object-oriented. Whatever method you use for software specifications, you will also have an overall process or method of implementing the software. That's what I mean by *software development methodology.*

The most common method is called the waterfall approach, so named because each stage in the software implementation process proceeds step by step from the previous stage, as shown in figure 1.17. First, you write the project specifications by analyzing the user's needs and business processes. Next, you write the design, then do the actual coding and implementation of the software, and finally, you test and debug the program. After testing, you deliver the final product to your users.

The waterfall method is really a carry-over from the engineering field. It is similar to the way buildings, bridges, and other physical structures are designed and built. It can work for certain types of software where the design specs are very static and well understood (e.g., a word processor or real-time software for operating a factory). When implementing database and groupware applications, however, this approach does not work at all well for two major reasons:

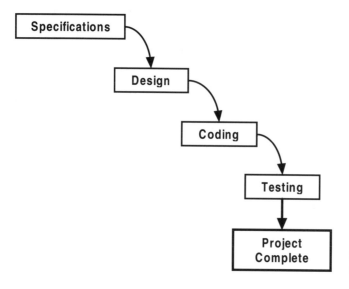

Figure 1.17   The waterfall software design method

1 *User requirements are not static*   A groupware application usually models or auto-mates some existing business process, but as an organization grows, these processes can change. User's needs change all the time, sometimes even over the length of time it takes to develop a product; as a result, database applications can be obsolete by the time they are finished.

2 *It's extremely difficult to specify a design accurately enough to get it exactly right on the first crack*   No matter how skilled the designers are, they can still run into prob-lems. For example, many users are not able to accurately vocalize or describe exactly what their job is, or precisely what they need the software to do. Once you give them a usable product they can be much more helpful, telling you what parts of the program are useful to them, what areas are confusing or difficult to use, what needs to be changed, and so on.

Recently another software design method called the *whirlpool method* has gained popularity. Unlike the linear waterfall approach, the whirlpool method is iterative—as the name implies, the process goes around and around until the product reaches a place the users are happy with. The testing phase must include actual users of the software. Once the testing is complete, the process can return to any previous stage proceed again from that point, as shown in figure 1.18.

This method solves both of the major difficulties raised in the waterfall method. First, the whirlpool method can handle changing requirements, even if the requirements are changing during the software development process. If requirements change or grow, you go back to the specifications or design stage.

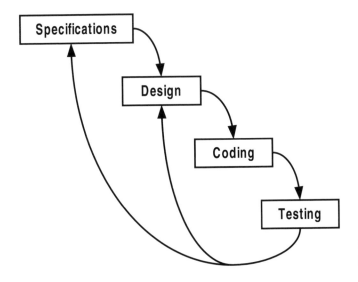

Figure 1.18 The whirlpool software design method

Even more importantly, the whirlpool method provides a way for the initial requirements analysis and design specifications to be improved over time. User feedback with actual software enables the designers to fine tune the specifications until they are exactly right. The process does not end until the users are satisfied with the product.

Users love this method because it produces results, and they get software that's really useful to them. The process puts the users' needs as the first priority. Programmers usually like it, too because it provides a simple, efficient, and reliable way to specify, design, and implement high quality applications. You may find, however, that managers aren't as keen on it. The method does not allow the deadline-oriented approach to project management that some managers prefer to use. It takes a real commitment to meeting the user's needs for a company to choose the whirlpool method. It may be worth pointing out that since it is a user-driven process it does tend to create happy customers. And when used with a Rapid Application Development (RAD) tool like Notes, the process really isn't that expensive because the coding stage goes so quickly—at least it will once you've finished this book!

1.17 Summary

You've been introduced to all the components of a Lotus Notes application. Don't worry if you don't fully understand all of them; the usage of each one will be demonstrated in the tutorial in part 2 of this book. And in chapter 2, I'll take a more detailed look at the LotusScript programming language.

C H A P T E R   2

LotusScript basics

This chapter covers the basics and foundations of LotusScript programming. It is intended for new programmers who are unfamiliar with LotusScript. If you already know this material—from using LotusScript or compatible languages like Visual Basic—you can probably skip this chapter and go on to chapter 3.

In this chapter you'll learn:

- Why Lotus added LotusScript to Notes, and when you should use it
- How to use the LotusScript code editing window
- About LotusScript variables and data types
- How to use the Notes looping and logic statements such as `if/then/else` and `while` loops
- How to use the Notes class libraries to manipulate Notes-specific objects like documents and views
- The difference between front end and back end classes, and why you need to use them
- How to use event-based programming to write code that responds to user activities, such as opening or saving a form
- How to use functions and subroutines to keep your programs modular and easy to maintain
- How to use Notes 4.5 LotusScript libraries to write functions that are available throughout a database
- About the various kinds of agents—triggered agents (e.g., when new documents are added to a database), manually run agents, and scheduled agents—and how to process the documents an agent has found
- How to handle text and manipulate strings in LotusScript
- How to use the class browser to get help on language statements and classes
- How to use the interactive LotusScript debugger to find and fix bugs in your code

2.1 Why LotusScript?

It may not be immediately obvious why Lotus added LotusScript to the collection of programming tools included with Notes. The Notes formula language is very complete, and is much closer to a full-featured programming language than most macro tools. But there are some fundamental capabilities of LotusScript that would have been very difficult to tack onto the formula language. In this section we'll look at some of these differences and explore what kinds of functions are best suited to each of these two languages.

First, let's take a look at the kinds of functions the two programming languages are designed to implement. The formula language is simpler than LotusScript, and it's usually pretty easy to get formulas working the way you want. Formulas are used in many areas where a simple, straightforward function is what you need:

- Simple functions, such as quickly getting the current user's user name.
- Manipulating the current document in various ways:
  - Using formulas to fill in a default value for a field, and for input translation and validation.
  - Using hide/when formulas for hiding fields conditionally.
  - Setting a form's window title.
  - Using a subform formula to choose which subform to insert programmatically. (For example, the mail template uses this to allow a user to choose the letter-head.)
  - Designating computed fields values. This is a special kind of field that displays the result of a formula as a read-only field on a document.
- Keyword formulas to programmatically determine the items for display on a pick list or radio button.
- Accessing or manipulating the Notes user interface (e.g., displaying a menu or a message, opening another document, etc.).
- Simple list processing, such as reading a list of values from a view and extracting a particular entry.
- Replicating a subset of a database.
- Determining which documents to show.
- Displaying calculated column formulas in a view.

As you can see, formulas are used a lot in Notes for many different purposes. But there are several important areas where formulas fall short, for which a full featured programming language like LotusScript is needed.

When you are working with objects like lists, arrays, and document collections you often need looping constructs such as `while` and `for/next` loops. For example, if you are creating a report to email to someone, you may need to extract information from a number of documents and paste the results into a new document. LotusScript, a VB-compatible scripting language, has all the standard looping structures as well as some additional ones to make it even easier to process Notes collections of documents.

Another advantage of LotusScript is that it has a full complement of data types. You can declare and use simple, general purpose variables in formulas, but sometimes you need more control than that. LotusScript has all the data types you would expect in a VB-compatible language as listed below:

- Numbers (integer, long, and floating point)
- Arrays and lists
- Date/Time values
- Variants (can hold any type of data)
- Strings
- User-defined (i.e., the equivalent of defining a record in C or Pascal)

In combination with loops, these variable types allow you to accomplish virtually any programming task in LotusScript.

Another important reason for adding LotusScript to Notes was to give the programmer access to the Notes object model. LotusScript features classes and object reference variables to allow you to program Notes in a object-oriented way. For example, all access to Notes data objects (documents, views, etc.) is done through a set of predefined classes that are included with LotusScript. To manipulate documents you first declare a variable of the type NotesDocument. You would then assign this object variable to a particular document. This might be the current document the user is working on, or a document that you have retrieved from a particular database. Then you can access the elements of the document through the object's properties, or you can manipulate the document using the object's methods. I'll cover this topic in more detail later in this chapter.

As well as accessing predefined classes, you can create your own new classes. You can also access predefined LotusScript Extension classes using the UseLSX statement. For example, Oracle provides a set of classes, via such an extension, to allow you to interact with Oracle directly from LotusScript.

Another reason LotusScript is useful is because Notes is a multiplatform, client/server application. This means that you can run a Notes application on any operating system, regardless of the platform on which it was developed. With Notes 4.5 and Domino, Lotus has added the Web as another platform, allowing users to run Notes applications on standard Web browsers like Netscape and Microsoft Internet Explorer. In many ways, the Web is just another platform. Just as you can develop a Notes application under Windows, and it will run fine on MacOS or UNIX, the majority of your applications will also work on the Web. All this means, that there are now several different types of Notes applications:

- Standard Notes (user has the Notes client)
- Notes and Web mixture (i.e., some users accessing the application via the full Notes client, some accessing it through their Web browsers)
- Web only (e.g., using Netscape over the Internet)
- Other interface (phone, pager, fax, etc.)

Because some interfaces are more limited than others, it is very useful to know that you always have LotusScript available to run tasks on your Domino server. This means you can always add intelligence and groupware features to your application because LotusScript is always available on the server, even if the user has only a minimalist user interface such as a phone keypad or a fax machine.

2.2 The LotusScript code editor

LotusScript is a VB-compatible scripting language. Like VB, LotusScript is interpreted by Notes at runtime so you do not have to compile your programs. You simply attach your code where you want it to run (i.e., to forms, buttons, etc.) and Notes will run it when the user activates that item. One of the big advantages of LotusScript is that it is a multi-platform language. This means that you can develop Notes applications with LotusScript running under Windows 95, for example, and users can run your program on any Notes-supported operating system: Windows 3.x and NT, MacOS, UNIX, OS/ 2, and so on. In chapter 12, you will even learn how to run LotusScript functions from a Web browser like Netscape or Microsoft Internet Explorer.

To start, let's take a look at how you enter LotusScript code into Notes in the Lotus-Script code editor. First, you may want to create a sample database that you can use to try out LotusScript as you go through this chapter.

1 From the Notes workspace, select the File|Database|New menu.
2 Under Title enter LotusScript Testing.
3 Under File Name enter Testing.nsf.
4 Select the Discussion (R4) template.
5 Deselect the Inherit future design changes option. This is a new development database that will have a modified design, and you don't want it overwritten with the Discussion template.
6 Click on OK to save and open the new database.

Close the About Discussion window. You'll be in the All Documents view, and you'll see a number of Action Bar items that allow you to create new main topics, responses, and so on. Now, go into the view editor and add a button to which you can attach LotusScript code.

1 Select Design|Views in the views pane on the left side of your screen.

2 Double click on the `*($All)` view to load it in design mode.

   Notes: `*($All)` is a special view name Notes uses internally to represent the All Documents view that always shows up at the top of the views pane. The `*` in front of it indicates that this is currently the default view, which means it will be used as a template for any new views you create in this database.

3 Select the Create|Action menu to create a new action button.

4 Under Title enter `LotusScript Test`, and select a Button icon.

5 Close the action properties window. You will now see the Notes programming pane shown in figure 2.1. Under the Run option notice that there are a few different options—you can attach Simple Actions, formulas, or scripts (i.e., LotusScript code). Select the Script button.

6 You will now see the LotusScript programming editor, with a default Click subroutine created for you that is run when the user clicks on the button. Enter the following line of LotusScript code into the editor:

```
Messagebox "Hello, world!", , "LotusScript Test"
```

7 Save the view (i.e., select the File|Save menu or press the save SmartIcon), and close it.

Now you can run your code by selecting the All Documents view and pressing the LotusScript Test button.

Tip

Under some operating systems you can use longer filenames, but remember that Notes is a multiplatform system. It's always a good idea to restrict your filenames to eight characters or less (plus three for the NSF extension) so that they'll work unmodified on all supported Notes platforms, including Windows 3.x.

Tip for UNIX Users

In the UNIX operating system filenames are case sensitive (e.g., TESTING.NSF versus testing.nsf refer to two different files) so you should be careful to always use case consistently.

2.3 Variables and data types

LotusScript features a full complement of data types that you declare using the `Dim` statement. For example, the following code declares an integer type variable named `i`:

```
Dim i As Integer
```

You can declare multiple variables on one line, but you must specify the type of each variable. For example, to declare two integer variables and one text string variable, use:

```
Dim i As Integer, j as Integer, Temp as String
```

As in Visual Basic, it is possible to declare variables implicitly in LotusScript just by using them. You can create the `j` variable just by assigning it a value, with no prior `Dim` statement:

```
j = 1
```

However, it is strongly recommended that you disable the implicit declaration facility, because it can cause a lot of unnecessary bugs in your programs if you don't. For example, if you are using a variable many times throughout a function and you misspell

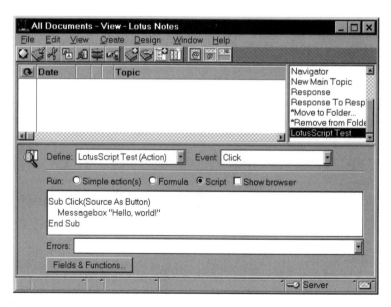

Figure 2.1   The LotusScript code editor

it once, LotusScript will not generate an error message: it will simply create a new variable with the misspelled name. That part of your code will then have a bug because you expect the variable to have the value you assigned to it, but because it is a new, uninitialized variable it does not.

Disabling implicit declaration is easy. Go back into the LotusScript code editor (i.e., Design|Views, double click on ($All), select the View|Action Pane menu and click on the LotusScript Test action). At the top of the programming pane you'll see an item titled Event. Use the drop down menu to select (Options). Enter the following line of code:

```
Option Declare
```

Now, if you misspell a variable name, LotusScript will flag it as an error when you save the script.

The following is a list of standard data types you can declare using the Dim statement:

1 Numbers
- *Integer*   2-byte integer, range: −32,768 to 32,767
- *Long*   4-byte integer, range: −2,147,483,648 to 2,147,483,647
- *Single*   4-byte floating point, range: −3.402823E+38 to 3.402823E+38
- *Double*   8-byte floating point, range: −1.7976931348623158E+308 to 1.7976931348623158E+308
- *Currency*   8-byte currency, range: $−922,337,203,685,477.5807 to $922,337,203,685,477.5807

2 *Other* data *types*
- *String*   length ranges from 0 to 32,768 characters, uses two bytes per character storage
- *Variant*   generic variable allows storage of any type of data

You can also declare arrays of variables. For example, the following line of code declares an array of ten string variables:

```
Dim Temp(10) As String
```

Later in this chapter I'll show you how to declare variables for specific types of Notes objects, such as documents, databases, views, and so forth.

2.4 Looping constructs

LotusScript has a full complement of looping constructs that allow you to add flow control and advanced logic to your Notes applications.

2.4.1 If/Then/Else

The most basic and common form of logic control in LotusScript is the If statement. It allows you to conditionally execute blocks of LotusScript code. For example, the following code executes the Messagebox statement only if the user types "Yes" into the prompt that the Inputbox$ function displays.

```
Dim Temp As String
Temp = Inputbox$("Do you want to see the test message?", "Test")
If Temp = "Yes" Then
     Messagebox "Hello, world!", , "LotusScript Test"
End If
```

The End If statement is required to end the block, because you can execute as many lines of code as you want in an If block. You can add an Else statement if there is code you want to execute when the condition is not TRUE.

```
If Temp = "Yes" Then
     Messagebox "Hello, world!", , "LotusScript Test"
Else
     Messagebox "You're not very cooperative!"
End If
```

If you have a series of conditional code, you can use the Elseif statement to add more conditions, as in the following code:

```
Dim Sales As Currency
Dim Discount As Single
REM … set the value of the Sales variable
If Sales > 1000 Then
     Discount = 0.1
Elseif Sales > 500 Then
     Discount = 0.05
Elseif Sales > 250 Then
     Discount = 0.025
Else
     Discount = 0
End If
```

There is another looping construct, called the Select Case statement. It provides the same logic as a multiple If/Then/Elseif statement like the one above, but in a more readable and easy to use manner. For example, here is the `Select Case` statement equivalent to the code presented above:

```
Select Case Sales
    Case Is > 1000: Discount = 0.1
    Case Is > 500: Discount = 0.05
    Case Is > 250: Discount = 0.025
    Case Else: Discount = 0
End Select
```

You can have multiple lines of code executed for each case. This example simply shows the abbreviated syntax for executing a single line of code for each case.

2.4.2 *While loops*

The `While` statement is a useful construct that allows you to execute LotusScript statements until a logical condition is reached. The following loop executes until the user enters "Yes" or the loop has been executed five times. In addition to the `While` loop, this code introduces the logical operator `And`. `Or` is the other commonly used logical operator; both can be used in any conditional statement (e.g., like the `If` statements discussed in the previous section).

```
Dim Temp As String
Dim Count as Integer
While Temp <> "Yes" And Count < 5
    Temp = Inputbox$("Are you tired of seeing this prompt yet?","Test")
    Count = Count + 1
Wend
```

A slightly different form of the `While` statement is called the `Do` statement. The `Do` statement is a bit more flexible, because it allows you to choose whether you want the logical condition checked at the beginning or the end of a loop. For example, the following code is identical in function to the previous example:

```
Do While Temp <> "Yes" And Count < 5
    Temp = Inputbox$("Are you tired of seeing this prompt yet?","Test")
    Count = Count + 1
Loop
```

But you may feel more comfortable expressing the logic in a more English like manner, as follows:

```
Do
    Temp = Inputbox$("Are you tired of seeing this prompt yet?","Test")
    Count = Count + 1
Loop Until Temp = "Yes" Or Count = 5
```

As you can see, with the Do loop you can specify either "while" or "until," depending on which way you want to express the logic. Use whichever is more comfortable for you. The other difference is that you can specify the condition to be checked at the end of the loop rather than the beginning, which means the loop always runs at least once, regardless of the value of the variables. A While loop is only executed if the condition is TRUE.

2.4.3 For/Next statements

The For statement allows you to execute a block of LotusScript code a given number of times. The following code displays the numbers 1 to 5 in five separate message boxes.

```
Dim Count As Integer
For Count = 1 To 5
    Messagebox Count
Next
```

Note that you can nest loops within each other, as many times as you want. The loops are ordinary LotusScript statements, so they can be used anywhere, including inside other loops. For example, the following code executes the loop five times, but displays a message only when Count is less than 3.

```
Dim Count As Integer
For Count = 1 To 5
    If Count < 3 Then
        Messagebox Count
    End If
Next
```

2.4.4 Goto and exit

The final flow control statement available in LotusScript is the infamous Goto statement. I say *infamous* because you have probably heard that you shouldn't use the Goto. It is blamed for a lot of "spaghetti code," especially in old Cobol and Basic programs, programs that are very difficult to read and maintain. Generally, the advice not to use the Goto is wise. Your programs will be more readable and less error prone if you use the other looping statements presented in this chapter, and there's nothing you can do with the Goto that can't be accomplished with these other statements. Occasionally, however, use of the Goto is warranted. Usually, it is when you have a large block of code that does not require any looping, but once in a blue moon there is some condition that requires you to go back and reexecute part of a loop. You'll see just such a case in the sequential number generator in this book, where a very rarely occurring record-locking conflict requires reexecution of part of the number generation code. The syntax of the `Goto` statement is simple, as shown in the following code:

```
Goto my_label
    Messagebox "This statement is never executed."
my_label:
    Messagebox "But this statement is."
```

One place you may be tempted to use the `Goto` is to exit a loop prematurely based on some condition. But this is not necessary in LotusScript because the `Exit` statement is provided for this purpose. For example, the following `For` loop is exited if the user enters "Yes" at the prompt.

```
Dim Temp As String
Dim Count As Integer
For Count = 1 To 10
    Messagebox Count
    Temp = Inputbox$("Do You want out of this loop?")
    If Temp = "Yes" Then
        Exit For
    End If
Next
```

You can use `Exit` on any type of LotusScript code block, even a function or subroutine.

- `Exit For`
- `Exit Do`
- `Exit Function`
- `Exit Sub`

2.5 The Notes class libraries

Now that we've covered the basic programming elements of LotusScript, we can move on to more interesting ground—how to access and manipulate Notes-specific objects like databases and documents.

LotusScript is an object-oriented (OO) language which uses classes and methods to manipulate items of various kinds. Don't be intimidated by OO terminology like *classes*, *methods*, and *properties*; just think of it as another syntax for calling subroutines and accessing data variables. In fact, the reason Lotus implemented the language in an OO style is because it makes it easier and simpler for you, the programmer. Working with

OO classes and objects is much easier and faster to program than working through old-fashioned subroutine interfaces.

A class is simply a type of object. For example, there's a NotesDatabase class that lets you declare a database variable. An object has methods and properties. Properties are like variables. For example, the NotesDatabase class has properties like Title, FileName, Server, and so on. And a method is just a subroutine or executable code that operates on the class. For example, you can call the FTSearch (full text search) method of the Notes-Database class to perform a text search through a database.

The syntax of using object classes is very simple, as shown in the listing 2.1 code that displays the title of the current database in a message box:

Listing 2.1 Displays current database

```
1  Dim db As NotesDatabase
2  Dim session As New NotesSession
3  Set db = Session.CurrentDatabase
4  Messagebox db.Title , , "Database Title"
```

Listing Notes

1 A Notes object variable (i.e., an instantiation of a class) is declared using the normal Dim statement. The line declares a variable called db that can hold a NotesDatabase type object.

2 NotesSession is another Notes class that contains information about the current user's session, including a reference to the current database. The New keyword initializes the variable to an instance of the NotesSession class.

3 This line introduces two important concepts. The first is the Set statement, which is what you use to initialize an object variable. The second concept is accessing a property. Here, the CurrentDatabase property of the NotesSession object is assigned to the db variable.

4 This line also accesses a property, in this case, the Title property of the db NotesDatabase object.

Calling a method—that is, calling a function related to an object—is just as easy as accessing an object's property. For example, in listing 2.2 the NotesUIWorkspace class is used to compose a new document. NotesUIWorkspace is a class that represents the current workspace window and allows you to accomplish some user interface functions.

Listing 2.2   Compose a new document

```
1  Dim workspace As New NotesUIWorkspace
2  Call workspace.ComposeDocument("", "", "Main Topic")
```

Listing Notes

1 Notice the use of the New keyword to initialize the workspace variable.

2 This line shows the syntax for accessing a method. The Call keyword indicates that you are calling a method. The method is called ComposeDocument and takes three parameters: the server, the name of the database file in which to compose, and the name of the form. (The first two parameters are optional; if they are left out, the compose occurs in the current database.)

It's also possible to call a method using the Set statement, because some methods return a value that you can use. For example, in listing 2.3, the ComposeDocument method returns an object variable of the type NotesUIDocument. NotesUIDocument is a class that allows you to manipulate and access the document currently on the user's screen. In the following code, it is used to send the focus of the cursor to the rich text Body field instead of the default Subject field.

Listing 2.3   ComposeDocument method

```
   Dim workspace As New NotesUIWorkspace
1  Dim uidoc As NotesUIDocument
2  Set uidoc = workspace.ComposeDocument("", "", "Main Topic")
3  Call uidoc.GoToField("Body")
```

Listing Notes

1 Declares a variable in the NotesUIDocument class.

2 Calls the ComposeDocument method, and returns the result to the uidoc variable.

3 Calls the GotoField method of the uidoc NotesUIDocument object to move the cursor to the Body field.

Tip

If the method returns a simple text or numeric value, you do not need to use the Set statement. For example, you can use the following code to retrieve the text value of a field into a text variable:

```
SubjectValue$ = source.Fieldgettext("Subject")
```

2.6 Front end versus back end classes

You will often hear Notes programmers talking about *front end* and *back end* classes. Front end classes are ones that can be used to manipulate or interact with the user interface in some way, such as the NotesUIDocument class used in listing 2.3. Back end classes are used to manipulate Notes documents and databases programmatically, without any interaction with the user. Because it is possible to run LotusScript agents in the background on the server, it is important to know which back end classes you can use in these types of agents.

The following are commonly used front end classes:

- NotesSession represents the current Notes environment. It is used to access environment variables, the "current" database, the user's name and address books, and so on. NotesSession can also be used on back end code run on the server. (That is, usually it is used to obtain access to the current database.)

- NotesUIDatabase represents the current database open on the screen, and is used for event-based programming (for example, executing a LotusScript program when the database is opened or closed).

- NotesUIDocument represents the document currently open on the user's screen. It contains a wide variety of methods for manipulating the document under program control.

- NotesUIView represents the currently open view, and like the NotesUIDatabase class, it is used for event programming (covered in more detail in the next section of this chapter).

- NotesUIWorkspace represents the current Notes workspace window, and has a variety of methods for interacting with the user interface (for example, composing a document).

The following list shows the most commonly used back end classes:

- NotesDatabase represents a Notes database. Your back end programs will often begin by using this class to open a Notes database.

- NotesDateTime represents a Notes date and time field. It can be used by front and back end classes to manipulate date/time values.

- NotesDocument represents a notes document. This is the class you use to access or edit a Notes document programmatically (i.e., without user interaction).

- NotesDocumentCollection represents a collection of documents in a database. The collection can be a set of documents manually selected by the user, or a selection of documents queried by an agent. (See the section on manipulating document collections later in this chapter for more details.)

- NotesRichTextItem is used to manipulate rich text fields.
- NotesView represents a Notes view, and is often used in back end processing to get access to a document or group of documents.

Note that a program working through the front end (i.e., one that interacts with the user interface in some way) often makes use of back end classes as well to manipulate or access Notes data. But the reverse is not true—an agent running on the server, for example, can use only the back end classes.

2.7 *Event programming*

You've already seen how LotusScript code can be attached to a button in a view. But it's probably at least as common to attach code to an event, a technique that allows you to trigger the LotusScript program based on some action by the user. For example, you can enter code that's run every time a document is saved. Or for Notes 4.5 users, you can enter LotusScript code that runs every time a database is opened or every time a user deletes a document. (The database events were added in Notes 4.5, so they're not available in earlier versions.)

Attaching code to events is easy (as shown in figure 2.2):

1 Open the LotusScript Testing database.

2 Select Design|Forms, then double click on the Main Topic form to open it in design mode.

3 In the programming pane you'll see a menu called Event. Use the drop down list to select the Querysave event.

4 Under Run select the Script option and enter the LotusScript code in listing 2.4.

Listing 2.4   Querysave event

```
1  If Source.IsNewDoc Then
     Messagebox "Saving this new document for the first time!", , "New
   Document"
   Else
     Messagebox "Re-saving an old document.", , "Old Document"
   End If
```

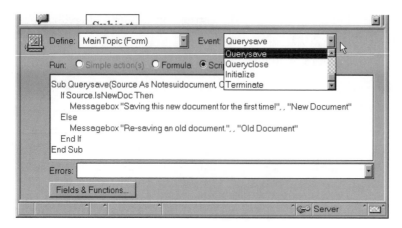

Figure 2.2   The event menu in the form designer

Listing Notes

1 Many events have default variables preassigned to convenient values. In this example, the Querysave event provides a NotesUIDocument called `Source` that is already initialized to the current document. In this line of code, we use the `IsNewDoc` property of this `NotesUIDocument` object to determine whether the document is being saved for the first time.

Here is a brief summary of the events to which you can attach code. Code can be attached to forms and fields (all 4.x versions of Notes), and to view and database level events (Notes 4.5 only).

Forms

- Options is a special event where you set LotusScript options for the form, such as the `Option Declare` statement to force declaration of any variables used in the form.

- Declarations is where you include any global variables for the form. Variables declared here will maintain their values until the document is closed.

- Queryopen is called before the form is opened or initialized with Notes data.

- The Postopen event is called just after the form is opened and initialized. This is a good place to put LotusScript code that is needed to calculate default values (i.e., when the default value is too complex to be calculated using a formula).

- Querymodechange is called just before a document switches from view mode to edit mode (or vice versa).

- Postmodechange is called after a document enters edit mode (or vice versa).
- The Postrecalc event is called after a document is refreshed.
- Querysave is called before a document is saved; this is a good place to do any pre-save processing like LotusScript-calculated field values.
- Queryclose is called just after the document is saved, before it is closed.

Fields

- The Entering event is called when the cursor moves into a field.
- Exiting is called when the cursor leaves a field.
- Databases (Notes 4.5 only):
  - Database events are accessed by clicking on Design|Other and double-clicking on the Database Script item.
  - Postopen is called after the database is opened.
  - Queryclose is called just before the database is closed.
  - Querydocumentdelete is called just before a document is deleted.
  - Postdocumentdelete is called after a document is deleted.
  - Querydocumentundelete is called just before a document is undeleted.
- Views (Notes 4.5 only):
  - Queryopen is called before the view is opened or initialized.
  - Postopen is called just after the view is opened on the user's screen.
  - Regiondoubleclick is called in a calendar style view when a region is double clicked.
  - Queryopendocument is called after a user double clicks on a document in a view, just before the document is opened.
  - Queryrecalc is called before a view is refreshed.
  - Queryaddtofolder is called before a document is added to a folder.
  - Querypaste is called before a document is pasted into a view.
  - Postpaste is called after a document is pasted into a view.
  - Querydragdrop is called before a drag drop operation is completed.
  - Postdragdrop is called after each drag drop operation.
  - Queryclose is called just before a view is closed.

2.8 Functions and subroutines

You can declare functions and subroutines that can be called from other scripts. The only difference between the two is that functions return a value and subroutines do not. When should you use them? A good rule of thumb in modular programming is that no single code module should be longer than one printed page in length. If it is longer than that, it will be difficult to maintain and debug, so it's probably a good idea to use some functions and subroutines to break it up into smaller, more manageable chunks.

Creating a function or procedure is simple. If you type the function declaration into the code window above or below any of the predefined events, Notes will automatically add an item to the Event menu for accessing the code in the future. For example, if you wanted to create a customized message box function for the Main Topic form, simply go into any event (such as Querysave), type the following line of code after the end of the Querysave subroutine and press Enter:

```
Sub MainTopicMessage (temp as String)
```

Notes will automatically add an `End Sub` statement and will add an entry for the MainTopicMessage subroutine to the Event drop down menu. Then you just add your subroutine code. For example:

```
Messagebox temp, , "Main Topic Form"
```

You call the subroutine simply by typing its name and adding its parameters in brackets:

```
MainTopicMessage("Display this text.")
```

You can pass as many parameters as you want to a function or subroutine. The only difference between functions and subroutines is that functions return a value. As an example, you could write a function that displays a standard prompt to the user and then returns the value the user entered, as follows:

```
Function MainInputBox (prompt As String) As String
    Dim temp As String
    temp = Inputbox$(prompt, "Main Topic Form")
    MainInputBox = temp
End Function
```

Note that the function itself has a type, declared after the function parameters. This is the type of value the function will return. To set the actual return value, a string is assigned to the function's name using the `MainInputBox = temp` statement. When you call `MainInputBox` you can assign the result to a value:

```
Dim user_input as string
user_input = MainInputBox("Please enter a value: ")
```

It's important to understand the scope of functions and subroutines. If you define a function on a form, as in the example in this section, then it can only be called and accessed from that form and its events. You can't, for example, attach LotusScript code to a button or agent that calls this function. In the next section, I'll show you how to use LotusScript libraries to create global database subroutines and functions that can be accessed from anywhere in the database.

2.9 LotusScript libraries

LotusScript libraries are a very useful feature that have been added to Notes 4.5 (not available in Notes 4.0 or 4.1). By using a library, you can define functions, subroutines, and variables that can be called by all objects within a database. As a simple example, you might want to have a customized message box function that displays the name and version number of your application in the window title bar. It will be much easier to maintain by creating one global procedure that contains the title and version information.

You need Notes 4.5 to enter this example:

1 Select the Create|Design|Script Library menu.

2 Select the Edit|Properties menu and enter `Application Message Box` under Title. Close the properties window.

3 Enter the following line of code into the programming pane and then press Enter.

```
Sub MyMessagebox (temp As String
```

4 Notes will automatically add the `End Sub` command and create an item in the Event menu called `MyMessagebox`. Enter the following line of code:

```
Messagebox temp, , "Your Application Name 1.0"
```

5 Save and close the script library.

6 Select Design|Forms and double click on the Main Topic form.

7 Under Event select Options and enter the following line of code:

```
Use "Application Message Box"
```

Tip for Notes 4.5 Users

For a more detailed look at the practical uses of libraries see the section "LotusScript libraries" in chapter 14.

You must enter this line of code into any object from which you want to use the script library.

8 Under Event select Querysave and enter the following code:

```
If Source.IsNewDoc Then
     MyMessagebox "Saving this new document for the first time!"
Else
     MyMessagebox "Re-saving an old document."
End If
```

9 Save and close the Main Topic form.

You should use a script library anytime you want to have a centralized library of code or variables that you want to access throughout a database.

2.10 *Agents*

Agents provide you with another very powerful and useful way to run formulas and LotusScript code. Agents provide you with four important techniques. First, they allow you to run code in response to certain events. For example, you can create an agent that processes all new documents that are added to a database. Second, agents can be scheduled to run hourly, daily, weekly, or monthly. This can be very useful for creating reports and so on. Third, your users can manually run agents, from a button, that automatically will search for a particular collection of documents to be processed. And last, but not least, agents provide you with a way to run LotusScript code from applications running on the Internet via Domino.

It's also important to understand that agents in Notes are a true client/server tool. You can run agents on the user's workstation, but you can also set up agents to run in the background on the server (i.e., these are the kinds of agents that only use back end classes, as discussed earlier in this chapter). In the following sections, I'll discuss each kind of agents in a bit more detail. For examples of various types of agents, see chapter 18.

2.10.1 *Triggered agents*

Triggered agents are run in response to some user activity, such as adding documents to a database. You can select the Create|Agent menu top see the options available, as shown in figure 2.3.

You can set the agent to run if new mail has arrived (usually only used in mail databases), if documents have been created or modified, or when documents have been

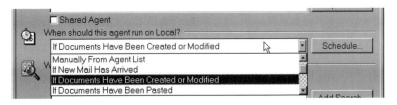

Figure 2.3 Triggered agent options

pasted into the database. In the programming pane, you can select whether the agent should run formula or LotusScript code. When the specified action has occurred Notes automatically runs the agent. By default, the agent runs on your local workstation. To run it on a server click on the Schedule ... button and select the server on which you want to run it.

2.10.2 Scheduled agents

Like triggered agents, scheduled agents can be run on local workstations or in the background on the server. You select the schedule you want under the "When should this agent run?" menu. There are four choices, each of which has a customized options screen (accessed via the Schedule ... button) to fine tune the schedule:

- *On Schedule Hourly*   These can be run once every thirty minutes, hour, or every two, four, or eight hours (see figure 2.5), and you can define the time of the day at which the schedule starts and ends. With scheduled agents you can also set the dates when the agent will be active.

▼ **Agent Manager**

Agent Restrictions	Who can -
Run personal agents:	
Run restricted LotusScript agents:	Joe McGinn/Joe's Place
Run unrestricted LotusScript agents:	Joe McGinn/Joe's Place

Figure 2.4   Server Agent Manager section

Tip

To run an agent on a server you must have permission in the server document in the public Name and Address Book (NAB). To determine if you have permission to run an agent:

1 Select the Files|Tools| Server Administration menu.

2 Select the Servers| Server view item, and then double click on the server on which you want to run an agent.

3 The users who can run agents are specified under the Agent Manager section, as shown in figure 2.4.

Unrestricted agents have access to all LotusScript commands. Restricted agents, on the other hand, cannot access any commands that interact directly with the operating system. This includes directory commands, running external programs, low level file I/O, setting the system date/time, making calls to a C application, making OLE calls, and using environment variables. It is probably a good idea to attempt setting access to Restricted first, and then move it up to Unrestricted on a case-by-case basis when you need to access the restricted functions.

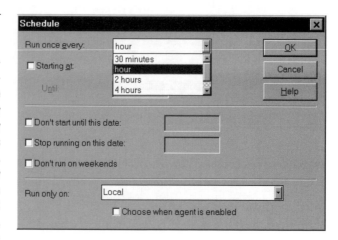

Figure 2.5   Schedule options for hourly agent

- *On Schedule Daily*   You can specify the time at which the agent is to be run.
- *On Schedule Weekly*   You can specify the day and time to run the agent.
- *On Schedule Monthly*   You can specify the day of the month and time to run the agent.

2.10.3 *Manually run agents*

One other option available under the "When should this agent run?" menu is to run an agent manually, either from the Actions menu or the agent list. These are generally one of two types of agents. They either process a collection of documents that the user has selected manually, or they search for a set of documents to process based on search criteria the user specifies when creating the agent. When you create a manual agent, you get a "Which documents should it act on?" menu on the agent screen, as shown in figure 2.6.

You can choose from the following options:

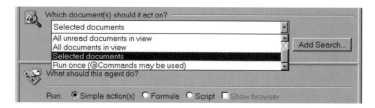

Figure 2.6   Which documents menu

- All documents in database
- All new and modified documents since last run
- All unread documents in view
- Selected documents
- Run once (@Commands may be used)

For all types except run once you can also add search parameters to the agent to narrow down the collection of documents that are processed by the agent. The run once selection is a special type of agent that can run the user interface @formula commands, but this kind of agent can be run only on a local workstation, not a server. When you click on the Add Search ... button you will see the Search Builder dialog box in figure 2.7.

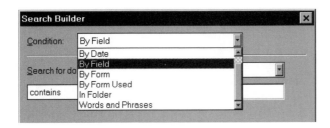

Figure 2.7   Search Builder

Using the Condition menu you can construct your search in a variety of powerful and flexible ways:

- *By Author*
- *By Date*   (allows you to select a range of dates)
- *By Form*   (pulls up the form graphically so you can specify a query by example)
- *By Form Used*   (specifies on which forms the agent should work)
- *In Folder*   (selects the documents in a specific folder)
- *Words and Phrases*   (allows you to specify keywords for which to search, including combinations of words)

You can even combine these techniques for a single agent simply by clicking on the Add Search ... button again and specifying additional search criteria using the Search Builder.

You can also run a manual agent from a button by using the following formula command:

```
@Command([ToolsRunMacro]; "Agent Name")
```

This has two uses. First, it allows you to chain agents to cooperate on completing a task. Second, it allows you to run LotusScript agents from a Web browser. (You can't run LotusScript code directly on a Web browser since the browsers don't contain the Lotus-Script interpreter).

In the next section, I'll show you how to access the agent's selected documents in LotusScript code.

2.11 Using the class browser

There is a quick and easy way to get help on all LotusScript commands and classes. In any LotusScript code window, you can click on the option Show browser, as seen in figure 2.8.

You can use the panes on the window to expand it, and you click on the twisties (i.e., the small triangles) to expand a section, as shown in figure 2.9. By itself the browser seems to be of limited utility, because it only presents the most basic syntax of commands. But you can access full help and examples by clicking on any item and pressing the F1 key on your keyboard. Notes will open up the corresponding help document.

You can also use the browser to view the Notes class libraries. This allows you to quickly and easily get information on the properties, methods, and operation of any Notes class. To access it, click on the drop down menu at the top of the class browser and select Notes: Classes, as shown in figure 2.10. As with commands, you can access the full help on a class by clicking on it and pressing F1.

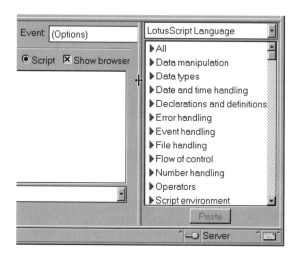

Figure 2.8   The class browser

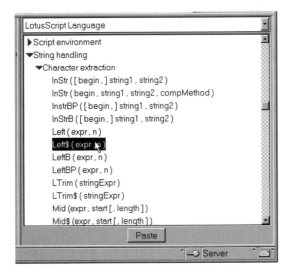

Figure 2.9   The class browser expanded

2.12 Debugging LotusScript code

Debugging LotusScript programs is fairly easy because Lotus has included an interactive debugging tool to assist you. To turn the debugger on you select the Files|Tools|Debug LotusScript menu. (This is a toggle command—to turn the debugger off just select it again.) Turn the debugger on, and then try running the Display Subjects agent again. As

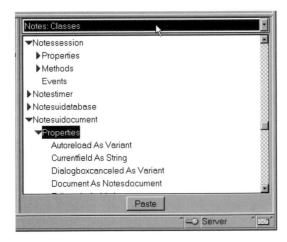

Figure 2.10   The Notes classes

Tip

Not only can you examine variables, you can actually set their values. Just click on the variable you want to change and enter the value in the New Value area, then continue running the script. This can be useful for testing code against unusual or uncommon values.

soon as the agent begins, you will see the debugger screen shown in figure 2.11.

At this point you have a number of options. You can press the Continue button to run the script normally. Or perhaps more usefully, you can press the Step Into button to step through the script one line at a time. Try pressing this button a few times. Notice how variables, once they are initialized, show their values in the Variables tab on the bottom half of the screen, as in figure 2.12. This makes the single-step execution mode extremely useful, since you can actually watch the values of variables as your script is executed a line at a time.

Of course, you don't have to single step through the entire program to see variable values. If your script encounters a LotusScript error (e.g., you try to access a document variable before initializing it), then the debugger screen is displayed and you can examine the values of variables to identify the problem.

You can also set breakpoints—points where you want to see the debugger window whether there's an error or not. Simply click on the line of code where you want to see

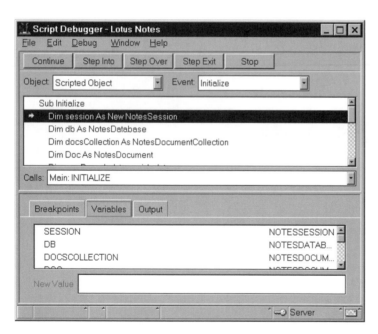

Figure 2.11   The LotusScript debugger screen

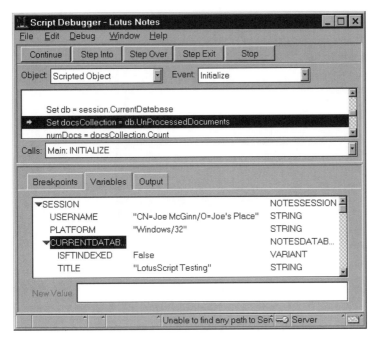

Figure 2.12   Viewing LotusScript variables

the debugger and select the Debug|Set/Clear Breakpoint menu (or press F9). When your script gets to that line (but before the line is executed), the debugger will be displayed and you can examine variables, step through the program, and so on.

There may be times where you want to see the output of a program but without using breakpoints (e.g., if the value is changing many times inside a loop and you don't want to break on every change). You can use the LotusScript `Print` statement and then view the output by clicking on the Output tab in the debugger, as shown in figure 2.13.

Note that the debugger can be used on LotusScript programs no matter where they are running—in agents, attached to buttons, or even on events such as attached to the Querysave event on a form. The only exception is code running in a dialog box via the `@DialogBox` statement: the debugger will be disabled while code is running in a dialog box.

2.13 Manipulating document collections

Usually an agent processes a number of documents. No matter what search criteria you specify you use the same code to access the collection of documents, even if it's a group

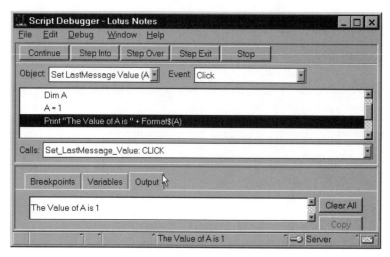

Figure 2.13   Viewing LotusScript output

of documents manually selected by the user. The NotesDocumentCollection class allows you to work with a collection of documents in an easy way. As an example, we'll create a simple agent that displays the subject field of all selected documents on the screen:

1 Open the LotusScript Testing database, and select the Create|Agent menu.

2 Under name enter `Display Subjects`.

3 Under When should this agent run? select Manually From Actions Menu.

4 Under Which document(s) should it act on? select Selected Documents.

5 Under Run select Script, and under Event select Initialize.

6 Enter the code in listing 2.5, then save and close the new agent.

Listing 2.5   Accessing a document collection

```
    Dim session As New NotesSession
    Dim db As NotesDatabase
1   Dim docsCollection As NotesDocumentCollection
    Dim Doc As NotesDocument
    Dim numDocs As Integer, j As Integer
2   Set db = session.CurrentDatabase
3   Set docsCollection = db.UnProcessedDocuments
    numDocs = docsCollection.Count
4   For j =1 To numDocs
5       Set doc = docsCollection.GetNthDocument(j)
6       Messagebox doc.Subject(0)
    Next
```

Listing Notes

1 A `NotesDocumentCollection` variable is used to access a set of documents.

2 Gets the current database.

3 Sets the `docsCollection` variable to the `UnProcessedDocuments` property. This is how you access the agent's selected documents.

4 Loops through the document collection once for each document.

5 `GetNthDocument` retrieves a specific document from the collection.

6 The document can now be processed normally.

Tip

If you modify a document, you must remember to save it as follows:

```
doc.Subject = "New Value"
flag = doc.Save(False, True)
```

To run the agent, select some documents and select the Actions|Display Subjects menu.

2.14 Text handling and string manipulation

You often need to manipulate text and strings in LotusScript programs. The most basic manipulation is adding strings together to create meaningful messages. For example, in the agent in the previous section you might want to display a message box showing how many documents have been selected. You can't just display the number because the user won't know what it means, so instead you concatenate two strings together to produce a readable message:

```
Messagebox "You have selected " + Format$(numDocs) + " documents.", ,
"Selected Documents"
```

This code shows two techniques you will use a lot, string concatenation and the `Format$` function. As you can see, concatenation is done by simply adding the strings together using the + sign. The `Format$` function converts the `numDocs` integer variable into a string. The following is a list of the most commonly used string manipulation functions:

- `Format$(x)` returns the variable x as a text string.

- `Left$(string, n)` returns the left n characters of `string`.

- `Mid$(string, start, end)` returns a subset of `string` from character number `start` to character number `end`.

- `Right$(string, n)` returns the right n characters of `string`.

- `Len(string)` returns the length of `string`.

- `InStr(string1, string2)` searches `string1` for the first occurrence of `string2`. Returns an integer specifying the position at which `string2` was found (returns 0 if not found).

Using combinations of these functions, you can perform sophisticated string operations. For example, consider the following lines of LotusScript code:

```
Dim session As New NotesSession
Dim db As NotesDatabase
Dim DB_Name as String
Set db = session.CurrentDatabase
DB_Name = Left$(db.FilePath, Instr(1, db.FilePath, db.Filename, 1)-1) +
"DocNums.NSF"
```

The purpose of this code is to reference another database called `DocNums.NSF`, a database which is in the same subdirectory as the current database. (For full details and explanations of this code, see chapter 3.)

The `db.FilePath` variable is the current databases file name; it might be set to something like `C:\NOTES\DATA\TESTDIR\Sales.NSF`. The `db.Filename` variable would be set to `Sales.NSF` in this case. The `Instr` statement (`Instr(1, db.FilePath, db.Filename, 1)-1`) returns the position at which the filename occurs (i.e., just to the right of the \ character). The `Left$` function then extracts everything to the left of the filename and appends the new filename `DocNums.NSF` to it. The result is the value of the `DB_Name` variable:

```
C:\NOTES\DATA\TESTDIR\DocNums.NSF
```

Here are some other string functions that you probably won't use as often as the above ones, but which are useful nonetheless:

- `Trim$(stringvar)` removes leading and trailing spaces from `stringvar` and returns the result as a string.

- `Ltrim$(stringvar)` removes leading spaces from `stringvar` and returns the result as a string.

- `Rtrim$(stringvar)` removes trailing spaces from `stringvar` and returns the result as a string.

- `Lcase$(stringvar)` returns `stringvar` converted to lowercase letters.

- `Ucase$(stringvar)` returns `stringvar` converted to uppercase letters.

2.15 Summary

In this chapter, you've learned the basics of how to use the LotusScript programming language.

You have learned how to use the LotusScript code editing window, and we have covered all the basics of LotusScript development, such as declaring variables and using loops and logic. We have looked at how to use the LotusScript classes to access Notes objects, and have discussed the differences between front end and back end classes.

You have learned how to use event-based programming and subroutines and functions, including the use of LotusScript libraries to create global functions that can be accessed from anywhere in a database. We have covered the various kinds of agents and implemented a sample one.

Lastly, you have learned how to use the Notes class browser and the interactive debugger to debug and maintain LotusScript code.

C H A P T E R   3

Directory and filename management

Many Notes applications consist of multiple databases, and you often have to code access references back and forth between them, in both LotusScript and formula programming. I continually read questions posted on Internet newsgroups about how to reference external databases without hard-coding server names and filenames. This is because you usually want your Notes application to be able to run on any server, regardless of what the server is named. You will often, for example, develop an application on one server and run it as production code on another. And of course, if you are developing a commercial application that will ship to as yet unknown customers, your program needs to be flexible enough to adapt to a customer's server name.

This is a classic problem in computer science that rarely seems to be provided for directly in programming languages. In Notes, the problem is even more complex because your application needs to reference not only other databases, but also needs to do so correctly both when connected to the network and when running as a remote client (e.g., a laptop that is not directly connected to the server). For example, Figure 3.1 shows the server and filename combinations you would need to access a database called Sales.NSF in a variety of situations—when the application is running on your development server, your production server, and on a laptop that is not always connected to a server. It can be a challenge to write code that evaluates to the correct names in all situations, keeping in mind that you don't always know the server names in advance. Nevertheless, the formula programming language and LotusScript are flexible enough to allow for solutions to these problems.

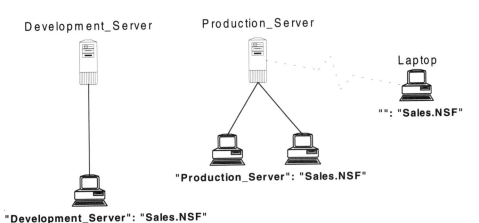

Figure 3.1 Accessing the Sales.NSF database

In this chapter you will learn:

- How to specify filenames using environment variables.
- How to make your applications more generic by specifying the current server name.
- How to solve all filename conflicts and related issues by storing your applications in subdirectories underneath the main Notes data directory.

3.1 Specifying filenames using environment variables

One technique is to use environment variables that allow the user to specify the filenames and server names for your databases. For example, to open a log database using a hard-coded server and filename reference, you would use the code in listing 3.1. Notes always requires that you supply both a server name and a filename to open a database. (You might be connected to more than one Notes server, so a filename by itself is not sufficient to identify a Notes database.) If you are on a system not currently connected to a server, you use the empty quotes " " to tell Notes to use the database stored on the local hard drive.

Listing 3.1 Open a database

```
@Command([FileOpenDatabase]; "My_Server": "Logdb.nsf")
```

The code in listing 3.2 allows the user to specify the server and database filename via the LogDatabase environment variable. In this case, the variable would be set to "My_Server": "Logdb.nsf" (including the quotes).

Listing 3.2 Open a database via environment variable

```
@Command([FileOpenDatabase];@Environment("LogDatabase"))
```

Now the database name is no longer hard-coded into your application, and you can allow the customer to input a server name.

It is easy to create a button that allows the user to edit the environment variable. The formula code in listing 3.3 shows a clean, simple formula that can be attached to a button to allow a user to edit the value of an environment variable. In this example, the environment variable is called `LogDatabase`. It will be blank the first time you press the button. It will remember the current state of the environment variable, and display it as the default value on subsequent edits.

Listing 3.3   Edit an environment variable

```
1  @Environment("LogDatabase ";@Prompt([OKCANCELEDIT]; "Log Database
   Name";"Enter the name of the log database:";@Text(@Environment("LogData-
   base"))))
```

Listing Notes

1   The second parameter of the `@Environment` statement is the value to be saved into the variable. Note how formula commands can be nested. Here we use a `@Prompt` statement to get the value for the variable from the user. The second parameter to `@Prompt` uses a nested formula again, this time to use the previous value of the environment variable as the default value for the prompt.

There are a couple of drawbacks to this technique. It can work all right if you only have one or two databases, and not too many users. But it becomes cumbersome to administrate on more complex systems, especially on a multiuser system having remote users. The problem is that the environment variables must be defined on each workstation, which is a lot of work if you have more than a few users. The other drawback is more serious: it's difficult to create a setup that will work for both network and remote database access without creating even more administration for users. To open a database on the server you supply the server name. But to open a local database (e.g., on an unconnected or remote laptop), you have to supply an empty string as the server name. The users would have to edit the environment variable every time they switch from connected to unconnected use (i.e., when they pull their laptops off the network and go home with them), a solution that is error prone and not very user friendly.

3.2 Specifying the current server

A somewhat better technique is to use a formula to specify the current server, that is, the server on which the database you are currently in is running. The formula in listing 3.4 will return the server name for a connected user, and the empty string for an unconnected user working on a local database, which is exactly what you want. This code in will work correctly for both networked and remote users.

Listing 3.4   Specify the current server

```
1  @Command([FileOpenDatabase];@Subset(@DbName;1): "Logdb.nsf")
```

Listing Notes

1 As you can see, this method still requires hard-coding of filenames or coding them into environment variables. But the current server name is accessed using `@Subset(@DbName;1)`. The nice thing about this method is that you can always access the correct version of the database as long as the databases and replicas reside in the NOTES\DATA directory (which, happily, is the default location for both local and remote databases). It returns the current server name if you are on a server directly, and an empty string if you are not. In both cases, it accesses the database you want it to.

Listing 3.5 shows how to get the current server name in LotusScript code for the equivalent LotusScript functionality. It also shows how to trap gracefully for a database not found error.

Listing 3.5   Getting the current server name

```
   Dim session As New NotesSession
   Dim db As NotesDatabase, other_db As New NotesDatabase("","")
   Set db = session.CurrentDatabase
1  If ( Not (other_db.Open(db.Server,"Logdb.nsf"))) Then
      Messagebox "Database " + db.Server + ":Logdb.nsf not found."
2     Exit Sub
3  End If
```

Listing Notes

1 The argument `db.Server` is what provides the current server name.
The `If` statement tests to make sure the database exists. Like the formula version, it will work whether or not you are connected to the server.

2 Exits the subroutine if the database was not found.

3 At this point, the database is open and ready for processing.

The advantages of this method are that it is maintenance free, easy to implement in both formulas and LotusScript, works on any server name even if you don't know it in advance, and supports both connected and remote users. It sounds almost perfect. *Almost?*

Well, if you're an "in-house programmer," where you have some control over the configuration of Notes and the databases and filenames to which users have access, this method might be fine for you. But applications that are being distributed to large numbers of users could still face problems with this method. For example, what if another application used the same technique and a filename that you used? It is not unlikely, because most Notes programmers limit their filenames to 8:3 characters so that they'll be compatible with all operating systems (including Windows 3.x, which does not support long filenames). If another programmer used the same technique and chose the same filename you did, then the two applications will be incompatible. And another problem for commercial applications: what if the users want to create a separate training copy of your application, or perhaps backup and archive copies that are still functional?

If it sounds like a mess too big to solve, don't despair. With just slight modifications to the technique presented in this section, you can solve these remaining difficulties.

3.3 Specifying the current server and directory

It is possible to specify the current directory name in addition to the current server name. Rather than storing your databases in the NOTES\DATA directory, you store them in a subdirectory under the DATA directory. Thus, if you have a Sales application, you would set up your directories on the server as follows, where each directory contains a complete set of the databases that make up your application:

```
Notes\Data\S_Live\
Notes\Data\S_Trai\
Notes\Data\S_BkpMay\
Notes\Data\S_BkpJune\
```

With the techniques I'll present in the next two listings, you will have a comprehensive directory management system that is:

- Foolproof. It will work for any directory names and any number of applications.

- Appropriate for both connected network and remote, local access to databases within subdirectories (the local replicas should be in subdirectories, too, of course).

- Compatible with all other Notes applications. Since your files are always in their own directory, there is no chance of filename conflicts.

- Manageable: the only administration is done at the server level, creating directories and copies of the databases. This is an acceptable level of administration since it only has to be done once when you install your application, and is more reliable than requiring individual users to administrate environment variables. Even for applications having several databases and many users, it works quite well.

The formula code in listing 3.6 uses the current server and directory to open the `Dblog.nsf` database. It's best to break the formula down into two or more lines to keep it more readable.

Listing 3.6 Specify the current server and directory

```
1  SubDir:=@LeftBack(@Subset(@DbName;-1);"\\");
2  DB_Name:=@If(SubDir="";"";SubDir+"\\") + "Dblog.nsf";
   @Command([FileOpenDatabase];@Subset(@DbName;1):DB_Name);
```

Listing Notes

1 This statement gets the current subdirectory. `@LeftBack(@Subset(@DbName;-1);"\\")` provides the current directory, but without a trailing backslash, for example, `Notes\Data\S_Live`.

2 This statement constructs the full filename we want to reference. If the `SubDir` variable is empty it means the database is in the default Notes DATA directory, so we add nothing to it. If there is a subdirectory, the `+"\\"` adds a backslash to it so that we can then append the filename `Dblog.nsf`. This allows it to work even if a database is in the Notes Data directory and not a subdirectory.

3 If this example is run in a database in the `S_Live` directory, `DB_Name` is set to `Notes\Data\S_Live\Dblog.nsf`. If it is running in the `S_Train` directory, then `DB_Name` evaluates to `Notes\Data\S_Train\Dblog.nsf`. Note that you still have to specify the current server using `@Subset(@DbName;1)`, so that it will work on both connected and remote systems.

Last but not least, the corresponding code in listing 3.7 gets the current server and subdirectory in LotusScript.

Listing 3.7 Specify the current server and directory in LotusScript

```
   Dim session As New NotesSession
   Dim db As NotesDatabase
   Dim DB_Name As String
1  Set db = session.CurrentDatabase
2  DB_Name = Left$(db.FilePath, Instr(1, db.FilePath, db.Filename, 1)-1) +
   "Dblog.NSF"
   REM Open the Dblog.NSF database
   Dim log_db As New NotesDatabase("","")
```

```
3   If ( Not (log_db.Open(db.Server, DB_Name))) Then
        Exit Sub
    End If
```

Listing Notes

1 Gets the current database, which is where the database filename, filepath, and server name of the current database are stored.

2 Removes the filename from the right side of the filepath, and then appends the name of the database we want to reference. For example, if the current database is

   `C:\NOTES\DATA\S_TRAIN\Sales.NSF`

   the result will be: `C:\NOTES\DATA\S_TRAIN\Dblog.NSF`.

3 When referring to a database, such as in this open command, always supply the current server (`db.Server`) in addition to the database directory and name. This way the database will work correctly on both servers and remote (i.e., laptop) client systems.

3.4 Summary

You have learned how to create a comprehensive directory and filename management system. It solves all of the critical issues for both in-house and commercial Notes application development. You should always use this safe method of organizing and referring to databases, even if your application is small and simple at first. If you get into this habit, your database "relationships" will always work, and you'll be relieved of a lot of support calls from your users.

Tutorial—building a Notes 4 application

Part 2 is a tutorial that steps you through the process of building a complete Notes application. The instructions will show you how to build a complete, professional quality, multidatabase Notes 4 application, one menu click, database, form, and view at a time. Don't worry if you don't fully understand a particular component or setting. Just like learning to ride a bike, by the time you've finished the tutorial you'll be comfortable with all the tools.

The program you will build is a customer support application, for customer support call tracking and recording information about your customers. This will involve building three databases and creating relationships among them.

Last but not least, you'll learn how to fine tune your user interface, distribute your finished Notes applications, and set up a basic quality assurance program using Notes.

C H A P T E R   4

A customer support application

In this chapter you will build the basic components of a customer support application. A customer support application needs to do several things:

- Maintain contact information (phone numbers, addresses, etc.) on the customers you are supporting. A customer can be a company, an organization, or an individual.

- Allow your customer support staff members to record the details of calls and conversations they have with customers. This includes the ability to attach notes about future calls to an existing problem report.

- Generate sequential document numbers for new calls, so that the users of your application can give a customer a reference number.

The application will consist of the following three databases:

1 Customer information (Customer.NSF). Contains contact and related information on your customers, both individuals and companies.

2 Logged support calls (Calls.NSF). Contains the customer support calls. The Calls database will be related to the Customer database, so that the user of the Calls form can specify which customer is calling without having to exit the form.

3 Document numbers (DocNums.NSF). This database is used to generate a unique, sequential document number for each customer problem report. It contains the Last Used Number, Prefix, and Suffix codes needed for sequential document number generation. (For full details on the design and implementation of this database and other aspects of generating sequential numbers, see chapter 17.)

The application will be designed so that if a customer calls back on the same incident, the follow up call can be attached to the original; thus, the support database can show a history of customer interaction by incident or by customer. Figure 4.1 shows the relationships among the three databases that make up this application.

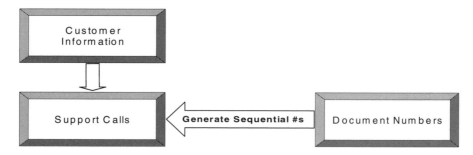

Figure 4.1 The customer support databases

In this chapter you will learn:

- How to create and use database subdirectories.
- How to create a multidatabase application, including defining relationships among the databases.
- How to create a number of different kinds of forms and views.
- How to add sequential document number generation to a Notes application.
- How to manage the generation of sequential numbers over a WAN.

4.1 Creating a database directory

Tip

If you are running Notes on a system that supports long file-names (e.g., Windows95, Windows NT, OS/2, etc.) you can use a more descriptive subdirectory name such as:

CUSTOMER_SUPPORT.

Before creating the databases, you must create a directory for them. If you don't, they will be stored in the Notes DATA directory. They will still work, but it's good practice to store your applications in a subdirectory so that you do not run into filename conflicts when you distribute your application to other systems. (See chapter 3 for a more detailed explanation of application directories.)

1 If you are running Notes on Windows or OS/2, open a DOS command window. If you are running another operating system, open the equivalent utility or program that will allow you to create directories.

2 Change into the Notes DATA directory. The DOS command is:

    CD \NOTES\DATA

3 Create a subdirectory under DATA called CUSTSUPP:

    MKDIR CUSTSUPP

4 Type EXIT to close the DOS prompt window.

You will use this subdirectory for all the databases you create for the customer support application.

4.2 The document numbers database

In a customer support database, you need to generate sequential document numbers to use as a tracking code. The users of the application will give this code to the customer after logging a customer call, so that the customer can refer to the tracking number if he or she must call back. The Document Numbers database contains the pieces needed to generate sequential document numbers. As well as generating numbers, you will have the ability to attach user-defined prefix and suffix codes to the numbers you generate.

1 Create a new, empty database by selecting File|Database|New.

2 Under Title enter `Document Numbers`.

3 Under File Name enter `DocNums.nsf`.

4 Click on the directory icon beside the file name.

5 Select the CUSTSUPP directory.

6 Do not select any template for this database; you want to start with an empty database.

7 Your screen should look like figure 4.2. Click on OK to save and open the new Document Numbers database.

Tip

It's always a good idea to keep your Notes database filenames no longer than eight characters. This will ensure that they will work on all supported Notes platforms, including Windows 3.1.

You need to create just one form and one view in the Document Numbers database. First, create the Document Number form.

1 Create a new form by selecting the Create|Design|Form menu.

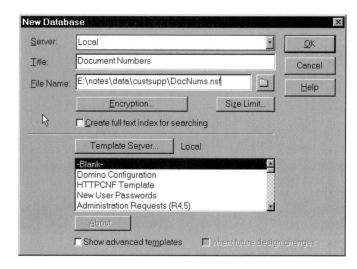

Figure 4.2   Creating the document numbers database

2 Select Design|Form Properties, and name the form Document Number.

3 You must to create several fields on this form. Don't worry about the visual appearance or style of the fields for now.

4 Create the following fields on the form using the Create|Field menu. Under Name enter `DatabaseTitle`. Under Type set this field to be Text, Editable.

5 Repeat step 4 to create the following two fields:
- Prefix: Text, Editable
- Suffix: Text, Editable

6 Select Create|Field one more time and create a field named `LastUsedNumber`. Under Type select Number, Editable.

7 Close the field properties window, and click on the programming pane. You should be in the programming pane for the LastUsedNumber field, for the `Default Value` event. Enter `"0"` (including the quotes) as the default value for this field.

8 Click the mouse cursor to the left of each field, and type in the text of the field name as a prompt so that the user can see which field is which when working on this form.

9 Save and close the Document Number form.

Now you need to create the All Documents view:

1 Click on Create|View, and name the view `($All)`. This is a special name that appears as the All Documents view to the user of your application.

2 Select the Shared option, and select OK to save the new view.
Click on Design|Views, and double-click on the `($All)` view to load it in design mode.

3 Click on the # column, and press the Delete key to delete this column. When Notes asks you if you want to "Permanently delete the selected columns from the view?" select Yes.

4 Select Create|Append New Column. In the programming pane, select Field and click on DatabaseTitle. When asked "Existing action will be lost. Do you want to continue?" select Yes.

5 You must set the DatabaseTitle column to be sorted. Select the Design|Column Properties window. Under name enter `Database Title`. Click on the Sorting tab. Under Sort select Ascending, then close the column properties window.

6 Select Create|Append New Column. In the programming pane, select Field and click on LastUsedNumber. Select on Design|Column Properties, and enter Last Used Number under Title.

7 Save and close the All Documents view.

8 Close the document numbers database.

9 Go into the Access Control List (File|Database|Access Control…) and give all of your users at least Editor access to the Document Numbers database (or you can just specify the default access as Editor). This does not affect the rest of your application security—access to your customer lists and customer support calls is controlled through the separate ACLs of those databases.

The Document Numbers database is now complete. Later in this chapter, you will add code to the Calls database to actually generate the document numbers.

4.3 The customer database

The Customer database is basically a database of person and company contacts, so it will be based on the Name and Address Book template included with Notes 4.x. Fortunately, this template provides all the necessary fields and forms for storing contact information on companies and individuals.

1 Create a new database by selecting File|Database|New.

2 Under Title enter Customers.

3 Under File Name enter Customer.nsf (*Customer* is eight characters long, so it is a better file name than *Customers*, which has nine characters).

4 Click on the directory icon beside the file name.

5 Select the CUSTSUPP directory and press OK.

6 Select the Personal Address Book template.

7 You must deselect the option Inherit future design changes. This is a new development database that will have a modified design, and you don't want it overwritten with a future version of the Personal Address Book template.

8 Click on OK to save the new Customer database.

You can now add some test customers to the database. You should add some companies by selecting the Companies view and clicking on the Add Company button. Then click on the People view and add some people by pressing the Add Person button. You will need these documents to test the Calls database later in this chapter.

The only other modification needed in the Customer database is a new view, which will be used in the Calls database to select the customer for the current call.

1 Create a new view using the Create|View menu.

2 Under View Name enter `Customers`.

3 Click on the Shared option so that all users of your application can see this view.

4 Under selection conditions you will see `SELECT Type = "Person"`. Change this to:

```
SELECT Type = "Person" | Type = "Company"
```

5 Press OK to save the new Customers view.

6 Click on Design|Forms, and then double-click on the Customers view to load it in design mode.

7 Click on the Name column, then select the Create|Insert New Column menu.

8 In the programming pane select Formula, and enter the following formula:

```
@Text(@DocumentUniqueID)
```

9 Select Design|Column Properties. Under Title, enter `Universal ID`.
The Universal ID is a default Notes property automatically assigned to all documents that is guaranteed to be unique for each document. By creating a view with a Universal ID in it, we can now create relationships between the other database (in this case, the Calls database) and the Customer database.

10 Click on the Sorting tab, and under Sort select Ascending. Close the column properties window.

11 Click on the Name column. Replace the existing formula for Name with the following one:

```
@If(Type="Person";@Trim(@Subset(LastName;1))+@If(Firstname !="";",
"+@Trim(@Subset(FirstName;1)); "");CompanyName)
```

This slight modification will cause this view to show the person's name for person type documents; otherwise, it will show the `CompanyName` field. The reason for this

---

Tip

Once you have tested your application, you can return to this view and hide the Universal ID column, since it is confusing to many users. It will still work for the purpose of relations, but it won't be visible to users. To hide this column:

1 Click on Design|Views, and double click the Customers view to load it in design mode.

2 Double click on the Universal ID column to display the column properties window.

3 Select the Hide Column check box, then close the properties window.

4 Save and close the Customers view.

---

is so that this one view can be used to select either People or Companies (i.e., when being referenced from the Select a Customer button on the Calls form, shown later in this chapter).

12 Save and close the Customers view.

If you look at the Customers view, you will see the unique 32-character Universal ID of the documents are displayed in the first column, and people/company names in the second. This view will be used to create a database "relation" from the Calls database.

The Customers database is now complete, so you can close it. Whenever you have an application that needs to store contact information, you should use the Personal Address Book template.

4.4 The calls database

The bulk of the customer support application is in the Calls database. After creating this database, you will add a form to log customer support calls, and a second response form to log related calls (i.e., if a customer calls back on an problem reported earlier). You will also add document number generation code, so that your users can give tracking numbers to customers for future calls on the same problem. Last, you will add a new view to look at support information broken down by customer and by incident.

First, you must create the Calls database. There is no perfect template for this database, but the Discussion (R4) template is a good starting point as it contains the basics of a main form, a response form, and basic views upon which to build.

1 Create a new database by selecting File|Database|New.

2 Under Title enter `Calls`. You can leave the File Name as `Calls.NSF`.

3 Select the Discussion (R4) template.

4 Click on the directory icon beside the file name.

5 Select the `CUSTSUPP` directory.

6 You must deselect the option Inherit future design changes.

7 Click on OK to save and open the new Calls database.

4.5 Customer support call form

You will use the Main Topic form to record customer support calls.

1 Click on Design, Forms and double-click on the Main Topic form to load it in design mode.

2 Double-click on the Subject field to display the field properties window. Click on the Options tab and change the Help description to read:

`Enter a short description of the problem.`

3 Open the field properties window for the Body field, and change the help description to:

`Enter a detailed description of the problem.`

4 Depending on the nature of your business, you may want to add more text or rich text fields above the Body field for storing more detailed information. For example, if you are supporting a software product, include fields for the customer's hardware and software configuration, software name and version, and so on.

The one feature this form still needs is a way for the user to indicate who is calling. Here you will create a relational field that creates a link to the Customer database.

1 Click to the right of the Categories field, and press Enter to create a new line on the form just below the Categories field.

2 Type `Customer:`, and then select Create Field. Name the new field `CustomerName`, Type Text, Editable. Close the field properties window.

3 Click to the right of the `CustomerName` field and press Enter again, and then select Create|Field. Name this one `RelatedDocument`. Click on the hide/when tab (the tab with the key on it, second from the right) and make it a hidden field by selecting all options. (You do not need to select the option Hide paragraph if formula is true.) Close the field properties window.

4 Click to the right of the RelatedDocument field, press Enter to get another blank line, and add a button using the Create|Hotspot|Button menu. Under Button Label enter `Select Customer`.

5 Click on the hide/when tab for the button and put checkmarks on the options Previewed for reading, Opened for reading, Printed, and Previewed for editing. Deselect the options Opened for editing and Hide paragraph if formula is true. This will cause the Select Customer button to be displayed only when the document is in edit mode.

6 In the programming pane for the button, select Formula, and enter the formula code from listing 4.1.

7 To the left of the CustomerName fields, select the text "Customer:" using the mouse. Then select the Create|Hotspot|Action Hotspot menu. In the formula

pane for this hotspot, enter the following code (for full listing notes, see listing 19.2):

```
FIELD RelatedDocument:=RelatedDocument;
SubDir:=@LeftBack(@Subset(@DbName;-1);"\\");
DB_Name:=@If(SubDir="";"";SubDir+"\\") + "Customer.NSF";
@Command([FileOpenDatabase];@Subset(@DbName;1):DB_Name;"Customers");
@Command([OpenDocument]; "0"; RelatedDocument);
@Command([OpenView]);
@Command([FileCloseWindow])
```

When the user clicks on this hotspot with the mouse, this code will open the related customer document (i.e., after a related document has been selected using the Select Customer button you created in step 4). This will enable your customer support representatives to quickly and easily get at contact information (e.g., a phone number) for any problem report in the Calls database.

8 Save and close the form.

Listing 4.1 Code for select a customer button

```
    SubDir:=@LeftBack(@Subset(@DbName;-1);"\\");
1   DB_Name:=@If(SubDir="";"";SubDir+"\\") + "Customer.NSF";
2   Choice:=@PickList([Custom];@Subset(@DbName;1):DB_Name; "Customers";"Select
    A Customer";"Select the customer who is calling.";1);
3   Chosen_Customer:=@Subset(Choice;1);
4   @If(Chosen_Customer ="";"";@Do(
5     @SetField("RelatedDocument"; @Text(Chosen_Customer));
6     @SetField("CustomerName";@DbLookup("":"NoCache"; @Subset(@DbName;1)
    :DB_Name; "Customers"; Chosen_Customer;2))));
    @Command([ViewRefreshFields])
```

Listing Notes

1 This code builds a pathname for Customer.NSF using the directory of the current database (i.e., in this case, Calls.NSF). The reason for this is so that a multidatabase application like the one you are now building can be stored in any subdirectory under NOTES\DATA. This prevents file name conflicts with other Notes applications, and provides you with a means of creating separate training and backup versions of your application just by creating new directories. See chapter 3 for a more detailed explanation of application directories.

2 The @Picklist command displays the Customers view as a menu from which the user can select a customer. The choices the user makes are stored in the Choice variable. The last parameter, in this case 1, indicates which column in the view is to be returned by @Picklist. You specify 1 here to retrieve the Universal ID column from the view you created in the Customer database.

Note that when referencing an external database, the current server name is specified in addition to the name of the customer database and the current directory, that is, @Subset(@DbName;1):DB_Name.

@Subset(@DbName;1) specifies the current server. The reason for specifying the current server is so that the application will work correctly both when running on a server and when running in a local directory on a remote client.

3 Ensures that only a single customer is selected.

4 If the Chosen_Customer variable is empty, it means the user pressed Cancel, so the function does nothing (indicated by the empty string ""). Otherwise, the @Do command executes the two @Setfield commands.

5 Sets the hidden RelatedDocument field to the Universal ID of the selected customer document. This hidden field is used by the Customer: hotspot to load and display a customer record.

6 Uses the customer documents Universal ID to look up the customer's name (i.e., the second column) from the Customers view in the Customer database. Stores it in the CustomerName field. This field is for display purposes, so the user can see to which customer the call document is related, without having to launch the customer form.

Test the form by adding a new document (click on the All Documents view, then New Main Topic). Test the Select a Customer button. Then test the Customers hotspot—it should open the related customer document on the screen. Don't worry about the physical appearance of the Calls form, we'll clean it up in chapter 6—Finishing Touches.

4.6 Generating document numbers

A customer support application is just the sort of situation where you need a way of generating unique, preferably sequential, document numbers. When the users of your application are on the phone with the customer, they'll want to be able to give the customer a reference number for tracking purposes. If the customer has to call back about the same problem, the support staff can attach the new call to the original one rather than entering it as a new incident.

For a detailed explanation of how the number generation code works and how to adapt it for particular situations, see chapter 17—Generating sequential numbers.

1   In the Calls database select Design|Forms, and double click on the Main Topic form to open it in design mode.

2   Click to the right of the timeComposed field near the top of the form, and press the Enter key to create a blank line on the form. Use the Create|Field menu to create three new fields on the same line, with the following field names and types:

   • Name: Prefix, type Text, Editable.
   • Name: DocumentNumber, type Number, Editable.
   • Name: Suffix, type Text, Editable.

3   Click to the left of the Prefix field, and enter `"Document #:"` as a prompt.

4   Click on the form (i.e., not on a field) so that the programming pane shows the events for the Main Topic form. Under the Define item it should say "Main Topic (Form)"; if it doesn't use the drop down list to select Main Topic.

5   Under Event select `Querysave`. This is the event that gets run just before a document is saved.

6   Select Script. When asked "Existing action will be lost. Do you want to continue?" select Yes.

7   Enter the LotusScript code in listing 4.2 into the `Querysave` code window. For detailed code listings see listing 17.1 in chapter 17—Generating sequential numbers. Because of the length of this code, I'll only comment on the most important elements here.

Listing 4.2   Querysave code for Main Topic form

```
    Dim session As New NotesSession
    Dim db As NotesDatabase
    Dim numbers_db As New NotesDatabase("","")
    Dim view As NotesView
    Dim doc As NotesDocument

    Dim workspace As New NotesUIWorkspace
    Dim PrefixCode
    Dim SufficCode
    Dim NextDocumentNumber As Long
    Dim Database_Path As String
    Dim New_Document_Number As String, DB_Name As String

    Set db = session.CurrentDatabase
1   DB_Name = Left$(db.FilePath, Instr(1, db.FilePath, db.Filename, 1)-1) +
    "DocNums.NSF"
2   Start_Lock:
    Set doc = source.Document
```

Listing 4.2 Querysave code for Main Topic form (continued)

```
REM Only generate the number if the field is blank
If doc.DocumentNumber(0) = "" Then
  REM Open the document numbers database
  If ( Not (numbers_db.Open(db.Server, DB_Name))) Then
    REM If the numbers database does not exist (i.e., on a laptop)
    REM then do nothing.
    Exit Sub
  End If

  REM Get the document number for this database
  Set view = numbers_db.GetView("($All)")
3   Set doc = view.GetDocumentByKey(db.Title)
  If doc Is Nothing Then
    REM No LastUsedNumber document exists for this database, so create
one
    Set doc = New NotesDocument(numbers_db)
    doc.Form = "Document Number"
    doc.DatabaseTitle = db.Title
    doc.LastUsedNumber = 0
    Call doc.Save (True,True)
  End If

4   PrefixCode = doc.Prefix(0)
  SuffixCode = doc.Suffix(0)
  NextDocumentNumber = Clng(doc.LastUsedNumber(0))
  NextDocumentNumber = NextDocumentNumber + 1
  doc.LastUsedNumber = NextDocumentNumber
  New_Document_Number = PrefixCode & Format$( NextDocumentNumber) &
SuffixCode

  REM Save the incremented LastUsed value
5   flag = doc.Save(False, False)
  If flag = False Then
    REM This means another user edited the LastUsedNumber while we were
trying to, so
    REM goto the beginning of this function and try again.
    Goto Start_Lock
  End If

6   Call Source.FieldSetText("Prefix", PrefixCode)
  Call Source.FieldSetText("DocumentNumber", Format$( NextDocumentNumber))
  Call Source.FieldSetText("Suffix", SuffixCode)
End If
```

Listing Notes

1 Uses the safe database referencing method from chapter 3 so that `DocNums.NSF` can be found even in the `CUSTSUPP` subdirectory. Always use this technique when accessing external databases in LotusScript.

2 The beginning of the document number generation process. See listing note 5.

3 Retrieves the DocNums.NSF document for the current database, so that the `Last-UsedNumber` (and the optional Prefix and Suffix codes) can be retrieved.

4 These lines get the Prefix and Suffix code, retrieve and increment the `LastUsed-Number`, and combine these pieces into the New_Document_Number variable.

5 This line is the key to record locking, which is what guarantees that the generated document numbers will be unique. If the Save method returns False, it means another user updated the `LastUsedNumber` while this script was running. To avoid generating a duplicate number, this script executes the `Goto Start_Lock` statement which goes back to the beginning of the function and retrieves the next available number.

6 Writes the Prefix/Suffix codes and the newly generated document number to the `DocumentNumber` field in the current form. Note that we're using the `Notes-UIDocument FieldSetText` method, so that the changes appear immediately on the user interface when the user saves the document.

You can now test your document number generator. Save and close the Main Topic form. Add a few new documents and the Document Numbers will be generated (starting at number one). Notice that you do not have to close a form to generate a document number—just press the Save action bar item and the number will appear on your screen.

Now try experimenting with some of the other features of document number generation, such as prefix and suffix codes. Open the Document Numbers database, and you'll see that a `DocNums.NSF` document for Calls has been created. Double-click on it and double-click on a field to edit it. Try entering some text in the Suffix and Prefix fields, press Save, and then go back to the Calls database and enter a few more records to see the difference.

4.7 *Customer support related call form*

When a user calls back regarding a previous incident, you will want to log the current call as being related to the original one so that you can correctly track problem resolution. You don't want the second call recorded as a new incident.

The Response form will be used to record related calls to an existing problem. The customer support staff asks the user for the problem reference number (i.e., the Document Number). With this number they can search for the original call document and then press the Response button to create a related call document.

1 Select Design|Form, and double click on the Main Topic form to open it in design mode.

2 In the Main Topic form, use the keyboard or mouse to select the Customer hotspot, and the CustomerName and RelatedDocument fields. Then select Edit|Copy, and close the Main Topic form.

3 Double click on the Response form to open it in design mode.

4 Put an empty line between the timeComposed field and the yellow line, and select Edit|Paste.

5 Click on the CustomerName field. Select the Default value event, enter `Customer-Name` as the formula. This will cause this field to be inherited from the parent document.

6 Click on the RelatedDocument field. Under Default value, enter `RelatedDocument` as the formula.

7 Save and close the Response form.

Try adding a few response documents. Notice that the customer information (including the link to the customer document) is inherited from the original call, it does not have to be reentered. Using this form your customer support representatives can add an unlimited number of comments or follow up calls to any incident.

4.8 Calls by customer view

You should create a view that takes advantage of some of the new fields, so that you can analyze your customer support data. In particular, it can be very helpful to have a view that allows you to look at problems broken down by customer.

1 Click on Design|Views, and click on the By Category View (but don't open it).

2 Select the Edit|Copy menu, then Edit|Paste.

3 Double-click on the Copy of By Category view to load it in design mode.

4 Select the Design|View Properties menu, and name the view Calls By Customer. Delete the "By Category" text in the Alias field.

5 Click on the leftmost column. The programming pane should have the field Categories selected. Select the CustomerName field instead.

6 Click on the leftmost column again. Select the Edit|Copy menu, then the Edit|Paste menu.

7 Click on the second column from the left. In the programming pane select the DocumentNumber field.

8 Save and close the view.

Try the Calls By Customer view. It is categorized by two fields, Customer Name and Document Number, which presents a detailed history of customer support interaction by customer and by incident.

4.9 Customer support over a wide area network

One of the challenges of building a customer support application is that it often must work over a WAN, so that your whole organization has access to the support logs. Yet each separate office also wants to be able to see a list of just their support calls, the ones they are responsible for. The problem is worsened by the fact that Document Numbers can only be generated across a LAN, otherwise duplicate numbers would be generated at different sites.

One solution is to make the DocNums.NSF database a separate copy, not a replica on each server, as shown in figure 4.3. In other words, create each copy of the DocNums.NSF database using the Notes File|Database|New Copy menu. Having done this, you can edit the Calls record in each DocNums.NSF database to specify a different suffix/prefix code for each office. For a more detailed explanation and a look at some other WAN options, see the Generating sequential numbers over a wide area network section in chapter 17 (Generating sequential numbers) and the Generating sequential numbers on the Internet section in chapter 12 (Internet LotusScript and agents).

If you are doing customer support over a WAN, you'll want to create a view that is categorized by Document Number, so that you can see the calls belonging to each office (i.e., each Notes server).

1 Click on Design|Views, and click on the Calls By Customer view (but don't open it).

2 Select the Edit|Copy menu, then Edit|Paste.

3 Double-click on the Copy of Calls By Customer view to load it in design mode.

4 Select the Design|View Properties menu, and name the view Calls By Document Number.

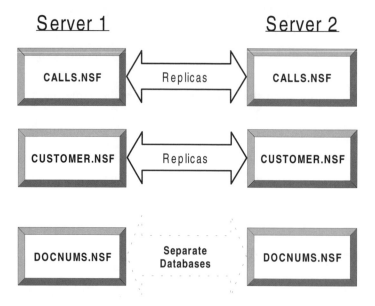

Figure 4.3 Database organization over a WAN

5 Click on the leftmost column and select the Prefix field in the programming pane.

6 Save and close the Calls By Document Number view.

This view is now categorized by your offices (i.e., each one has a different Prefix code) and document numbers.

The Customer.NSF and Calls.NSF databases should be replicated across all systems, so that everyone can access all calls and is working off of one, consistent customer database. But remember, as shown in figure 4.3, the DocNums.NSF database should be copied to other servers, not replicated.

4.10 Summary

You have built the core components of a multidatabase customer support application. You've learned how to create a multidatabase application in a subdirectory, and how to create safe and reliable references between the databases. You created a number of different kinds of forms and views, and added the important feature of sequential number generation to the customer support Calls form.

C H A P T E R   5

Improving the user interface

The difference between a good application and a great one is often simply taking the time to add some "nice to have" features to the program, even if they aren't absolutely required. The most effective way to do this is to see if there's some way to streamline the user's work, to reduce the number of steps he or she has to take to do a job.

In this chapter you will learn:

- How to add a search button to your views to allows users to easily find a customer support call by entering the document number.
- How to add a button to the Calls form that allows users to add new customers to the Customer database.
- How to display the customer's phone number on the Call form.
- How to add a status field to track the status of customer requests and problems.
- How to display the status as an icon in a view.
- How to add a navigator to a Notes application.

5.1 Find a call by document number

The first place to look when improving a program is the area of things that the users have to do a lot. If you can remove even one or two button presses and simplify a commonly done activity, it is worth the effort to do so, and your users will thank you for it.

One thing that some customer support staffs spend a lot of time doing is taking return calls from customers regarding a previously recorded incident. The customer gives the support staff the document number, and then the user has to find that document in the Calls database.

This process is actually fairly cumbersome using the built-in Notes searching tools. The user can't just search for the document number (e.g., 35) because there's a good chance that this number will be in many fields throughout the database, and the Notes searching works across all fields. You could have a long, unique prefix code, but then the user has to type that in every time.

The solution is to combine LotusScript and formula code to implement a column-specific search. This technique is explained in detail in the section "Search and Display a Document" in chapter 13 (see code listings 13.3 and 13.4).

You will build two agents, the first a LotusScript agent, the second a simple formula agent:

1 Select the Create|Agent menu item.
2 Name the agent Find Call Part 1.
3 Select the Shared Agent option.

4 Under When should this agent run? select the option Manually From Actions Menu.

5 Under Which document(s) should it act on? select the option Run once (@Commands may be used).

6 Under What should this agent do? select the Script option.

7 Under Event select Initialize, and enter the code in listing 5.1.

8 Save and close the agent.

Listing 5.1   Find Call Part 1

```
Dim session As New NotesSession
Dim workspace As New NotesUIWorkspace
Dim doc As NotesDocument
Dim db As NotesDatabase
Dim unid As String
Dim document_to_find As String
Dim collection As NotesDocumentCollection
```
1
```
document_to_find = Inputbox$("Enter the call # you want to find:", "Find a Call")
If document_to_find = "" Then
```
2
```
    Call session.SetEnvironmentVar("UNID","")
    Exit Sub
End If

Set db = session.CurrentDatabase
```
3
```
Set collection = db.Search( "DocumentNumber="+ document_to_find, Nothing, 0)

If collection.Count = 0 Then
```
4
```
    Messagebox "Call number " + document_to_find + " not found."
    Call session.SetEnvironmentVar("UNID","")
    Exit Sub
End If
```
5
```
Set doc = collection.GetFirstDocument
unid = doc.UniversalID
```
6
```
Call session.SetEnvironmentVar("UNID",unid)
```

Listing Notes

1 Asks the user to enter the Call number he or she wants to find.

2 If the user presses Cancel, this line sets the UNID environment variable to the empty string. This will prevent part 2 of the agent from displaying an error message.

3 Searches for the `DocumentNumber` that the user entered.

4 If the call number entered is not in the database, an error message is displayed.

5 Retrieves the document from the collection returned by the Search method.

6 Sets the `UNID` environment variable to the `Universal ID` of the found call. This variable will be used by part 2 of the agent to display the call.

Tip for Notes 4.5 Users

You do not need a second agent in Notes 4.5: you can display the document directly using the improved NotesUIWorkspace EditDocument method. Simply remove the SetEnvironmentVar statements and add the following line to the end of listing 5.1:

```
Call workspace.EditDocument(False, doc)
```

For Notes 4.0 and 4.1 users

You need to add to the second agent, a formula to display the document found in part 1.

1 Select the Create|Agent menu item.

2 Name the agent Find Call Part 2.

3 Select the Shared Agent option.

4 Under "When should this agent run?" select the option Manually From Actions Menu.

5 Under "Which document(s) should it act on?" select the option Run once (@Commands may be used).

6 Under "What should this agent do?" select the Formula option.

7 In the programming pane enter the following formula code:

```
@If(@Environment("UNID")!="";@Command([OpenDocument]; "0";
@Environment("UNID"));"")
```

8 Save and close the agent.

Last, you need to create a Find Call # button:

1 Click on Design|Views, and double-click on the ($All) to load it in design mode.

2 Select the View|Action menu.

3 Select Create|Action, and Title it Find Call #.

4 Select a button icon, and then close the action properties window.

5 Select Simple Actions in the programming pane.

6 Click on the Add Action button.

7 Under Action select Run Agent, and under Agent select the option Find Call Part 1, then press OK.

8 Click on the Add Action button again.

9 Under Action select Run Agent, and under Agent select Find Call Part 2 and press OK.

10 Save and close the view.

Click on the All Documents view and test the Find Call # button. You don't have to enter the document prefix, just the number itself, since it uses the DocumentNumber field to find the document.

5.2 Add a new customer from call form

Another area to look for usability enhancements is anything that might inconvenience or distract the users from their primary goal, which in this application is recording a customer support call. One situation that could be bothersome is if the person calling is a new customer, not yet in the customer support database. It would be nice if the user could add a new customer record without leaving the call-taking form. The solution is to put an "Add New Customer" button next to the "Select Customer" button in the Main Topic form, so that the user can easily add the customer record without having to open another database.

1 In design mode, open the Main Topic form in the Calls database.

2 Click the mouse to the right of the Select Customer button.

3 Select the Create|Hotspot|Button menu. Under Button label enter `Add New Customer`.

4 Insert the code from listing 5.2 into the code window for the button.

5 Save and close the form.

Listing 5.2   Code for Add New Customer button

```
  SubDir:=@LeftBack(@Subset(@DbName;-1);"\\");
  DB_Name:=@If(SubDir="";"";SubDir+"\\") + "Customer.NSF";
1 Form_To_Use:=@Prompt([OkCancelList];"Select a Form";"Do you want to add a
  Person or a Company?";"Person";"Person":"Company");
2 @Command([Compose];@Subset(@DbName;1):DB_Name; Form_To_Use)
```

Listing Notes

1 Prompts the user to select the Person or Company form to add a new customer.

2 Composes the new customer document using the specified form.

When the user presses the Add New Customer button, he or she is given the option of creating a Person document or a Company document. Once it is added, he or she can link the customer to the current call using the Select Customer button.

5.3 Display the customer phone number

When your customer support staff members need to phone customers, they can press the Customer: hotspot on the Calls form to open the customer document. It is helpful to display the most commonly used field (probably the phone number) directly on the Calls form, so that they don't need to press the hotspot.

Fortunately, the phone numbers are already displayed in the Customers view in the Customer database. If you want to display other fields, you may have to add them to this view first.

1 Open the Calls database.

2 Click on Design, Forms, and double-click the Main Topic form to open it in design mode.

3 Click to the right of the CustomerName field, and press Enter to create a new, blank line on the form.

4 Type `Phone Numbers:` on the line.

5 Select the Create|Field menu. Name the field `PhoneNumbers`, Type Text, Computed for Display.

6 Select the "Allow multi-values" option. This will allow this field to display multiple phone numbers.

7 Click on the Options tab, and under "Display separate values with:" select New Line.

8 Close the field properties window, and enter the code in listing 5.3 in the Value event of the PhoneNumbers window.

9 Click on the Select a Customer button. Add a semicolon to the end of the last line of the formula code for this button, press Enter, and then enter the following code:

```
@Command([ViewRefreshFields])
```

This will cause the PhoneNumbers field to be refreshed when a customer is selected.

10 Save and close the Main Topic form.

Users will now be able to see the customer's phone numbers directly on the call-taking form. Because the field is Computed for Display, it is recomputed whenever the form is opened or refreshed. This means that the current phone number will always be displayed, even if it's been edited since the contact was linked to the document.

Listing 5.3 Code for PhoneNumbers value event

```
   FIELD RelatedDocument:=RelatedDocument;
   SubDir:=@LeftBack(@Subset(@DbName;-1);"\\");
   DB_Name:=@If(SubDir="";"";SubDir+"\\") + "Customer.NSF";
 1 temp:= @DbLookup("";@Subset(@DbName;1):DB_Name;"Customers";
   RelatedDocument;3);
 2 @If(@IsError(temp);"";temp)
```

Listing Notes

1 The @DbLookup command looks up the phone numbers of the customer related to the current call.

2 The result from the @DbLookup must be passed through the @IsError function to prevent a Notes error message in the case where the related customer has not yet been selected.

5.4 Status field

You will probably want a way to indicate which support calls require further action and which have been completed. This is easy to achieve using a status field:

1 Open the Calls database.

2 Click on Design, Forms, and double-click the Main Topic form to open it in design mode.

3 Click to the right of the Subject field, and press Enter to create a new, blank line on the form.

4 Select the Create|Field menu. Name the field Status, Type Keywords, Editable.

5 In the Choices section, enter the following choices:

- Unassigned
- Being Worked On
- Problem Resolved

6 Click on the tab between Basics and Options (the keywords options tab), and under Interface select Radio Button. Under Frame select None.

7 Close the field properties window, and set the default value to Unassigned.

When a new call document is created, the default Status value is Unassigned. If the person answering the phone is not the one responding to the problem, he or she would leave the status as Unassigned. When someone's working on a problem they select Being Worked On, and then they select Problem Resolved when the customers problem has been fixed.

You also need a few fields to keep track of the response to the problem, and to assign the problem to one of your staff members.

1 Click to the right of the Status field, and press Enter to create a new line on the form.

2 Use the Create|Field menu to create the following fields:

Tip

There may be situations where you want the values for check box or radio fields to be edited by end users. For example, some users might want to add a Need More Info status when they don't have enough information to solve the customer's problem. For details on implementing editable key list fields see the section "Dynamic Check Boxes and Radio Buttons" in chapter 19.

- AssignedTo: Authors, Editable. Under Choices select the option Use Access Control List for Choices.

  The AssignedTo field is used to select the user (from your support staff) who is working on the problem. The selection list from which to choose a name is taken from the database's Access Control List.

- ActionsTaken: Rich Text, Editable. This field is used for the support staff to indicate how the problem was resolved. The field is rich text so that the user can include graphics or document links if necessary.

3 Save and close the Main Topic form.

5.5 Display status as an icon

The status information is very important to people looking at the database, so you should probably include it in most of your views. For important information like this, you may want to have the status displayed as icons in the view, so that users of the system can quickly see calls that need help.

1 Open the Calls database.

2 Click on Design, Forms, and double-click the ($All) view to open it in design mode (i.e., this is the All Documents view to the end user).

3 Click on the Document Number column and then select the Create|Insert New Column menu.

4 In the programming pane, select Formula, and enter the following code:

```
@If(@IsResponseDoc; 0;
Status="Unassigned"; 160;
Status="Being Worked On";83;
Status="Problem Resolved";82;0)
```

5 Select the Design|Column Properties menu and select the item Display values as icons. Close the column properties window.

6 Select the right side of the column header and shrink the column down to be one or two characters wide.

7 Save and close the view.

Click on the All Documents view, and notice how easy it is to see which items need attention, which are being worked on, and which have been completed, as shown in figure 5.1.

Tip

If you would like to use different icons, the numbers to be used for any given icon are derived from a chart on page 241 of the Notes 4 Application Developer's Guide (in the section "Displaying an icon in a column").

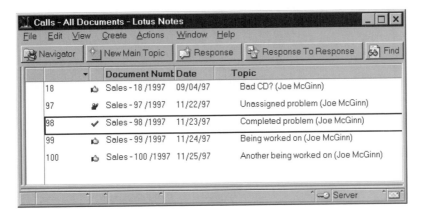

Figure 5.1   Status displayed as an icon

5.6 Adding a navigator

Your applications should always include a navigator to help nonexpert users to easily access the database. The Discussion database on which Calls is based already has a basic Navigator. You can turn it on by selecting the Navigator button in any view. You can also set up the Navigator to be turned on by default in the database's Launch properties (i.e., in the Launch tab of the database properties window).

The default navigator is set up using icons, but you can also create buttons and other graphic elements. In this section you'll add a simple enhancement to the Navigator, a button to open the Customers database.

1 Select Design|Navigators and double-click on the Main Navigator.

2 Select the Create|Button menu, and use the mouse to draw a button at the bottom of the Navigator.

3 Under Caption enter `Go to Customers`.

4 Close the properties window, and select Formula in the programming pane. Enter the following code:

```
SubDir:=@LeftBack(@Subset(@DbName;-1);"\\");
DB_Name:=@If(SubDir="";"";SubDir+"\\") + "Customer.NSF";
@Command([FileOpenDatabase];@Subset(@DbName;1):DB_Name)
```

5 Save and close the Navigator.

The navigator will now appear as shown in figure 5.2. Clicking on the Go to Customers button opens the Customer database.

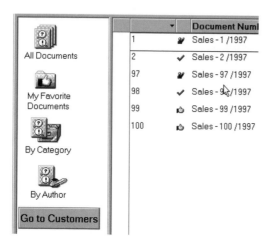

Figure 5.2 Calls navigator

5.7 Summary

You have streamlined the user interface by adding several buttons and functions for activities that the users of the customer support application need to do frequently. You have added a button to easily search for documents, and another button that allows users to create a new customer document while recording a call. You have learned how to display related fields from another database (e.g., displaying the customer phone number). You have added a status field for tracking purposes, and learned how to add an icon column to a view to display status values graphically. And last, you have added a Navigator to the customer support application.

In the next chapter, you'll learn how to improve the graphical appearance of your application and add other finishing touches.

C H A P T E R 6

Finishing touches

Your application is almost finished. The core functionality is done, and the user interface has been fine tuned. Now you need to create a graphical design for your forms so that they are visually appealing, and so that they have a standardized look. This important step is often ignored by programmers, but it can make your applications much easier to market and sell. Even for in-house applications, you'd be surprised how much more accepting users are of a new application if it is visually appealing.

In this chapter you'll learn:

- How to create a graphical header for your forms to make them more attractive and readable.
- How to use tables to organize fields and other information on your forms, and how to best take advantage of table's visual properties.
- How to effectively use hidden fields to make your forms less cluttered.
- How to use Lotus Components to extend the functionality of Notes (Windows95 users only).

6.1 Graphical design

The complete study and practice of graphical design is beyond the scope of this book. It is a difficult art to master, which perhaps explains why some programmers ignore it, or perhaps simply don't have the time to learn it. Notes 4 is a powerful layout and design tool, which in many cases means it gives you "enough rope to hang yourself." I have seen some truly ugly Notes applications.

The best solution to this problem is to find a Notes application whose look you like and copy it. For example, the Personal Address Book template that you used to create the Customers database in chapter 4 is an example of good graphical design. See the Person form in figure 6.1.

It has enough color, but does not overuse it, which is a common mistake. The most important information, the person's name, is displayed prominently so that the eye can find it quickly.

The form in figure 6.1 also makes subtle but effective use of fonts and tables. In the remainder of this chapter you will go through these techniques one by one, using the Calls form in the calls database.

Tip

You should avoid changing the background color of your forms. Notes fields are "transparent", meaning their background color is the same as the form's, making the fields hard to read for most background colors other than white.

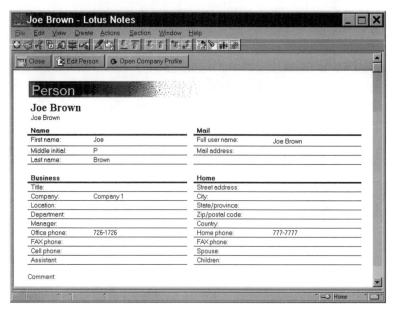

Figure 6.1   The Person form

6.2 Graphical form header and color

I didn't pay much attention to graphical design when building the customer support database. If you're like me, your Calls form probably looks something like the rather unappealing form in figure 6.2.

We can do much better than this. A little bit of color goes a long way in making a form attractive. You'll start by creating a color layout region similar to the one in figure 6.1. You'll need access to the LAYOUT.PCX graphics file from the *Inside Lotus-Script* CD.

1 Open the Calls database.

2 Click on Design|Forms and double-click on the Main Topic form to open it in design mode.

3 Click just above the Body field. This is where you'll start building the new form.

4 Select the Create|Layout Region|New Layout Region menu.

5 Select the bottom-right corner of the layout region with your mouse and drag it up to make the region smaller.

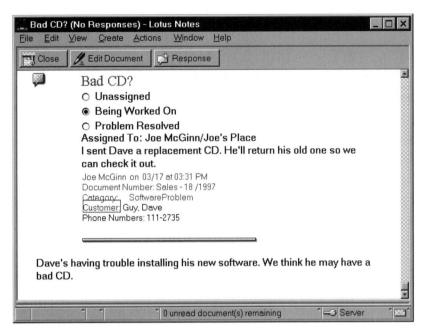

Figure 6.2   The Calls form

6   Double click on the layout region and deselect the Show Border option. Close the properties window.

7   Open a graphics program and load the LAYOUT.PCX file from the *Inside Lotus-Script* CD. Copy it to the clipboard.

8   In the Notes form designer, select the Create|Layout|Region|Graphic menu. Drag the graphic to the top left corner of the layout region.

9   Select the Create|Layout Region|Text menu, and drag the text item to the top left of the region so that it is on top of the graphic you created in step 6.

10 Double click on the text object and under Text enter call. Click on the fonts tab and set the text's color to yellow and its size to 14. Close the properties window.

11 Save the Main Topic form.

It can balance the form out and add a nice bit of color if you add a phone icon or a small logo for your business. If you have other development tools like Visual Basic or a C compiler, they usually come with a collection of icons. You can also use the WORLD.PCX from the *Inside LotusScript* CD. To add an icon to the form:

1   Load the icon in a graphics program (like Windows Paintbrush) or an icon viewer.

2 Select the icon in your graphics program (there is usually a Select All item under the Edit menu), and then select the Edit|Copy menu.

3 Return to the Main Topic form, and click on the layout region. Select the Create|Layout Region|Graphic menu. Slide the graphic icon over to the right. (You may have to go into the Layout properties and expand its width to five inches or so.)

4 Save the Main Topic form.

The part of the form you've been working on should look something like figure 6.3.

6.3 *Using tables to display fields*

Using tables to line up fields on your forms can greatly improve their readability and appearance. Careful use of table properties can also give structure to a form. Before using tables, though, we'll move the Document Number field. It should be a prominent field so that the user finds it easily.

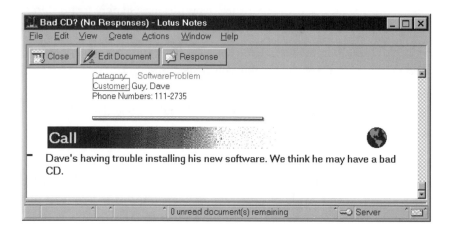

Figure 6.3 The graphical form header

1 Open the Calls database. Click on Design|Forms and double-click on the Main Topic form to open it in design mode.

2 Select the Document # prompt and the Prefix, DocumentNumber, and Suffix fields, and then select the Edit|Cut menu.

3 Click just above the Body field.

4 Select the Edit|Paste menu.

5 Select the Document # prompt and fields again and then the Text Properties window. Change the font size to 12 and select gold (dark yellow) as the color.

Now you will begin using tables to organize fields:

1 Click to the left of the Body field.

2 Select the Create|Table menu. Enter one row and one column as the table dimensions.

3 Select the tmpFrom, DateComposed, and time-Composed fields. Press the Edit|Cut menu.

4 Click your mouse cursor inside the table you created above the body field, and select Edit|Paste.

5 Select the tmpFrom, DateComposed, and time-Composed fields again and open the text properties window. Change the color from cyan to dark blue. Dark blue has more contrast against the white background, so it is easier to read.

6 Select the Table|Properties menu. On the Cell Borders tab, select None on the top, left and right sides, and Double on the bottom (if you're using Notes 4.5, you select 0 instead of None and 2 instead of Double).

Now you will create a table for the customer contact information:

1 Click to the left of the Body field.

2 Select the Create|Table menu. Leave the table dimensions at the default, two rows by two columns.

3 Select the Table|Properties menu. Click on the Layout tab, and enter 1″ as the Column 1 width.

4 Cut and paste the Customer hotspot into the top left cell of the table.

5 Cut and paste the Phone Numbers prompt into the bottom left cell, and the PhoneNumbers field into the bottom right one.

6 Select the CustomerName and RelatedDocument fields, and the Select a Customer and Add New Customer buttons, and cut and paste them into the top right cell. (Don't worry, the table cells have no trouble handling multiple items.)

7   Use the text properties window to change the color of the Customer hotspot and Phone Numbers prompt to dark blue.

8   Click your cursor above the table and enter From. Color the text black, change the size to 9, and the style to bold.

9   Select all cells in the table, and select the Table|Table Properties menu. Set the cell borders on the left and right side to None (or 0 in Notes 4.5).

10 Select just the top row in the table, and set its top cell border to Double (or 2).

You need one more table, this one to hold the problem status and response information:

1   Click to the left of the Body field.

2   Select the Create|Table menu. Select four rows and two columns.

3   Select the Table|Properties menu. Click on the Layout tab, and enter 1″ as the Column 1 width.

4   Use cut and paste to move the Categories, Status, AssignedTo, and ActionsTaken prompts and fields into the new table. Put the prompts in the left column and the fields in the right one.

5   Select all the prompts in the left column. Use the text properties window to change their color to dark blue, size to 9, style to plain.

6   Select all the fields in the right column. Use the text properties window to change their color to black, size to 9, style to plain.

7   Select all cells in the table, and select the Table|Table Properties menu. Set the cell borders on the left and right side to None.

8   Select just the top row in the table, and set its top cell border to Double.

9   Click your cursor above the table and enter Problem Status. Color the text black, change the size to 9, and the style to bold.

Now you just need to do a little clean up work on the form:

1   Use cut and paste to move the Subject field to just above the From table.

2   You now must delete the empty area of the form having the two little blue boxes (one of them has a picture of a lock on it) and the blue line above the colored layout region. These objects are in a table, so it's a little tricky to select them.

Start by clicking (and holding down) your mouse cursor to the right of the red hidden field just above the blue boxes. (This should be the NewsLetterSubject field.) Then, still holding the mouse button down, slide the mouse down until you have selected the blue boxes, the red "This document was marked…" text, and the blue line just below it. Let go of the mouse button and select the Edit|Clear menu.

Your Calls form should now look something like figure 6.4. As you can see, this is a remarkable improvement over where you started in figure 6.2. Graphical design isn't really a lot of work, once you have a good look and design with which to work.

6.4 *Making effective use of hidden fields*

Notes makes it very easy to hide fields under various circumstances. For example, in the Calls form you could hide the phone number field when it's empty. This makes the form easier to read, as it isn't cluttered with empty prompts when no information is available. Of course, you need to show all fields when the form is in edit mode.

1 Open the Calls database. Click on Design|Forms and double-click on the Main Topic form to open it in design mode.

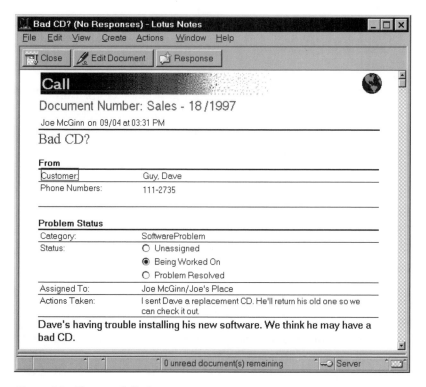

Figure 6.4   The new Calls form

2 Double-click on the PhoneNumbers field to open the properties window.

3 Click on the hide/when tab. It is the one with the line and key on it, second from the right. Click the checkbox Hide paragraph if formula is true, and enter the following formula:

```
PhoneNumbers = "" & !@IsDocBeingEdited
```

The `@IsDocBeingEdited` formula ensures that the field is displayed when in edit mode. (The character ! means NOT in a formula; thus this field is hidden if it's blank and it's not in edit mode.)

4 Click on the Phone Numbers prompt. Enter the same formula for its hide/when criteria, and select the checkbox Hide paragraph if formula is true.

5 Save and close the form.

You can try creating a Call document that has no phone number. Save it, and open it up again in read mode. The PhoneNumbers field and prompt will not be displayed. When you edit the document, they are displayed again.

6.5 Lotus Components

There's one other way to jazz up your user interface—by using Lotus Components.

Lotus Components are currently available only on the Windows95 platform. Fortunately, they require no changes or additions to your Notes applications, as they work directly on any rich text field. You don't have to worry about adding platform-specific features to your application, because you don't have to do anything at all in your databases to support Lotus Components (other than have a rich text field on your forms).

Components are an add-on product based on an enhanced version of Microsoft's ActiveX (formerly known as OCX) component technology. A user who has installed Lotus Components will get the Lotus Components menu on his or her toolbar. You can then insert components into a rich text field in any Notes database. The components in the Lotus package include a spreadsheet and 3D charter, a project scheduler, and a comment tool.

For an example, see the email memo form in figure 6.5. I've inserted a Comment and Draw/Diagram component.

Once you've inserted a component into a document, it can be viewed and printed by any Notes user, regardless of whether or not he or she has Lotus Components installed on the computer. The user must have Components installed if he or she wants to create or edit components.

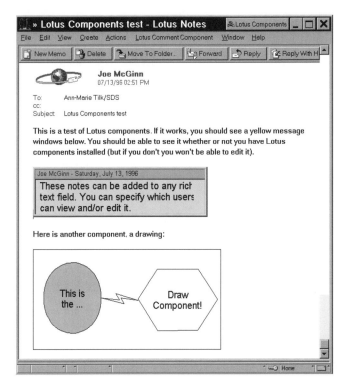

Figure 6.5   Lotus Components

6.6 Summary

In this chapter, you've learned how to spruce up the appearance and graphical design of your forms. This is a critical step in making your Notes applications look professional and polished. You have learned how to add graphical headers to the form, and how to use layout regions. You have also learned how to use tables to improve both the organization and visual appearance of your forms. We have explored the benefits of conditionally hidden fields, and looked at using Lotus Components to extend the Notes user interface.

In the next chapter we'll look at the final step of Notes development, distributing your Notes applications.

C H A P T E R 7

Distributing Notes applications

Your application is finished. Just one task remains to complete a project: you must distribute the application to your users. Notes templates provide an easy way to do this, but there is more to distributing an application than that. You need to test your application to make sure that all forms, views, navigators, and buttons function as intended. Just as importantly, you need to verify that your application really meets the users' requirements. Both of these tasks are part of quality assurance, which I will discuss in some detail later in this chapter.

In this chapter you will learn:

- About Notes templates and how they allow you to distribute application updates electronically

- The basics of a quality assurance program, and why you need to have one

- How to set up a quality assurance process with a Notes database, including automatic email notification

- How to set up useful views for a groupware application like quality assurance

- The quality assurance roles for various members of your software development team

7.1 Notes templates

A template is a special kind of Notes database that is used to create regular Notes databases. You can think of a template as a cookie cutter; it can be used to cut many applications having the same shape. When you create a Notes database from a template you have the option of inheriting template design changes. This means that if you change a form or some LotusScript code in a template, these changes will be replicated to all databases based on the template.

This makes templates an ideal way to maintain the source code for an application. When future versions of the application are released, only the template need be updated. All copies of databases based on the template will be updated, but the user's data will remain unaffected. You normally ship your application to users as a template (or a set of templates for a multidatabase application). The users can create as many copies of the application as they want, but the source code for all of them is maintained in just one place, the template.

Tip

Normally, the design of the databases on your server are updated automatically when the DESIGN program is run on the server at 1:00 A.M. For local databases, you can refresh the design manually by selecting the database and pressing the File|Database|Refresh Design menu.

To convert a database on which you have finished development into a template use the following steps:

1 Click on the database on the Notes workspace, and select the File|Database|New Copy menu.

2 Change the file name suffix from NSF to NTF, and select OK.

Note: Unlike databases, templates must be stored in the main Notes DATA directory, not a subdirectory.

3 Select File|Database|Properties to open the properties window for the new database.

4 Click on the Design tab. Select the option Database is a template.

5 Enter a Template Name.

Note: Once your users have started creating databases from a template, you cannot change this name. This is used to maintain the relationship between a template and the databases based on it.

That's all there is to it. Your template can now be used to create new databases, and you can upgrade the source code in all of these databases simply by providing a new template.

7.2 *Securing a database using Access Control Lists*

The primary means of providing security in a Notes database is through the database ACL. The ACL specifies what access each user has to the database. You can see the ACL for any database by selecting the File|Database|Access Control menu (or by right-clicking a database icon on the Notes workspace and selecting Access Control from the popup menu). Figure 7.1 shows the ACL for the Calls database.

The most important setting in the ACL is the Access menu, which you use to specify the type of access the user has. The following are the access roles available, from the least access to the most:

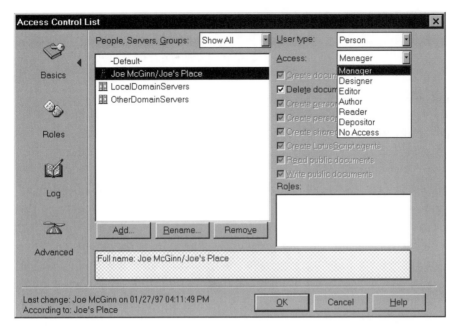

Figure 7.1 Calls database ACL

- *No Access*   The specified users cannot access the database at all.

- *Depositor*   Users can create documents only; they cannot see any documents even if they have created them. This is useful for customer surveys or feedback databases where the user fills out a form but does not have access to see documents in the database.

- *Reader*   Users can read all documents, but they cannot create or edit documents.

- *Author*   Users can read documents and create documents, and they can edit documents that they have created. This is the most common access level used for interactive databases like discussion databases.

- *Editor*   Users can read, create, and edit any documents.

- *Designer*   Users can modify database design elements like forms, views, and navigators.

- *Manager*   The manager can basically do anything to the database, including editing ACLs.

Tip

When you convert a database into a template, you should set the default ACL properties as follows:

- Default: Reader
- LocalDomainServers: Reader
- OtherDomainServers: Reader
- Your user name: Manager

7.3 A simple quality assurance program

The primary purpose of a quality assurance (QA) program is to make sure that you don't release an application that has lots of bugs in it. A secondary purpose is to maintain a consistent quality level for all software that you produce.

There are two things you want your QA program to do—first, to track bug reports. The QA process must ensure that all bugs found by the software testers are reported to the programmers, and then verify that the programmers have fixed the problems. Second, end user beta testing should be going on as you are testing your application. QA has to make sure that end user feedback and problem reports are also resolved. When all problems and reports have been resolved to the satisfaction of your QA standards, the software (i.e., your template) can be shipped to the users.

You should select someone on your programming team to be the quality assurance administrator. It should be someone who has a good understanding of both the technology and the users' requirements, but it should also be someone other than the lead programmer. Quality assurance is like editing a book, and it can be difficult for a writer or a programmer to edit his or her own work.

It is important to understand that quality assurance is a software release process. It is a process that by definition supersedes the "release it at the deadline" technique used in many businesses. It is important to explain the benefits of quality assurance to management, and to get them to support the process. You will need this support late in the project when the program's not quite done, but the users and marketing staff are howling for it to be released. As you've probably experienced, these pressures can be quite extreme. The reason for having a QA release process is so that these and other pressures do not compromise the quality of software that you deliver (whether it be to users in your company or for sale).

Fortunately, the groupware capabilities of Notes make it easy to implement a simple quality assurance process. In the next section you will construct a mail-enabled groupware database to manage this process.

7.4 A groupware quality assurance database

The purpose of the database you will build in this section is to allow you to manage the QA process as effortlessly as possible. When a programmer has completed a database template, and is ready to send it to QA for testing, the programmer adds a new document in the QA database. The document will include a link to the template, the template name, version number, and other information needed to test and release the database.

One of the easiest ways to make a Notes database into a groupware application is to use automatic email notification. For an important process like quality assurance, this ensures that nothing falls through the cracks. It also makes the process easier on everyone, since the users don't have to continually monitor the QA database for new information.

In the QA database you'll create in this section, automatic email notification is sent to:

- The QA administrator when a new database template is added to the QA database by a programmer

- The programmer when any problem report or feedback is entered against the template

- The person who entered the problem report if the programmer sets the problem's status to Need More Info

- The QA administrator when the programmer sets the status of the template to All Problems Resolved. There is an additional status field for the administrator to verify the status, in an access controlled section that only the administrator can edit

All this allows the QA process to proceed with very little manual intervention. There is a view for programmers to see all tasks assigned to them. The QA administrator has a view to look at problems by status so that problem areas can be easily identified.

Once the QA administrator has verified the completion of all tasks, he or she sets the status of the database template to Released to Production, backs up the new database template, and begins distributing it (finished at last!). Once a database template is released to production, it should not be modified for any reason, because you always need to keep a copy of every version of an application you release for testing and customer support purposes. Bug fixes and new features should be made to a new, separate copy of the template. The specific procedures for programmers, testers, and the QA administrator will be laid out in detail later in this chapter, after you have built the database.

The QA database will be based on the Notes 4 Discussion template.

1 Create a new database by selecting File|Database|New.

2 Under Title enter Quality Assurance.

3 Set the File Name to Quality.NSF.

4 Select the Discussion (R4) template.

Tip

Before beginning this database, you should decide who will be your quality assurance administrator. You will need his or her Notes email address to complete the QA database.

5 Deselect the option Inherit future design changes.

6 Store the QA database in the default Notes DATA directory, if you want.

7 Click on OK to save and open the new Quality Assurance database.

The first thing you need to do is edit the Main Topic form to add fields to record database template information. This is the form that programmers will use to submit a new database template to QA. See figure 7.2.

Tip

You may want to practice using the form design techniques from chapter 6 as you go. Put the fields in a table, with the "standard" Notes look and feel, and your fields should look something like figure 7.2.

1 Click on Design|Forms. Double-click on the Main Topic form to load it in design mode.

2 Click just above the Body field.

3 Use the Create|Field menu to create fields with the following attributes:

- `TemplateName`: Text, Editable. Contains the name of the database template from the properties Design tab.

- `TemplateVersion`: Text, Editable. Enter `"1.0"` (with the quotes) into the Default Value event.

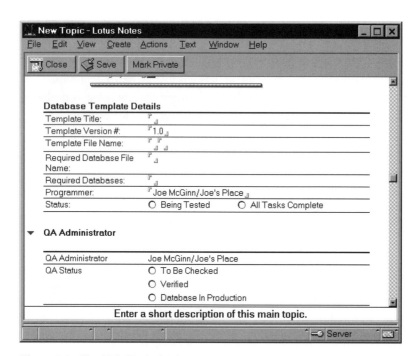

Figure 7.2   The Main Topic QA form

- `TemplateFileName`: Text, Editable. Contains the file name of the database template.
- `DatabaseLink`: Rich Text, Editable. Contains a Notes database link to the template.
- `RequiredDatabaseFileName`: Text, Editable. Contains the Notes database file (if any) that users need to enter when creating a database from this template. This is useful for multidatabase Notes applications where databases in a subdirectory need to have a certain filename to be correctly referenced by other databases in the application. (See chapter 3 for complete details on implementing multidatabase application links.)
- `RequiredDatabases`: Text, Editable. Contains the Notes database file names of any external databases that are needed for this template to function correctly. (For example, for the Calls template the `Customer.NSF` file name would be put in this field since it is used in the Calls database.)
- `ProgrammerName`: Authors, Editable. Under Choices, select Use Address dialog for choices. Under the Default Value event for this field, enter:

```
@Name([Abbreviate];@Username)
```

- `StatusText`: Keywords, Editable. In the choices window, enter:

```
Being Tested
All Tasks Complete
```

> Click on the Keyword Options tab (it's the one between Basics and Options), and select a Radio Button interface and None under Frame.
> Close the properties windows and enter "Being Tested" (with the quotes) as the Default Value for this field.

4 In a separate table on the form, create the following fields.

- `QAAdminName`: Text, Computed when composed. In the Value event for this field, select Formula and enter the email address of your quality assurance administrator. For example:

```
"John Smith/My_Server"
```

- `QAStatus`: Keywords, Editable. In the choices window, enter:

```
To Be Checked
Verified
Database In Production
```

> Click on the Keyword Options tab. Select Radio Button and None under Frame.

5 Select the table with the QAAdminName and QAStatus fields, and then select the Create|Section|Controlled Access menu.

6 In the section properties window enter `QA Administrator` under Title. Click on the Formula tab and enter the formula that identifies the QA administrator:

```
"John Smith/My_Server"
```

7 Enter text prompts for all the new fields.

Before closing the Main Topic form, you need to add some LotusScript code to implement automated email notifications.

1 Click on the form so that the form's events show up in the programming pane. Select the Declarations event. Enter the following line of LotusScript code:

```
Dim StatusValue As String
```

This global variable will be used to check when the programmer changes the templates status, so that the QA administrator can be notified.

2 Select the PostOpen event. This code gets the value of the documents Status field immediately after the document is opened.

```
Dim doc As NotesDocument
Set doc = Source.Document
StatusValue = doc.Status(0)
```

3 Select the QuerySave event, and enter the code in listing 7.1.

4 Save and close the Main Topic form.

Listing 7.1   Code for Main Topic QuerySave event

```
    Dim session As New NotesSession
    Dim db As NotesDatabase
    Dim doc As NotesDocument
    Dim newdoc As NotesDocument
    Dim rtitem As NotesRichTextItem

    Set db = session.CurrentDatabase
    Set doc = source.Document
1   If Source.IsNewDoc = True Then
2       Set newdoc = New NotesDocument(db)
        Set rtitem = New NotesRichTextItem (newdoc, "Body")
        Call rtitem.AppendText("A new template as been added to the Quality
    Assurance database. Double click on the link below to see it:")
        Call rtitem.AddNewLine(1)
        Call rtitem.AddNewLine(1)
```

Listing 7.1 Code for Main Topic QuerySave event (continued)

```
3   Call rtitem.AppendDocLink (doc, doc.Subject(0))
    newdoc.Subject = "New QA Database: " + doc.Subject(0)
    newdoc.SendTo = doc.QAAdminName
4   Call newdoc.Send (False)
    Else
5   If doc.Status(0) <> "Being Tested" And doc.Status(0) <> StatusValue Then
        Set newdoc = New NotesDocument(db)
        Set rtitem = New NotesRichTextItem (newdoc, "Body")
        Call rtitem.AppendText("The status of a template in the Quality
    Assurance database has been changed. Double click on the link below to
    verify the status change:")
        Call rtitem.AddNewLine(1)
        Call rtitem.AddNewLine(1)
        Call rtitem.AppendDocLink (doc, doc.Subject(0))
        newdoc.Subject = "QA Database Template Status Change: " +
    doc.Subject(0)
6       newdoc.SendTo = doc.QAAdminName
        Call newdoc.Send (False)
7       Call Source.FieldSetText("QAStatus", "To Be Checked")
    End If
End If
```

Listing Notes:

1 If it is a new document, the QA administrator needs to be notified that a new data-base template has been submitted to QA.

2 Creates a new email memo.

3 This line is the key to email notification. It appends a link to the current document in the body of the email message. When someone receives one of these email notifications, all he or she must do is double-click on the link to get to the relevant QA document.

4 Sends the new email memo.

5 If the programmer has changed the Status from Being Tested to All Tasks Complete the QA administrator is notified.

6 Sends the memo.

7 Resets the QAStatus field to To Be Checked, so that it has to be verified by the QA administrator.

Next, you need to modify the Response form to add problem reporting and track-ing fields. You'll also add LotusScript code to it to enable email notification to the pro-grammer when new problems are reported.

1 Click on Design|Forms. Double-click on the Response form to load it in design mode.

2 Click just above the Body field.

3 Use the Create|Field menu to create fields with the following attributes.

- `ReportType`: Keywords, Editable. In the choices window, enter:

```
Bug Report
Feature Request
To Be Documented
```

Click on the Keyword Options tab. Select Radio Button and None under Frame, and under Columns select 2.

- `StepsToReproduce`: Rich Text, Editable: Contains the steps needed to reproduce the problem. This is a Rich Text field so that users/testers can include screen captures or other relevant information.
- `AdditionalComments`: Text, Editable.
- `ProgrammerName`: Text, Computed when composed. In the Value event for this field, select Formula and enter:

```
ProgrammerName
```

This field will inherit its value from the parent document.

4 In a separate table, create the following fields:

- `ProblemStatus`: Keywords, Editable. In the choices window, enter:

```
Assigned
Being Worked On
Need More Info
Problem Resolved
```

Click on the Keyword Options tab. Select Radio Button and None under Frame. Select 2 under Columns.
Enter `"Assigned"` (with the quotes) as the default value for this field.

- `ActionsTaken`: Rich Text, Editable: Contains the programmer's response/fix to the problem.

5 Select the table having the ProblemStatus and ActionsTaken fields, and then select the Create|Section|Controlled Access menu.

6 Open the section properties and enter `Report Status` under Title. Click on the Formula tab and enter the formula to identify the `ProgrammerName` field:

```
ProgrammerName
```

All that remains to be done is to email-enable this form. The programmer is notified of new problem reports and feature requests. The person who reported the problem is also notified if the programmer sets the Status to Need More Info.

1 Click on the form so that its events show up in the programming pane. Select the Declarations event. Enter the following line of LotusScript code:

```
Dim CurrentProblemStatus As String
```

This global variable will be used to check when the programmer changes the problem status, so that the person who entered the problem can be notified if the programmer needs more information.

2 Select the PostOpen event. The following code gets the value of the document's Status field immediately after the document is opened.

```
Dim doc As NotesDocument
Set doc = source.Document
CurrentProblemStatus = doc.ProblemStatus(0)
```

3 Select the QuerySave event, and enter the code in listing 7.2.

4 Save and close the form.

Listing 7.2   Code for Response QuerySave event

```
    Dim session As New NotesSession
    Dim db As NotesDatabase
    Dim doc As NotesDocument
    Dim newdoc As NotesDocument
    Dim rtitem As NotesRichTextItem

    Set db = session.CurrentDatabase
    Set doc = source.Document
1   If Source.IsNewDoc = True Then
        Set newdoc = New NotesDocument(db)
        Set rtitem = New NotesRichTextItem (newdoc, "Body")
        Call rtitem.AppendText("A new problem report has been added to one of
    your databases in the Quality Assurance database. Double click on the link
    below to see it:")
        Call rtitem.AddNewLine(1)
        Call rtitem.AddNewLine(1)
        Call rtitem.AppendDocLink (doc, doc.Subject(0))
        newdoc.Subject = "New QA Problem Report: " + doc.Subject(0)
        newdoc.SendTo = doc.ProgrammerName
        Call newdoc.Send (False)
2   Elseif doc.ProblemStatus(0) = "Need More Info" And CurrentProblemStatus <>
    "Need More Info" Then
```

Listing 7.2   Code for Response QuerySave event (continued)

```
    Set newdoc = New NotesDocument(db)
    Set rtitem = New NotesRichTextItem (newdoc, "Body")
    Call rtitem.AppendText("A programmer has requested further information
or testing on the one of your problem reports in the Quality Assurance
database. Double click on the link below to see it:")
    Call rtitem.AddNewLine(1)
    Call rtitem.AddNewLine(1)
    Call rtitem.AppendDocLink (doc, doc.Subject(0))
    newdoc.Subject = "New QA Problem Report: " + doc.Subject(0)
    newdoc.SendTo = doc.From
    Call newdoc.Send (False)
End If
```

Tip

In any database that sends mail, you need to have a default view. If you don't, you will get a rather mysterious "Can't locate default view column name" error when you save the document and send the mail. Fortunately, once you know how it is easy to fix:

1 Click on Design|Views, and double-click on the ($All) View to open it in design mode.
2 Select the Design|View Properties menu. Press the Options tab.
3 Select the first option, Default when database is first opened.
4 Save and close the view.

Listing Notes

1 An email notification is sent to the programmer when a new problem report is entered. The email contains a link to the new QA document.

2 If the problem status has been changed to Need More Info since the document was opened, then the person who reported the problem is notified by email.

The basics of your QA database are now complete. Programmers can submit new templates for QA testing, and your users can submit bug reports and feature requests for it. No one has to monitor the QA database manually, because all important additions and changes to the QA database automatically notify the appropriate user by email.

You should clean up the All Documents view so that it shows buttons appropriate for QA:

1 Click on Design|Views, and double-click on the ($All) View to open it in design mode.

2 Select the View|Action Pane menu.

3 Double click on the New Main Topic action and change its title to `Add New Database Template`.

4 Double click on the Response action and change its title to `Add a Problem Report`.

5 Save and close the view.

7.5 Groupware views

There are a number of views you can add to the QA database to make it easier to use for the software development team. First, it's a good idea to add a graphical icon column that shows the status of problem reports.

1 Click on Design|Views, and double-click on the ($All) view to open it in design mode.

2 Click on the column to the right of the Date column and select the Create|Insert New Column menu.

3 In the programming pane select Formula, and enter the following code:

```
@If(Form != "Response"; 0;
ProblemStatus="Need More Info";160;
ProblemStatus="Being Worked On";34;
ProblemStatus!="Problem Resolved"; 81;
82)
```

4 Select the Design|Column Properties menu.

5 Select the option Display values as icons. Close the properties window.

6 Click on the right side of the new column and drag its size down to one or two characters wide.

7 Save and close the view.

The view will show icons that represent the status of problem reports, as shown in figure 7.3.

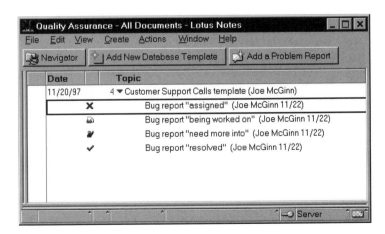

Figure 7.3   The QA view with Status icons

You can make the quality assurance database easier to use by creating specific views for programmer and QA administrator. For example, you can make a view for programmers to view only the database templates that they have authored.

1 Select the Create|View menu.

2 Name the view Your Problem Reports. Select the Share and "Personal on first use" options.

3 Press the Options button. Select the All Documents view and press OK.

4 Press OK again. Select Design|Views, and double-click on the "Your Problem Reports" view.

5 Click on the View area, so that the programming pane shows View Selection.

6 Click on Formula, and enter the following code:

```
SELECT (@Contains(ProgrammerName; @UserName))
```

7 Save and close the view.

A useful view for the QA administrator would be categorized by problem report status, so that it's easy to see which items need attention.

1 Click on Design|Views, and click on the By Category View (but don't open it).

2 Select Edit|Copy, then Edit|Paste.

3 Double-click on the Copy of By Category view to load it in design mode.

4 Select the Design|View Properties menu, and name the view By Problem Status.

5 Click on the left-most column, and select the ProblemStatus field in the programming pane.

6 Click on the Topic column and the select Create|Append New Column.

7 In the programming pane select Formula, and Enter the following code:

```
@Name([CN]; ProgrammerName)
```

8 Double click on the column header and enter Programmer Name as the Title.

9 Save the view but don't close it yet.

You'll want to change the selection criteria so that only problem reports show up in this view.

1 Click on the View area, so that the programming pane is showing View Selection.

2 Press the Add Condition button. Select By Form Used, click on the Response form, and press OK.

3 Save and close the view.

Your quality assurance administrator can use this view to analyze and manage problem reports. You may want to update the database's navigator to include buttons or icons for these new views.

7.6 Quality assurance roles

To conclude this chapter, let's summarize how the various members of your software development team contribute to the quality assurance process.

7.6.1 Procedures for programmers

First, the programmer's role. When you have a new database that is ready for testing, the first step is to convert it to a database template.

1 Select the database and press File|Database|New Copy. Change the filename suffix from NSF to NTF. Select OK to save the new template.

2 Select the database and select File|Database|Properties.

3 Click on the Design tab, and select the option Database is a template.

4 On that same tab, fill in the Template Name with a name for the template(e.g., Support Calls for the call logging database).

5 Open the Quality Assurance database and select Add New Database Template. Fill in every field in the Database Template Details section. Leave the Status at its default, Being Tested. The QA administrator will be notified about the new database template.

6 When bugs are reported to the database, the programmer of the template will be notified by email. When you are working on a problem, set its status to Being Worked On. This will let the QA administrator and customer support staff know what's happening. When you resolve a problem, change its status to Problem Resolved. If you need more information from the person who entered the report, change the status to Need More Info—the person who entered the report will be notified by email.

> **Tip**
>
> It is a good idea to create a separate tab on your workspace for the templates you have submitted to QA, so that you always make all code changes to the templates themselves.

7 When all outstanding tasks, testing, and bug fixes are complete, change the status on the Main Topic document to All Tasks Complete.

Note: Once you convert a database to a template, the template becomes your current source code. The old database used during development should be deleted (to avoid confusion), and all new testing databases must be created directly from the template. Any changes to the source code are done to the template, as they will then be replicated out to all testing databases.

New Versions: Once a template has been marked Database In Production, do not make source code changes to the database for any reason. If you need to implement bug fixes or new features, make a copy of the template and add a new QA document having a new version number. Any new revision, even a bug release, must be released through the QA process as a new database template.

7.6.2 Procedures for testers

Testers will use the quality assurance database when they have discovered a problem with a database, or when they want to record a new feature request.

1 Open the Quality Assurance database and select the document for the database you are working on. Then press the Add a Problem Report button.

2 Under Report Type, select whether this is a Bug Report or a Feature Request, or an item that needs To Be Documented.

3 Under Steps to Reproduce, enter the exact steps needed to reproduce the problem. If necessary, include graphics or document links to your test data.

4 Save and close the document. The programmer is automatically notified of the report just entered. The programmer will update this document when he or she resolves the problem. If the programmer needs more information to solve the problem, the tester is notified by email.

7.6.3 Procedures for quality assurance administrators

It is the responsibility of the QA administrator to make sure that all problems and features requests are resolved correctly.

- The QA administrator will receive email when a programmer adds a new template to the QA database. You must make sure that the necessary testing resources are applied to testing the template.

- QA will also be notified when a programmer changes the status of a template to All Tasks Complete. When satisfied that the new programmer status is correct, change the QAStatus to Verified.

- When the database template begins being distributed, change the QAStatus to Database In Production. At this point it is also very important that you make a backup of the database templates. Actually, you should make at least two backups—one stored on-site and one off.

Once a database template has been marked In Production by the QA administrator and backed up, it (or databases created with it) can be distributed to users. If further changes/enhancements are needed in that same database, you must create a new copy of the template, and begin the QA process again with a new version number. Each new release and new version must go through the same QA procedures. And once a template is moved to production, it should not be modified by anyone. (Your backups help ensure this.) All bug fixes and changes should be made to a separate copy, so that you always have a copy of each database and each version you release. You never know when you'll need an old version for support reasons.

7.7 Summary

You have learned how to use Notes templates to distribute Notes applications, and how to apply security to databases with the ACL. The basic principles and benefits of quality assurance were presented. You've built a quality assurance database, and learned how to add groupware features to a database using email notification. You have learned how to add useful views for a groupware database, and you have learned about the QA roles of the members of a software development team.

Tip

For your next few projects, you may want to use the tutorial as a guide, skimming through to the parts that you need for each application. Once you learn which techniques and parts you like to have in all your applications, it can be a real time-saver to pull those features into a Notes template to use as a base for your future projects.

Internet
programming

Part 3 covers everything you need to know about Internet programming using Lotus Notes. Chapter 8 introduces Domino, the Notes Internet server, and the Domino templates, and discusses some of the other issues to consider when programming for the Net. Chapter 9 shows you how to use the Domino templates to set up a complete, interactive Web site.

Chapter 10 shows you how user names and security are implemented for Internet applications. In chapter 11, we'll look at advanced user interface programming and getting input from a Web user. And last, in chapter 12, I'll show you how to create intelligent Internet applications by adding LotusScript agents to your application.

All of the instructions in Part 3 are based on using Notes 4.5 and the Domino 1.5a server. If you have older versions of Notes and Domino, you should download the latest one from the Domino Web site:

```
http://www.notes.net/welcome.nsf
```

C H A P T E R   8

Introduction to Internet programming

Lotus Notes is a platform-independent programming tool. This means, for example, that you can develop your application under Windows, and it can be run on a Macintosh or UNIX computer. With the introduction of Domino, Lotus has added the Web as the latest platform on which you can run your Notes applications. This means that users can run your application through Web browsers like Netscape or Microsoft's Internet Explorer, without the Notes client. You have access to the full spectrum of Notes tools—views, documents, forms, navigators, and hypertext links—for creating your Internet applications, making Notes the most powerful and easy-to-use Internet development system available.

In this chapter, you will learn about:

- Domino, the Notes Internet server. You'll learn how Domino works, and how it provides the most complete solution for delivering dynamic content over the World Wide Web.

- The differences between developing for native Notes clients and for the Web. We'll carefully look at both programming languages, forms, views, fields, and navigators so you know exactly what you can and can't do on the Web.

- The programming issues that arise due to the nature of the Internet (e.g., the fact that it is a relatively slow network, and what this means to you as a Web application developer).

- Ways of overcoming Internet networking issues, such as comparing delivery of text versus graphical information.

- How you integrate other Internet programming standards into Notes programming, such as Hyper Text Markup Language (HTML).

8.1 Domino

Domino is the Notes Internet server. Domino runs as part of your Notes server, and converts your Notes application to HTML in real time. HTML is the Internet protocol with which Web browsers like Netscape interact. Netscape sees the HTML data as standard Web pages, and is not even aware that there is a Notes server behind the scenes supplying the content. Figure 8.1 shows how Domino supplies data to a Web browser.

Domino has many advantages over other Web development tools, advantages which will save you a great deal of time and money in implementing your Web site. Most Web tools operate under a word processing paradigm. You create pages (i.e., files) one by one, marking them up with text and graphics, and then you manually create links between them. As you can imagine, this quickly becomes difficult to maintain even

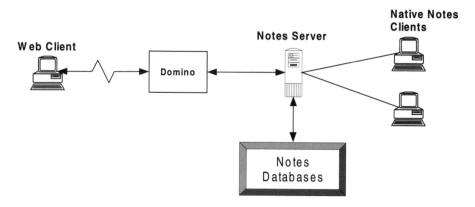

Figure 8.1   Notes server with Domino

for a modest Web site. And, then if you want to do anything interactive, you have to learn complex scripting languages like CGI just for developing the user interface. Domino, on the other hand, is a Web server designed to deliver dynamic, interactive content and applications to the Web user.

With Domino you have all the built-in high level capabilities of Notes. Links, for example, are created simply by using the Edit|Copy as Link menu on any Notes document, view, or database. Not only are links easy to create, they are also maintained by Notes automatically. This means that if you move a Notes document or database the link remains functional, whereas old-fashioned HTML-based manual links are dependent on filenames, and so can be broken just by moving or renaming a file.

Another major benefit of Domino is user interface access through Notes forms. You develop Internet forms just as you do Notes forms, using the interactive Notes form designer. You don't have to learn complex scripting languages like Common Gateway Interface (CGI) just to get a bit of input from the user. Users can create new documents or edit existing ones, just as if they were using a native Notes client. For example, see the Notes new user registration form in figure 8.2. In figure 8.3, we see the same form displayed in Netscape.

Almost as important as user interface access is that your Domino applications have full access to the object-oriented Notes database format. When Internet users create or edit documents, they are stored directly on your server as standard Notes documents. This is an enormous time saver, as previous generation net tools usually don't even have a database format. You would have to input information through CGI, and then most likely get out your C compiler or Visual Basic to write code that can save the data to a database file. Using Notes, you not only get access to the database format, but it is

New - Lotus Notes
File Edit View Create Actions Text Window Help
Registration Form
When you're finished filling out this form, click the submit button on the bottom. Thanks.
Fields marked with ★ are required.
First Name: ★
Middle Initial:
Last Name: ★
Internet E-mail: ★
Username: ★
[<Size = 40 Maxlength=80>]
Server

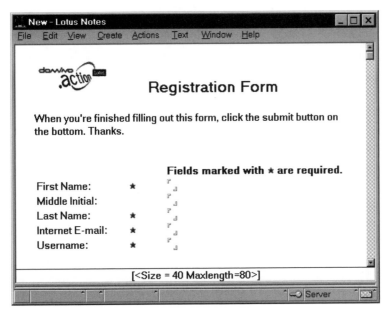

Figure 8.2 A Notes form

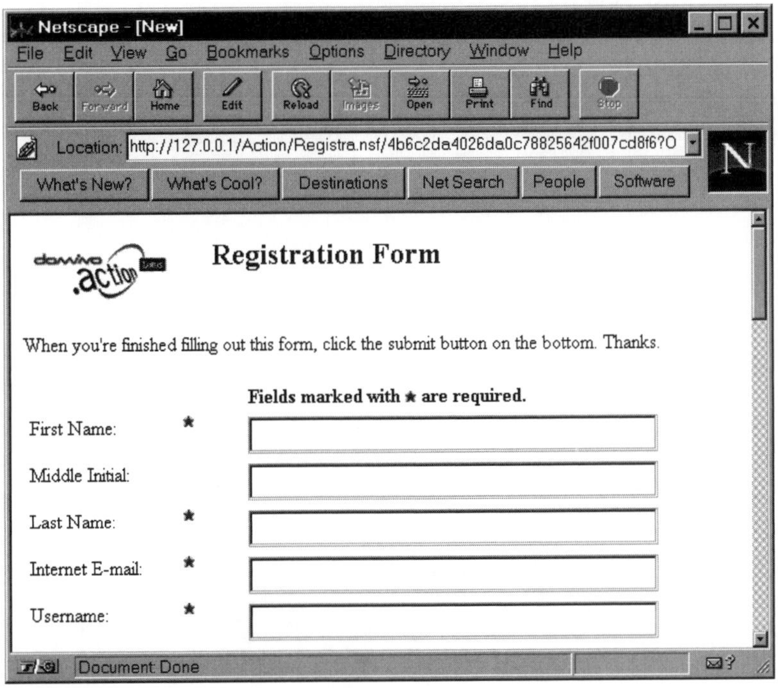

Netscape - [New]
File Edit View Go Bookmarks Options Directory Window Help
Back Forward Home Edit Reload Images Open Print Find Stop
Location: http://127.0.0.1/Action/Registra.nsf/4b6c2da4026da0c78825642f007cd8f6?O
What's New? What's Cool? Destinations Net Search People Software
Registration Form
When you're finished filling out this form, click the submit button on the bottom. Thanks.
Fields marked with ★ are required.
First Name: ★
Middle Initial:
Last Name: ★
Internet E-mail: ★
Username: ★
Document: Done

Figure 8.3 A Notes form in Netscape

virtually automatic. For example, to create a new document you simply issue a standard Notes compose command (e.g., telling Notes with which form to compose). Domino displays the user interface, and automatically saves the resulting data as a Notes document on your server.

You are not limited to form-based user interfaces, of course. You also have full access to views, calendar style views, and navigators in Web-based Notes applications. This means that your Domino Web site can be used to manage large volumes of hypertext-related documents, all with no programming. For example, figure 8.4 shows a calendar style view as seen through Netscape. All the view links—the hypertext jumps to documents and items in the view—are automatically maintained just as if the calendar were being viewed in the native Notes client.

By combining user interface access to views and forms, Notes database access, and some of the Notes templates, Domino allows you to have fully interactive threaded discussion databases on your Web site, as you can see in the example from the Domino Web site in figure 8.5. Document management and interactive databases like discussions

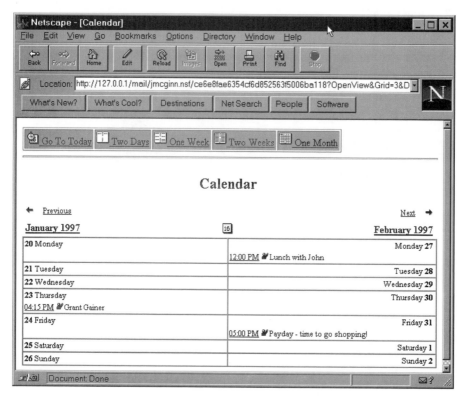

Figure 8.4 A calendar view in Netscape

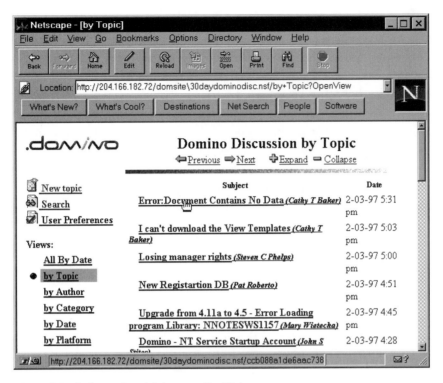

Figure 8.5   A discussion database on the Web

are extremely difficult to accomplish using traditional Internet tools; both were beyond the scope of any but the largest companies.

Domino applications also have access to Notes' powerful full text searching, with automatic (i.e., server-based) indexing.

With the advantages I've outlined so far, you are already miles ahead of competing Internet development tools, but Domino doesn't stop there. Notes is a true client/server tool, and you have the ability to make your Internet applications "intelligent" by taking advantage of this. Specifically, you can create LotusScript agents that run on your server to process documents that Web users have input or modified. One example of this (which I'll discuss in more detail later) is the registration database that is included with the Domino templates. The database allows Web users to register with user names and passwords for access to secure areas of your site. When a Web user adds his or her user name for the first time, a LotusScript agent on your server runs which copies the user name document into your Notes NAB (Name and Address Book) and automatically sets up the Internet password and other necessary information, so that the new user's registration is properly integrated into the Notes security system.

That brings us to the last (but certainly not the least) major benefit of Domino—security. Here is where Domino really shines, as it provides for all of the security needs for Internet applications. First, the Public NAB provides features for storing Internet users and passwords, either as individuals or groups. Then the ACLs for databases provide you with a high level of control over each database.

You can define anonymous access, to indicate how you want unregistered users to be treated for any database. (For example, you can give anonymous users read-only access, or depositor-only access.) You might allow anonymous users to deposit documents in a comments or feedback database, but you could require a registered user name for access to your online discussion databases. Just as in regular Notes databases, you can control access rights at the database, form, or field levels. You can define access based on user roles or groups. You can even present a different user interface depending on whether your application is accessed via the Web or the full Notes client.

Domino also supports the Secure Sockets Layer (SSL) that is used for server authentication and for encrypting data. This is very important for sensitive applications, since the Internet is a public network and you must assume that all Internet traffic is visible to anyone who really wants to see it. Encryption ensures that unauthorized users will not be able to interpret or read any data they intercept. I'll cover Domino security in more depth in chapter 10.

8.2 Web client versus full Notes client

Despite the power of Domino, there are still some limitations for Web-based Notes applications, compared to Notes applications running on the Notes client. Web browsers do not offer as rich an environment as the Notes client, so some features are just not possible. Lotus is actively participating in future HTML standards discussions to make future Web browsers more capable.

The most obvious examples of limitations are formulas and LotusScript, the two Notes programming languages. Because these are both part of the Notes client, they are not directly available to Web clients like Netscape. I say *directly* because you can still access them via the server as agents. You just can't run client-based LotusScript code (e.g., a LotusScript agent attached to a button or form event); you have to run all Lotus-Script tasks on the server. There are Domino features to simulate some front end Lotus-Script features. For example, you can have an agent that is run to process a document as the user is saving it (i.e., simulating the Querysave Notes client event). In the remainder of this section, I'll outline the rest of the differences you have to keep in mind for Web applications.

8.2.1 LotusScript and agents

LotusScript is available on your server to be used as a client server tool with Web applications, but it is not available in the Web browser itself, which places some restrictions on the use of LotusScript in Domino.

- The agent option to run If Document Has Been Pasted and the option to run the agent against Selected Documents are not available. Neither document pasting nor document selection are applicable to Web browsers.
- Attaching LotusScript code directly to form events, buttons, and action bar items are not supported, since all of these options require LotusScript to execute on the client. You can accomplish many of these functions using Domino agents, however. See chapter 12 for more details.
- Certain form action bar items (such as Edit Document and Categorize) are implemented via *system actions* which are not available on the Web. You should use the equivalent @ function formulas to implement these items.

8.2.2 Formulas

Many @ functions work fine in Web applications, with the following exceptions. Basically, these are formulas that are normally executed on the client (not the server). They cannot be made available on the Web, because Web browsers do not have a Notes formula interpreter to be able to run them:

- `@Certificate`.
- All of the `@DDE` functions.
- `@DocMark` and `@DeleteDocument`. The concept of marked or selected documents does not apply on the Web.
- `@IsCategory`, `@IsExpandable`, and `@Responses`.
- `@DialogBox`, `@Picklist`, `@Prompt`, and `@IsModalHelp`. For accessing the user interface for Web users, see chapter 11.
- `@GetPortsList`.
- `@Environment`, `@SetEnvironment`, and the `ENVIRONMENT` keyword. You can access the Web browser's environment via CGI variables.
- `@MailSend`.
- `@Domain`, `@MailDbName`, `@MailEncryptSavedPreference`, `@MailEncryptSendPreference`, `@MailSavePreference`, and `@MailSignPreference`.

- `@IsAgentEnabled` (e.g., not applicable since Web agents must run on the server, not the client).

- `@IsDocBeingMailed` and `@IsDocBeingRecalculated`.

- `@URLGetHeader` and `@URLGetHistory`.

- `@UserPriviliges`.

The following formulas are available only in view and column formulas; you can't use them on forms or in other contexts:

- `@DocChildren`

- `@DocDescendants`

- `@Doclevel`

- `@DocNumber`

- `@DocParentNumber`

- `@DocSiblings`

There are a few formulas that are supported, but that work slightly differently on Web clients as listed below:

- `@Now`, `@Today`, `@Tomorrow`, and `@Yesterday`. You should avoid the use of time-based calculations in Computed When Composed-type fields. Such formulas may be updated more than once in a Web transaction, so your computations may not always do what you want.

- `@UserRoles` is supported. $$WebClient is appended to the list of roles.

- `@Platform` is supported, but it returns the server's platform, not the client's.

A special type of formula, the `@Command`, is used mostly for manipulating the Notes client user interface, and so is generally not supported on the Web. The following very useful `@Commands`, though, are supported for Web applications:

- `@Command([CalendarFormat]` and `@Command([CalenderGoto])`.

- `@Command([Compose])`. You use this command to compose a new document, to allow the user to enter new data. The server argument is not supported.

- `@Command([EditClear])`. This command deletes the current document, and is supported only in forms (not in view action bar items).

- `@Command([EditDocument])`. This command edits the current document (supported only in forms).

- `@Command([EditInsertFileAttachment])`. This command is supported, which allows Web users to attach a file to a Notes rich text field.

- `@Command([FileOpenDatabase])`. This command is supported, but the server argument must be the empty string `""`, as if you were opening a local database in the full Notes client.

- You can open a database to a specified document by using the format `@Command([FileOpenDatabase]; "":"Database Name"; "View Name"; "Document Key")`. This must be immediately followed by `@Command([OpenDocument])`.

- `@Command([NavigateNext])`, `@Command([NavigatePrev])`, `@Command([NavigateNextMain])`, and `@Command([NavigatePrevMain])`. These are supported only in forms, not views.

- `@Command([OpenNavigator])` and `@Command([OpenView])`. These are fully supported.

- Like opening a database, you can open a view to a particular document using `@Command([OpenView]; "View Name"; "Document Key")`, followed by `@Command([OpenDocument])`.

- `@Command([ViewChange])`.

- `@Command([ViewExpandAll])`, `@Command([ViewCollapseAll])`, and `@Command([ViewShowSearchBar])`.

8.2.3 Forms

Most of Notes form features, including subforms, are available for Web applications running on Domino. The following features do not apply, or are available with some limitations:

- Merge replication conflicts, version control, and anonymous forms do not apply in Web applications.

- The automatically refresh fields feature is not available.

- Fields that inherit their values from a parent document are supported, except for rich text fields.

- The form composition option to inherit an entire document into a rich text field is not available.

- Storing forms in documents is not available.

- The option to launch a document's first attachment, OLE link, or document link is not available.

The following major form features do not apply to the Web or have some limitations:

- File attachments are supported, but the form requires a hotspot action item (i.e., one that contains the `@Command([EditInsertFileAttachment])` formula), since the user doesn't have the File|Attach dialog as in the native Notes client.

- Buttons are not supported, except for a custom Submit button on a form. You can simulate buttons by combining a graphic element with an action hotspot.

- Graphics are supported. Domino uses a platform-independent 256 color format for displaying Web graphics, so it might look slightly different than it does in the Notes client. If you use graphics, be sure to test your application with a Web browser to make sure it appears the way you intended.

- Layout regions are not supported (Lotus plans to add layout regions or some similar construct to a future version of Domino).

- Hotspots are supported. (A hotspot is a region on the screen where the user can click to run a formula or action you have programmed). Popup hotspots (i.e., the type you might see to define a word) are not supported.

- ActiveX and OLE components are supported, for Windows95 and Windows NT clients only.

- Tables are supported, but you don't have quite the level of control over borders that you do in Notes. The entire table has the same border style as its top left cell.

8.2.4 Fields

Most field types and capabilities are supported on the Web, but there are a few exceptions:

- Keyword fields are supported, but the entry helper interactive dialog popup option is not.

- Name fields are supported, except for the Notes server and user interface options Use address dialog for choices, Use view dialog for choices, and Use Access Control List for choices.

- Computed when composed fields are supported.

- Default value formulas are supported, except for the option of inheriting a value from a selected document in a view. (That is, there is no equivalent of selected documents in a Web browser.)

A few field options are not supported at all:

- Compute after validation.
- Field help (i.e., the help string that appears in the Notes client when the user is entering data in a field).
- Field level encryption.
- The option Give this field default focus.
- Signed fields.

8.2.5 Views

Most of the following properties of views are available for Notes Internet applications:

- Calendar style views are supported, which provides you with a sophisticated way of presenting date-stamped information to Web users. Some advanced features are not supported—conflict bars, clocks, scrolling through entries of a single day, and creating new appointments.
- Multiline column headings and rows are supported. To disable this feature go into the view properties and set the options Lines per heading and Lines per row to 1. (You'll find these options in the view properties window under the S tab.)
- Folders are supported as a way to access documents, but Web users cannot drag new items into a folder.
- The view options for On Open and On Refresh (found in the Options tag) are not supported. Show in View menu is also not fully applicable, since Web browsers don't have a View menu (but it can be deselected to make a view hidden even in the folders navigator).
- A number of view style options are not available—Beveled column headings, Show selection margin, style options for unread rows, and Alternate row colors.
- The view indexing options are not applicable. A Web user must manually refresh views to get the latest information.

The following view column properties are unsupported or have some restrictions for Web use:

- The option Click on column header to sort is not supported.
- Resizable columns (where the column is expanded or shrunk by clicking and dragging with the mouse) are not available.
- Collapsed and expanded categories are supported (but only one category at a time can be expanded).

- The option to Show twistie when row is expandable is not applicable; twisties (the triangles on which the user clicks to expand a row) are always displayed on the Web, they cannot be hidden.

8.2.6 Formatting in forms and views

A number of options for formatting text and paragraphs in forms and views have some limitations:

- Aligning paragraphs as left, right, and centered is supported. The Full justification (text that is even on both the left and right margin) and No alignment options in forms are not supported.

- A number of formatting aids are not available in Web browsers; using tabs, indents, outdents, and spaces will not work. Use tables to align fields on a form. (You can turn off table borders if you don't want the users to see them.)

- Line spacing is supported, except for Interline spacing.

- Bulleted and numbered lists are supported.

- Type fonts are supported, but due to the limitations of HTML they may look somewhat different in Web browsers than in the native Notes client. Test all text styles with a Web browser.

- Text sizes are marginally supported; only seven sizes are available in HTML.

- Text styles are supported, except for Shadow, Emboss, and Extrude.

- Text colors are supported.

- Graphic images are supported, but may not be sized correctly in some Web browsers (i.e., depending on whether the Web browser supports scaling).

8.2.7 Navigators

You can and should use navigators to make your Internet applications more user friendly. The following restrictions apply to navigators on the Web:

- The option to auto adjust panes at runtime is not available.

- The options Highlight when clicked and Highlight when touched are not supported.

- Graphics are supported but only as a graphics background; graphics buttons are not supported. You must create the entire GUI for your navigator in a paint program, and then use hotspots in the Notes navigator designer to make it interactive.

- Hotspot polygons and rectangles are supported. Graphics buttons, ellipses, text boxes, and other kinds of hotspots are not supported.

- Folders in navigators are not really applicable, because Web browsers do not support drag and drop to add documents to a folder.

8.3 Speed of delivery

As you've seen, there are restrictions on Notes functionality on the Internet due to the limitations of current Web browser technology and the limits of the HTML standard itself. Nevertheless, Domino is far and away the most advanced and flexible Web server available for presenting dynamic, interactive applications on the Web. These capabilities must be used with care, however. As the old saying goes, this much power gives you "more than enough rope to hang yourself," if you do not use it wisely.

By far, the most important issue in the development of user friendly Internet applications is speed of delivery. This is not really an issue with native Notes applications because they are usually run either on a LAN which is very fast, or on a remote machine where Notes applications and data are run from a local hard drive after being replicated from a server.

Internet applications, in contrast, are usually run on an extremely slow network accessed over public phone lines. I'm sure you've experienced Web sites that are agonizingly slow, some so much so that you probably cut off the download and skip the site completely. There are few things more frustrating to a user than a slow computer program, and if your user is frustrated, then your application is not user friendly, no matter how pretty it looks.

One issue to keep in mind when planning a Domino site is that Domino is a Web server for presenting dynamic, interactive Web applications. Most Web servers are little more than file servers, serving up HTML files that are interpreted by the Web browser client. Domino converts Notes databases and objects to HTML and serves them up in real time; this is what gives you so many powerful features, like interactive views, document management, database access, and client server agents. You may have heard the expression *TANSTAAFL, There Ain't No Such Thing As A Free Lunch*, and as in most computer applications it applies to Domino, too. This just means that all this functionality is not free; you must provide enough computing power to drive your Web site effectively. You may want to consider getting a powerful UNIX box to act as your Domino Web server, or at the least you should get the fastest PC you can manage and load it up with lots of memory (minimum 64MB). Keep in mind that the money you spend on a good server for Domino is saved over and over again in the extremely low cost of developing and maintaining Domino applications, applications that would take weeks or even months longer to develop using old-fashioned Web tools.

Aside from having a good server, the other way to keep your applications lean and mean is to minimize the amount of data that you send down the Internet pipe. We'll look at the two ways to do this in the remainder of this chapter.

8.4 Text versus graphics

By far, the most common mistake in Web site development is including too much graphical information. It may be true that a picture is worth a thousand words, but remember that the purpose of most Web sites is to deliver information, not fancy images. There's nothing wrong with including a small company logo or graphic to spiff up your site or a form, but do not go overboard. I've seen too many Web sites that use a large graphic for information that could be just as effectively communicated with text—more effectively, in fact, since the end users quickly and painlessly get the data they want.

Having said that, Lotus has included an extremely important feature in Domino to make applications that use graphics work better on the Web. If you open up a database properties you will see a new option under the Basics tab—Display images after loading (see figure 8.6). In well-designed Web sites, you have probably noticed that the page layout and text are loaded first, and then graphics images are loaded in a second pass. The Display images after loading feature allows you to accomplish the same thing for Domino applications. Be sure to turn this option on for any databases you are delivering over the Internet via Domino.

Tip

You cannot use the Display images after loading property if your databases are being accessed with a Notes 4.0 or 4.1 client. It is only available to Notes 4.5 clients and Web browsers.

8.5 Native Notes versus inline HTML and CGI

Another way to improve the performance of Domino applications is to minimize the amount of work the server has to do. Any formatting, data, and user interface presentation done using standard Notes objects are converted to HTML in real time by Domino. If you have many users accessing your Web site at one time, this may slow things down. Domino supports both inline HTML and CGI. HTML is a presentation format, and CGI is a user interface standard that you can use to present dialogs and so on to the user. Both are interpreted by the client, not the server, so using them can reduce the

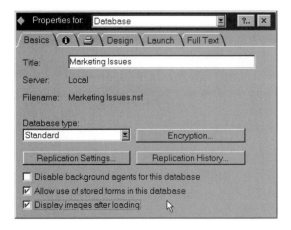

Figure 8.6   Display images after loading property

work load on your server, especially if there is a particular document or view that is used a lot on your Web site. You can also use them to access any features that the Web client supports that do not have an equivalent Notes structure supported by Domino.

8.6 The Domino templates

You may be starting to wonder how you're going to manage all this new Internet functionality. How are you going to tie it all together to create a useful Web site? If you had to do it all from scratch, it would be a lot of work, but fortunately the Lotus development team is one step ahead. They've provided a set of invaluable Domino templates that automates the process of creating and maintaining a complex Web site for your entire business.

8.6.1 Domino Action

The Domino Action template is a set of Notes templates that provide all the pieces you need to build a full featured corporate Web site:

- Home page.
- About The Company area.
- Policy and Procedure manuals.
- File download areas.
- Interactive discussion databases.
- Product and Services area.

- Job postings.
- Frequently Asked Question (FAQ) area.
- Document libraries.
- White papers.
- User feedback area.
- An automated Internet user registration database.

Domino Action does more than just provide the components of your Web site; it also provides all the necessary functionality to allow complete Web-based authoring. This means that authorized users can update areas on your Web site directly from their Web browsers. Changing text, graphics, and content on your pages is all done interactively on the Web and requires no programming. This is a major step in the evolution of Web development tools, as it allows the maintenance and growth of your Web site to proceed in an orderly fashion. For the first time, the maintenance of a Web site's content is separate from the more technical aspects of initial Web site construction and design. For example, you can allow your marketing and sales department, your public relations people, and product developers all to update the areas of the site for which they are responsible.

Among other benefits, this design allows you to maintain a consistent and standard look and feel across your entire site. It also allows you to manage authoring of your Web site in a secure manner, since only the users you specify as authors or contributors for an area are allowed to make changes (and they can change only the content, of course, not the design or format of the Web page itself).

Domino Action is also designed to automate workflow. You can assign content authors as distinct from content approvers, complete with automated email notification to keep the process flowing.

Last but not least, Action includes an automated Internet registration database. Your Web site can be set up to work with anonymous users, but it's also very useful to have the capability for registered users. This allows you to take advantage of Notes security; for example, you might require users to register before they see your price lists or certain product information. Registration also makes your discussion databases much more useful, since each message and response will include author information. Each registered user requires an entry in your NAB, including entries in the Internet address and HTTP Password fields (i.e., the user name and password Web users enter to identify themselves to your server).

With the Action registration database, you don't have to administer any of this manually. New users enter their names and passwords in a form, and then an agent is triggered on your server that automatically adds the appropriate document to your

NAB. Within a few hours, a new user can access your site as a registered user, without requiring any manual administration.

8.6.2 Domino SiteCreator

Domino SiteCreator is an extremely useful template that will save you an enormous amount of time. SiteCreator is an interactive application that completely automates the process of constructing a corporate Web site using Domino Action.

No programming is needed to use SiteCreator. You simply proceed through a number of forms, answering questions, and filling in the blanks, and then SiteCreator automatically generates your site. For example, in the first step you simply choose which sections you want your site to have and enter some basic information about your company, as shown in figure 8.7.

In just a few hours with SiteCreator, you can create a rich, interactive Web site that would take weeks or months to accomplish with competing tools. In the next chapter, I'll step you through this process of creating your company Web site.

Figure 8.7   Domino SiteCreator

8.6.3 Domino Merchant

Merchant is one of the most exciting developments to come out of the Domino team. Merchant allows you to add electronic sales and payment functions to your Domino Action site. This takes your Web site another level above an interactive site and allows you to conduct an almost entirely virtual business on the Net. Merchant provides all the pieces you need to conduct online commerce.

- Merchant provides a wide variety of means for conducting online transactions:
  - Electronic selling with secure credit card transactions using the Internet standard SSL so that all sensitive data are encrypted.
  - Support for the Cybercash system, which lets a user enter credit card information once and then use his or her Cybercash Wallet to make purchases.
  - Order routing to external approval and fulfillment systems. (For example, a purchase order can be automatically emailed to a credit approver.)
  - For intranet applications, integration with accounting systems to allow purchasing via purchase orders and a departmental charge-back system.
  - Support for delivery of no-fee items like product information, technical manuals, and so on.
  - Registration of your online store with the payment processing system.
- Merchant allows for automated delivery of electronic products such as software, so that no physical interaction or shipping is needed to deliver such products.
- For products that must be physically shipped, Domino can be integrated into your invoicing and shipping systems to allow for as much automation as possible.
- Domino Merchant allows distributed, secure web authoring of your product catalog. This means that your employees can update the product catalog directly using their web browser and any Internet connection.
- Different views of your products to different types of customers. For example, the prices of some products may be visible only to registered users.
- Domino Merchant provides tools to help you analyze your online store:
  - Customer surveys to help you gather information about your customers.
  - A full history of customer is maintained to allow a variety of reports for both you (i.e., demographics reports and analysis) and your customers. (For example, customers can look at their purchasing histories).
  - Order tracking reports to track orders for customer service purposes and for producing reports on pending orders.
  - Appropriate taxes are automatically calculated and added to the purchase price.

Predefined frameworks for common commerce like course registration and retail sales are provided. And, of course, prebuilt, professional-looking pages are provided to give your online storefront a consistent look and feel. Like Domino Action, all of this functionality is deliverable without custom programming, by integrating Merchant into the automated Domino SiteCreator. And Merchant is easy for your customers to use, with the provision of a *virtual shopping basket*.

Lotus and IBM are also exploring creative new ways of allowing businesses of any size to access Domino Merchant. As soon as it is feasible, they will provide Merchant as a *rentable application* for online businesses that are too small to afford their own server and Merchant application.

If you want to learn more about the Domino templates, including access to an interactive Domino discussion database, go to the Lotus Domino home page:

```
http://domino.lotus.com/
```

8.7 Summary

You've learned that Domino is a Web server designed to deliver dynamic, interactive World Wide Web applications. Much more than a simple Web server, Domino and Notes are a complete Web authoring and client server development environment, offering dozens of features not available in other Web tools. We've taken a detailed look at which Notes components and features can be used on the Web, and you've been introduced to some of issues involved in creating fast and effective Web applications.

In the next chapter, you'll create your first Domino Web site.

C H A P T E R   9

Creating a Domino Web site

In this chapter, I'll guide you through the process of creating your Web site. You'll be using two Domino templates, Action and SiteCreator. You'll learn how to:

- Install the Domino Web server.
- Use the Action and SiteCreator Domino templates to physically create your site.
- Set up your Name and Address Book Notes account for Web use.
- Set up your home page as the default starting location for incoming Web users.
- Initialize and maintain the content of your Web site.
- Create new hypertext links from your Web site to existing Notes documents, views, and databases. We'll cover both Notes-style links and HTML links.

You need the following hardware and software to complete this chapter:

- Notes 4.5 and the Domino 1.5a server. (If you don't have these I'll show you where to get them in the section on Installing Domino.)
- A Java-compatible Web browser, preferably Netscape 3.x or Internet Explorer 3.0. You can download these programs from the following Web sites:
  - Netscape Navigator: `http://live.netscape.com/cgi-bin/123.cgi`
  - Microsoft Internet Explorer: `http://www.microsoft.com/ie/download/`
- A computer that can run the Domino Notes server. The server can run on almost any platform that the client does, but it needs a lot more memory. I've found it quite comfortable doing Notes Internet development on a Pentium 200 PC with 48MB RAM under Windows95. You can get away with 32MB RAM, but with the Notes server, client, and a Web browser all loaded at once, you may experience a fair bit of disk swapping. If you have less than 32MB RAM, I strongly recommend that you acquire more memory.

9.1 Installing Domino

If you don't already have Notes 4.5 and the Domino 1.5a server, you should download them from the Domino Web site:

`http://www.notes.net/welcome.nsf`

You will have to register with the site to receive a password before you can download Domino. It will take a few hours for your registration to be processed. Once your account is up on the system, you can download Notes 4.5 and Domino 1.5a as a single file. It is about 35MB in size, which will take about six or seven hours to download for most Internet users, so you should probably start the download late at night before you go to bed.

Once you have downloaded the file, uncompress it by double-clicking on it. The install files will be put in a temporary directory (i.e., WINDOWS\TEMP for Windows users). Run the setup program from this directory by double-clicking on it. You may get a registry error warning message, which you can ignore. You will be prompted for your name and company, and then you'll see the Install Options screen. Select Customize features—Manual install, and then click on the Next button, as shown in figure 9.1.

On the Customize screen, make sure that Lotus Domino Server and the Domino.Action Templates items are selected, as shown in figure 9.2. You can deselect Notes Help Lite, as it is just a subset of the full programmer's Notes Release 4 Help. Click on Next, select a drive and directory to which to install, and proceed with the installation.

When the installation is finished, start Lotus Notes (not the Notes Server). You will be prompted for a password, and Notes will construct all your default files, such as your personal mail database and your server's Name and Address Book. Once these defaults have been set up, you're ready to try loading the Domino Server.

From the Notes folder run either Notes Server or Lotus Domino Server. (These both point to the same server program.) It will take a few seconds to initialize the server.

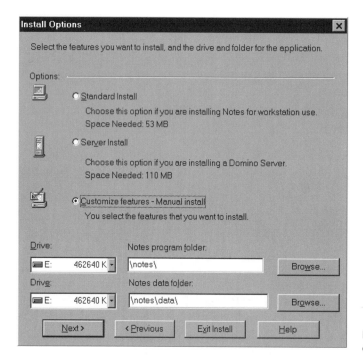

Figure 9.1 Install options

CHAPTER 9 CREATING A DOMINO WEB SITE

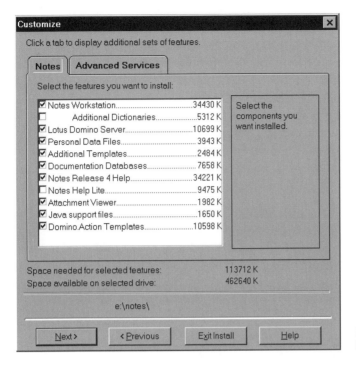

Figure 9.2 Customize installation screen

Once the server is up you have to start Domino by entering the following command in the server command window:

```
load http
```

You can unload Domino by typing:

```
tell http quit
```

You can also unload Domino when shutting down the server completely by typing:

```
exit
```

You can tell the Notes server you want Domino started automatically whenever the server starts by editing the NOTES.INI file, and adding the `http` protocol to the ServerTasks line, for example:

```
ServerTasks=Replica, Router, Update, Stats, http
```

Once the Domino server and the `http` service are running you should test the Domino server with your Web browser to make sure it's working correctly. All you have to do is load your Web browser and enter the following Web address:

`http://127.0.0.1/`

This is a special HTTP address that always points to your own computer. You do not need to be online with your Internet service provider to connect your Web browser to Domino. When you enter this address, you should see the a directory of your Notes databases on your server, as seen in figure 9.3.

Later in this chapter, once you've created your Web site, I'll show you how to configure Domino to automatically go to your corporate home page instead of to Notes server directory.

9.2 Creating your Domino Web site

Now that you have the Domino server, Notes 4.5, and your Web browser up and running, it's time to create your first site. You need to create two Notes databases, one based on the Domino Action template, the other based on SiteCreator. You may want to shut

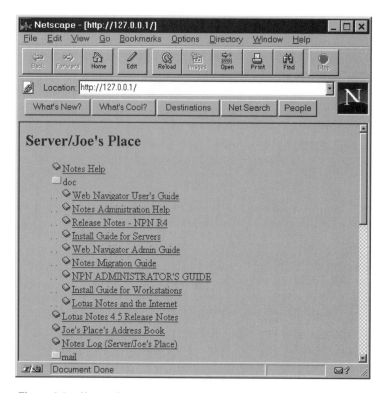

Figure 9.3   Notes directory via Web browser

down the Domino server (by typing `exit` on the server console) to preserve memory while generating your site.

1 Create a new database by selecting File|Database|New.

2 Under Title enter `LibAct`.

3 You should leave the File Name as LibAct.NSF, since that's the default filename for which SiteCreator will look when you construct your site.

4 Select the Domino.Action Library (1.0) template.

5 Click on OK to save the new database. You can close the Action database windows.

Now create the Domino SiteCreator database, as follows:

1 Create a new database by selecting File|Database|New.

2 Under Title enter `Site Creator`.

3 You can leave the File Name as SiteCreator.NSF.

4 Select the Domino.Action SiteCreator (1.0) template.

5 Click on OK to save the new database.

Read through the SiteCreator Overview document that is on your screen, then press the Launch Step 1 button at the bottom of this document (see figure 9.4).

You will now be in a document titled *Step 1: Configure Your Site*. Click on the Configure Your Site button to begin the configuration process. The first thing you must do is to decide which areas your site will include. Simply place a check in the boxes for the

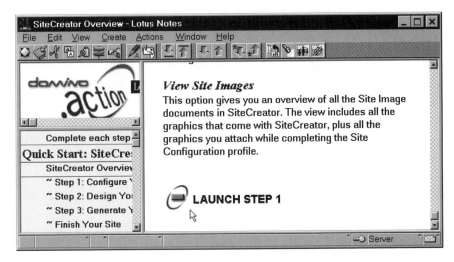

Figure 9.4   Launch Step 1 in the site creator

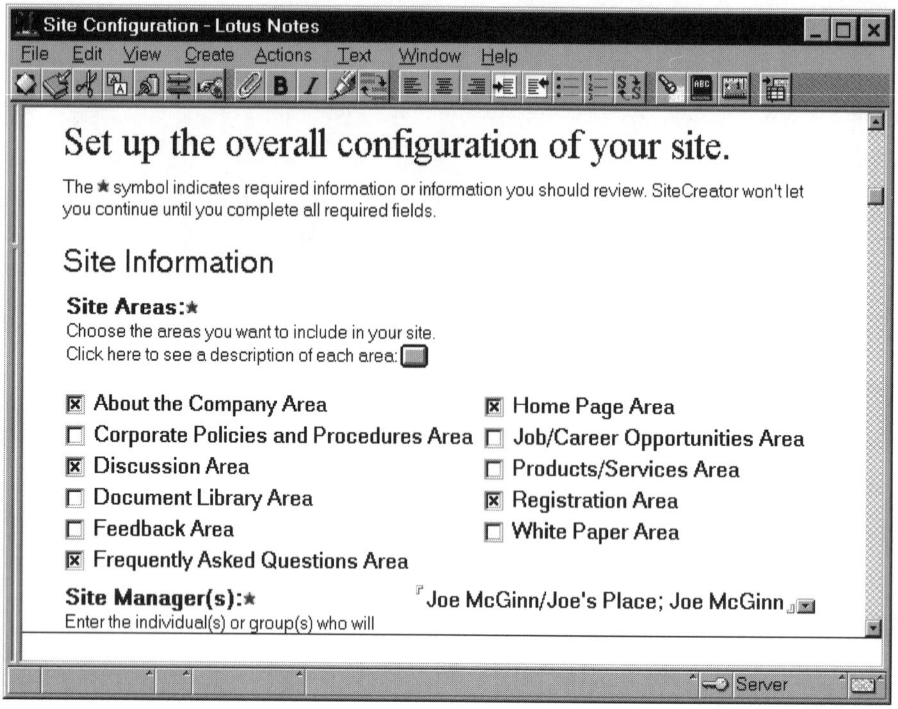

Figure 9.5 Select Web site areas

areas you want included, as shown in figure 9.5. You'll have to either double-click on the form once or press the Edit icon to put the site configuration document into edit mode.

Your user ID will automatically be filled in as the Site Manager, the person who has complete access to change any and all areas of the site, both the design and the content. If there are other people whom you also want to have this much access, just add them here (with semicolons between the user names).

Once you've selected the site areas, scroll down in the document until you see the company information screen (figure 9.6). Be sure to fill in this information as accurately and detailed as possible, as it will appear on many of your Web pages. (You can always make corrections and regenerate your site later on of course.) An important part of the configuration is the Attach Image button, shown in figure 9.6. This is where you attach graphics such as company logos or background images that you want to use in your site. For example, you can attach the Sandstone.bmp file from the Windows directory (for Windows95 users) as a background bitmap.

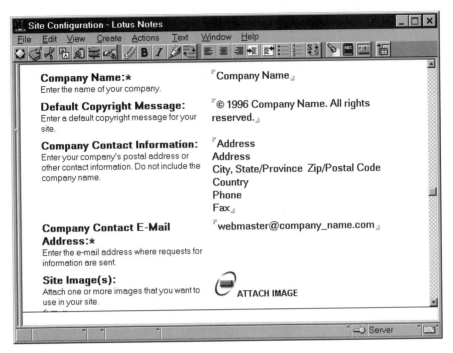

Figure 9.6   Company information and graphics

Once you have finished entering your company information and attached and imported your graphics files, scroll to the bottom of the document and click on the Continue icon (seen in figure 9.7) to proceed to *Step 2: Design Your Site*.

Scroll to the bottom of the Design Your Site document, and press the Custom Design button. SiteCreator will now ask you if you want to create the areas of your site, and for some details on each area. The first area you are asked to set up is the Registration Area. Internet users access this area to register a user name and password with your site.

Figure 9.7   Continue icon/button

Click on the Edit icon, and then click on Create under the Create This Area? question. Click on the Continue icon, and you will be asked for some more details about this page. Here you can design the look and feel of the page. For example, under Page Look there are two buttons, one that lets you choose from a variety of page styles, and another that lets you preview a graphic image of the page style you have selected, as shown in figure 9.8. You can also select the page's background color and image.

Figure 9.8   Page look preview

Click on the twistie (the little triangle) beside the word *Registration* to proceed with the Registration page setup. You can leave Registered Users Group at its default value. The Registration page needs to know the location of your Notes Name and Address book so that it can automate the registration process. The field defaults to NAMES.NSF, which should be fine as long as you didn't rename your public NAB when you installed the Notes server. If you have an Internet mail gateway address, enter it in the Internet Gateway Address field.

If you scroll down a bit further, you'll see an interesting section called Registration Custom Questions. Here you can enter customized questions that your site will present to a Web user when he or she registers with your site. This is a good example of how Domino Web sites are more interactive than traditional ones. For example, in figure 9.10 you can see the questions I've set up to ask visitors to my site about their levels of interest in *Inside LotusScript*.

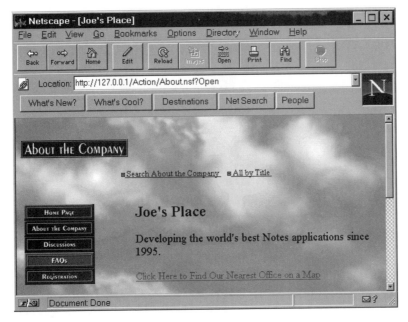

Figure 9.9 Page with a graphic background

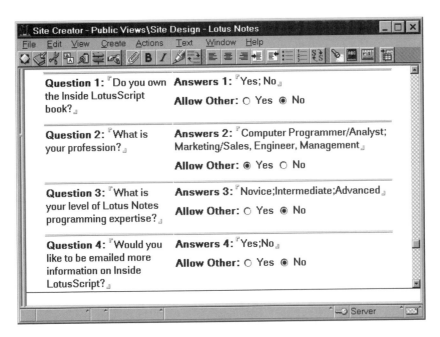

Figure 9.10 Registration custom questions

Now click on the Continue item at the bottom of the document to proceed to the security setup for the registration area. Edit the Content Composers field to add users who are authorized to edit the content of this page. (Your name will already be there as a default.) In the next field you can choose whether you want to allow anonymous access (i.e., access by unregistered Web users) to this page. You must leave this set to Yes for at least the registration page and your home page; otherwise, users will not be able to access the page to register. It's generally a good idea to allow anonymous access to all noninteractive parts of your Web site.

For interactive areas like the discussion database, you may want to require registration so that all messages posted include a user name. Or you can allow anonymous read-only access, and select No under the field Allow anyone to author. This means that anonymous users can read your discussion area but require a registered user name to enter new posts. Click on the Continue icon to finish setting up the Registration area and go on to the next area, setting up your home page.

For the home page, and for every other area you have selected to include in you site, you will go through the same process as you did for setting up the registration area—setting up the look and feel, security, and so on. On some pages you will have the option to set up content indexes. For example, in figure 9.11 I've added a few categories relating to this book for my discussion database.

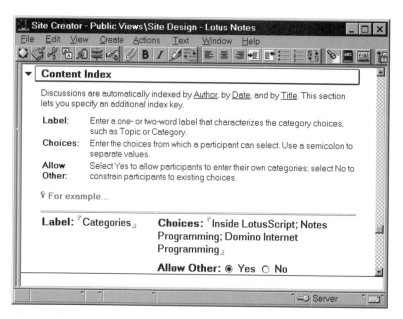

Figure 9.11 Discussion area content index

Once you have set up all the Web site areas on your site, it's time to generate your site. Scroll to the top of the document and click on the Generate Your Site icon. You will now see the *Step 3: Generate Your Site* document. Press the button at the bottom of your screen. SiteCreator will take a minute or two to set up some preliminary documents, and then you will proceed to the final step, Run AppAssembler. As it says on the bottom of the screen, it can take as long as an hour to physically generate your site, so once you press the Run button it might be a good time to break for lunch. Don't feel bad about the wait; if you were using competing Web tools, it would require several weeks or months of hard work to accomplish what SiteCreator will do while you eat your lunch! Press the Run button when you are ready to generate your Web site. After pressing this button you will be asked for your Notes password, so be sure to enter it before taking your break.

Once your site is generated, you must click on Finish Your Site in the SiteCreator navigator, and then click on the Finish Your Site icon. This may take another ten to fifteen minutes to run. This procedure applies some finishing touches to your site and makes sure that all your links are working properly.

9.3 Internet user IDs

Before you test your Web site, you have to set up your user ID in your Notes NAB. There are some special fields that have been added to the NAB where you have to enter your Web user name and password.

1 Open the NAB and click on the People view.

2 Double click on the person document for yourself.

3 Click on the Edit Person action bar button to put the document into edit mode.

4 In the Short name and/or Internet address field you can enter an abbreviated user name, such as your last name, that you can use to identify yourself to the Domino server from the Web.

5 In the HTTP Password field, as seen in figure 9.12, you must enter a password to use for Web browser access. This is the password you will enter when accessing your Web site using a browser. You may want to enter the same password you use for your Notes user ID so that it is easy to remember. Note that the password is encrypted on the screen so that it cannot be read by other users.

6 Click on the Save button, then close your person document and the NAB database.

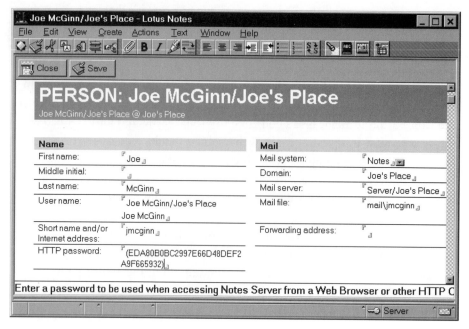

Figure 9.12   HTTP Web browser password

If your Notes server is already running, you should shut it down (using the `exit` command) and restart it to make sure it accesses your new password.

9.4 Testing Domino

Finally, it's time to test your Notes Domino web site by accessing it with a Web browser. First, start up your Notes server. If you haven't added the HTTP service to your NOTES.INI file, be sure to start HTTP by typing the `load http` command at the server console. Once your server is up and the HTTP service is running, start your Web browser (i.e., either Netscape or Microsoft Internet Explorer). You do not need to be connected to your normal Internet service provider; just ignore any warning messages your Web browser displays. Enter the following Web location:

```
http://127.0.0.1/
```

You should see a directory of your Notes databases, as shown in figure 9.3. If you don't, make sure that:

- Your Notes server is running.

- The Notes server HTTP service is running.
- In the server document in your NAB, look in the HTTP Server settings, and make sure the TCP/IP port number is set to 80, and that the TCP/IP port status is set to Enabled.

Once you have Domino and your Web browser working you can try browsing a Notes database, such as Notes Help. Note how all the basic Notes features—navigators, views, action bars, and documents—are all available through your Web browser, as shown in figure 9.13.

9.5 Creating a home page

Before you proceed to testing and initializing your Web site, you should set up a home page so that when you go to `http://127.0.0.1/` in your Web browser, your home page appears instead of your server directory.

1 Open your Name and Address Book.
2 Click on the Server twistie, click on the view named Servers, then double-click on your server document.

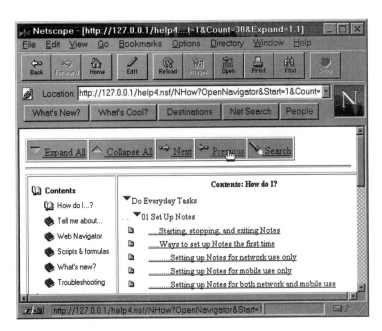

Figure 9.13   Notes help in a Web browser

3 Click on Edit Server, then expand the HTTP Server section.

4 Scroll down to the Mapping area, where you will see a field called Home URL. It should contain the text \?Open.

5 Enter Action\HomePage.NSF in the Home URL field, as show in figure 9.14. This is assuming you accepted the default home page database name, HomePage.nsf, and the default Web site directory, Action, when you configured your site in SiteCreator. If you changed either of these values, you'll have to change the location of your Home URL field accordingly.

Mapping	
HTML directory:	domino\html
Home URL:	Action\HomePage.nsf
CGI URL path:	/cgi-bin
CGI directory:	domino\cgi-bin
Icon URL path:	/icons
Path to icons:	domino\icons

Figure 9.14   Setting your Domino Home URL

9.6 Initializing your Web site

In your Web browser reload the http://127.0.0.1/ address. You need to initialize your Web site to "turn on" security. Because your home page is not yet initialized, you will get the Web user authentication screen seen in figure 9.15.

Enter your Notes user name and the HTTP password you entered in your person document. Instead of a listing of directories, you should now see your home page looking similar to the one in figure 9.16.

You have to visit, edit, and approve every area in your Web site. All of this is done directly from your Web browser, not the Notes client. To begin, click on the Edit/ Approve This Page icon on your home page. On the edit screen you can select a logo (i.e., if you added a company logo when going through SiteCreator), and set the Title and Subtitle text for the home page. Scroll down to the bottom of the edit screen and select the Process option. (Select Hold when you want to revisit the page later to finish your edits before the page is published.) The press the Submit button, as show in figure 9.17.

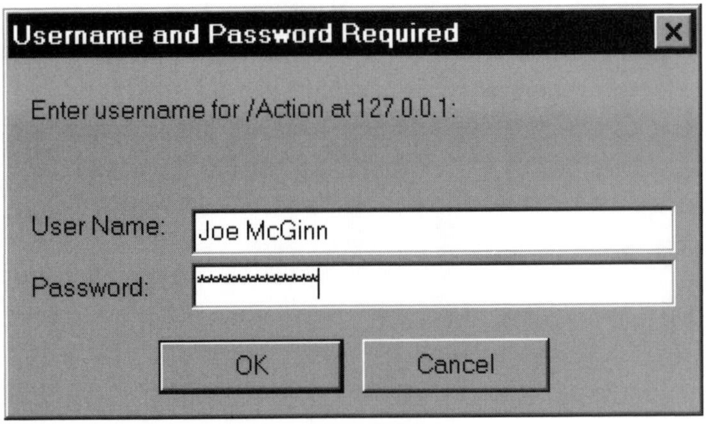

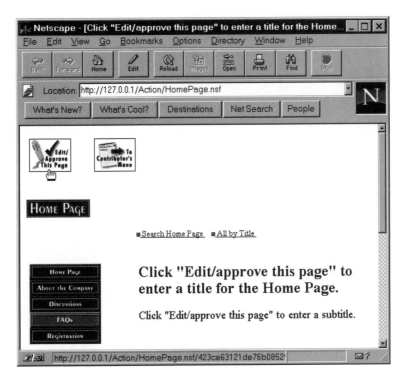

Figure 9.15 Web user authentication screen

Domino will present a message telling you the page is now available to the public, and then allow you to select a new area or return to the page you have just submitted.

Figure 9.16 Initial home page in Netscape

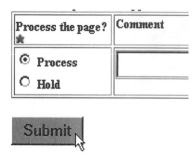

Figure 9.17 Process and submit your home page

That's all you have to do to publish a page; your home page should now look something like the completed page in figure 9.18.

You don't have to do anything to enable the graphical hypertext links to other parts of your site; they are all set up automatically by SiteCreator. Use the hypertext links on your home page to visit each area of your site, repeat the edit/approval process for each area, and your interactive, dynamic Web site is finished!

9.7 Creating hypertext links

One of the biggest challenges in traditional Internet programming is creating and maintaining hypertext links. Links are done manually by saving filenames and then creating URL links to them. Maintaining such links can be quite a hassle, because the link will be

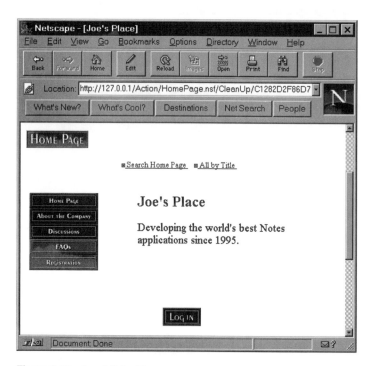

Figure 9.18 A published home page

broken if you change a filename. When a site gets large enough, it becomes very difficult to maintain, and errors—like broken links, for example—become common.

Fortunately, with Notes and Domino hypertext links are maintained without depending on physical details like filenames. You create links just as you would in Notes, using the Edit|Copy As Link command. And once pasted, the link is maintained via an object's Universal ID, which always remains constant, even if you physically move the object (i.e., document, view, etc.) on your disk. All links are maintained automatically by Notes and Domino, so you never have to worry about broken hypertext links.

You've created a complete Web site through the Domino Action SiteCreator template. Now, let's say that you have another database that contains the locations of your companies offices, and you want to link it to your About the Company page so that Web users can find the nearest office in their own states. First, we'll create an office location database based on the Discussion template. (We're not creating a discussion database here, but the Discussion template is a good starting point for a general purpose Notes database.)

1 Create a new database by selecting File|Database|New.

2 Under Title enter `Office Locations`.

3 Under File Name enter `Offices`.

4 Click on the directory icon beside the filename.

5 Select the Action subdirectory (i.e., the directory that contains your Web site) and press OK.

6 Select the Discussion (R4) template.

7 You must deselect the option Inherit future design changes.

8 Click on OK to save and open the new Customers database.

You'll want to create a graphical navigator showing the states on which users can click. For this you'll need a bitmap of your country. For the USA and Canada there are bitmaps included on the *Inside LotusScript* CD (USA.PCX and CANADA.PCX). If you are from another country, boot up your Web browser and go to the Alta Vista search engine at:

`http://www.altavista.digital.com/`

Enter `map countryname` as the search criteria and press Submit. Here you'll find a large selection of graphics images of your country. If you have a screen capture utility, use it to capture a map into a graphics format you can use on your computer. If you don't have a utility to capture images, go back to Alta Vista and search for `screen capture shareware download`, and you will find a large variety of shareware capture programs for all platforms. (You can add your operating system to the end of the search parameters to narrow it down.)

Now you are ready to create your graphical navigator in the Office Locations database.

1 Load your country bitmap into a graphics program, and use the text drawing tool to add the following text to the map (try not to cover up any states):

`Click on your state to find the office nearest to you!`

2 Save the image, then copy it to the clipboard using Edit|Copy. (You may have to use Edit|Select All or manually select the area of the image first.) Close the graphics program.

3 Open the Office Locations database. Use the New Main Topic button to create a document for each of your offices.

4 In the Office Locations database click on Design, Navigators, and select the Create|Design|Navigator menu.

5 Click on Design|Navigator Properties and enter `Country Map` as the name of the navigator. Select the option Auto adjust panes at runtime.

6 Select the Create|Graphic Background menu, and the map of your country will appear.

7 Use the Create|Hotspot Polygon menu to put hotspots around all the states in which you have offices. In the programming pane for each hotspot, you want to run a simple action—under Action select Open a Link.

8 For each office document you entered into the database.

   • Select the document for a given state in the All Documents view, and select Edit|Copy As Link|Document Link.
   • Go into the Country Map navigator, select the hotspot for the corresponding state, and press the Paste Link button in the programming pane.

Now it's time to create the link from your About the Company area to the graphical Country Map navigator. The first thing to do is set up the database launch properties so that the graphical navigator you created is opened when the user clicks on the link to it. You'll also have to set up the Access Control List so that anonymous Web users can access the map.

1 Close the Office Locations database. Click on the database on your workspace and select the File|Database|Properties menu.

2 Select the Launch tab. Under On Database Open select Open designated navigator, and then under Navigator select Country Map, as shown in figure 9.19. Now, when

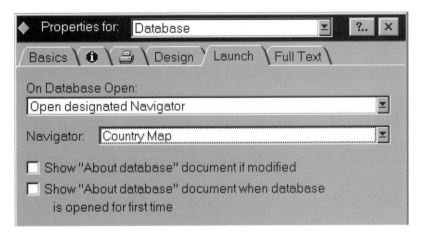

Figure 9.19 Database launch properties

you create a link to this database from your Web site, the Country Map navigator will open automatically.

3 Close the database properties window, and select File|Database|Access Control.

4 Press the Add button to add a new user. Type in a user named `Anonymous`, and make its Access type `Reader`, as shown in figure 9.20. This will assure that anonymous Web users have appropriate access to this database.

Now you will create the Office Locations link itself in your Domino Web site. Your Domino Web site links are HTML-based, because all site authoring is currently done

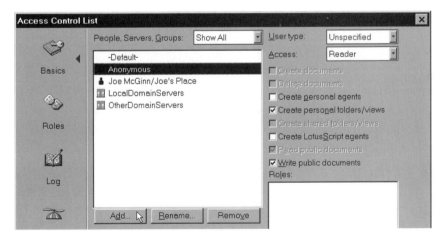

Figure 9.20 ACL for anonymous access

from Netscape. (Lotus is working on a new version of the Notes client so that the site can be edited by either a Web browser or the Notes client—check the lotus Web site at www.lotus.com to see if this is available yet.)

1 Make sure your Domino server is running, and then open your Web browser and point it at Domino on your system (http://127.0.0.1/—this will open your site home page).

2 You must press the Log In button at the bottom of this page, so that Domino will recognize your user ID and display the contributor buttons (Edit/Approve This Page, etc.) at the top of the Web pages.

3 Click on the About the Company link to go to your company description page.

4 Click on Edit/Approve This Page.

5 Enter the following HTML hypertext link code into the Web page content field:

```
[<a href=/Action/Offices.nsf?Open>Click Here to Find Our Nearest Office on a
Map</a>]
```

6 Scroll to the bottom of the page, click on Yes under Republish This Page, and press the Submit button.

Go to the published About the Company page, and you will see that you now have a hypertext link to the Office Locations database, as shown in figure 9.21.

When users click on this link, they will see the Country Map as shown in figure 9.22.

When the user clicks on a state, he or she will go to the document that you linked to that state. You should probably provide a way for the user to get back to your home page from the document. The easiest way to do this is with a database link to your home page in an action bar.

About the Company

▪ Search About the Company   ▪ All by Title

Joe's Place

Developing the world's best Notes applications since 1995.

Click Here to Find Our Nearest Office on a Map

Figure 9.21   Office locations hypertext link in Netscape

Figure 9.22 Country map navigator in Netscape

1 Open the Office Locations database. Click on View|Show|Folders so that you can see the design elements.

2 Click on Design|Forms, and double click on the Main Topic form to open it in design mode.

3 Select the View|Action Pane menu.

4 Double click on the Response action. (You don't need this action, so we'll modify it to use it as a return to home page action.)

5 Under title enter `Return to Home Page`. Under Button Icon select the letter `H`.

6 Close the properties window, and then replace the Compose formula in the programming pane with the following formula:

```
@Command([FileOpenDatabase];"":
"Action\\HomePage.nsf")
```

Note: You always specify the empty string as the server name for Domino Web site databases.

7 Save and close the Main Topic form.

Now, when a user clicks on a state on your country map, he or she will see a document similar to the one in

---

Tip

Here are some things you can do to clean up some little details in the Office locations database for Web use:

1 If you have a company logo graphic bitmap, you may want to edit the Main Topic form in the Office Locations database and replace the discussion logo with your company logo.

2 You may also want to remove the action bar items from the Main Topic form and from the All Documents view, since you don't want Web users to see these buttons in an information-only database.

---

figure 9.23, complete with a hypertext link to take him or her back to the home page. If you want, you can add more hypertext links in the same way—links back to the map, to the About the Company page, etc.

9.8 Domino universal resource locators (URLs)

In the previous section, you saw how an HTML hypertext link could be used to open a Notes database:

```
[<a href=/Action/Offices.nsf?Open>Click Here to Find Our Nearest Office on a
Map</a>]
```

The `Offices.nsf?Open` command is just one of the many extensions to Universal Resource Locators (URLs) that Domino supports. Using your Web browser, you can directly open any Notes object (i.e., database, view, form, document, navigator, etc.) by using these URL extensions. And as you've seen in the hypertext link above, these commands can also be included in an HTML hypertext link on a Domino Web page.

As in the example above, you can use a URL to open a database. The following URL opens the Offices.nsf database:

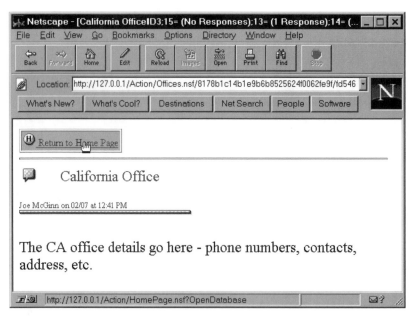

Figure 9.23 Form with link to your home page

```
http://127.0.0.1/Action/Offices.nsf?OpenDatabase
```

You can specify the full command—OpenDatabase—or just Open, which defaults to the appropriate open command for the object you are referencing. For example, the following two URLs are equivalent, and both open the By Author view in Offices.nsf.

```
http://127.0.0.1/Action/Offices.nsf/By+Author/?OpenView
http://127.0.0.1/Action/Offices.nsf/By+Author/?Open
```

Or you can create an HTML hypertext link to the All Documents view with:

```
[<a href=/Action/Offices.nsf/($All)/?OpenView>Click Here to go to the All Documents View</a>]
```

The other difference is that the Web browser doesn't know about special Notes objects like the All Documents view. In Notes, the All Documents view name is internally stored as ($All). This is done because Notes treats the All Documents view differently in the folders user interface (i.e., in the Notes client) to keep it apart from and above all other views. To reference the All Documents view from a Web browser you need to use its internal name; for example:

```
http://127.0.0.1/Action/Offices.nsf/($All)/?Open
```

The following list shows the other URL commands that are available to you:

- Open a form: ?OpenForm.

- Open a navigator: ?OpenNavigator.

- Run an agent on the server: ?OpenAgent.

- Open a specific document by specifying the Universal ID: ?OpenDocument. For example:

```
http://127.0.0.1/Action/Offices.nsf/AllDocuments/
ff863d8acb6e2210852561bd005867c7/?OpenDocument
```

- Open database about screen: $about. For example:

```
http://127.0.0.1/Action/Offices.nsf/$about
```

- Open database help screen: $help.

Tip

There are a couple of differences with using Notes object names in URLs that you need to be aware of. First, the URL syntax does not allow you to include a space; everything after the space gets ignored by the Web browser. Many Notes objects have spaces in their names, so you have to replace the spaces with plus signs. For example, I may reference the *By+Author* view in the URL, when the real name in Notes is *By Author*.

- Open database icon: `$icon`.

- Open a default search screen for a database: `$searchForm?`. For example:

```
http://127.0.0.1/Action/Offices.nsf/$searchForm
```

9.9 Summary

In this chapter you've learned how Domino works and how to install and set it up on your computer. You've created your first Domino Web site, set up your user ID to work over the Web, and tested accessing Notes and your Web site through a Web browser.

We've also gone through initializing your Web site and authoring content through a Web browser, setting up your default home page, and creating hypertext links between your Web site and a regular Notes database with a graphical navigator. We've covered hypertext links both as HTML and Notes document links.

In the next chapter we'll take a look Domino security, and you'll learn how to set up your Web site so that only authorized users can access the various parts of it.

C H A P T E R   1 0

Domino security on the Internet

One of the most important and powerful features of Domino is its wide range of security options for protecting your Web site against unauthorized access. The Internet is a public network, which means you cannot count on information that is sent over it remaining private. And, even if you are using Domino for an intranet (i.e., using Internet standards and software but on your own private network), you need a way of protecting sensitive information (e.g., salary figures in a personnel database).

In this chapter we'll look at all the security features available in Domino. You'll learn:

- How to create individual NAB person documents for Web users, including HTTP passwords to verify the identities of Web users.
- How to control database level access using Notes ACLs.
- How to handle anonymous users (i.e., users who are not registered in your NAB).
- How to secure individual views, forms, and fields.
- How to use the optional SSL to encrypt information that is transmitted over the Internet, so that anyone who intercepts it will not be able to read it.
- How Notes security differs from Domino Web security.

10.1 User registration

There are two ways of providing database access to Web users. You can set up your databases for default or anonymous access (we'll take a closer look at this in the next section), or you can create person entries for Web users in your Notes public Name and Address Book, just as you would for regular Notes users. Normally, you will use a mixture of both these techniques, for example, allowing anonymous access to your home page and other common pages, but perhaps requiring authenticated access for a discussion database.

A user will be challenged for a user name and password when he or she tries to access a restricted area or function. For example, you can allow a user anonymous access to read your discussion database but require a user name and password if he or she wants to post a new message. In this case, the user will not be asked for a password until he or she tries to compose a message. On the other hand, if you set up a database's anonymous security to "No Access" users will be challenged for a password as soon as they try to enter it.

Setting up the Internet Web fields in a person document in your NAB is quite easy. All you have to do is enter values in the User name and HTTP password fields, as shown

PERSON: Joe McGinn/Jo

Joe McGinn/Joe's Place @ Joe's Place

Name

First name:	⌐ Joe ⌐
Middle initial:	⌐ ⌐
Last name:	⌐ McGinn ⌐
User name:	⌐ Joe McGinn/Joe's Place Joe McGinn ⌐
Short name and/or Internet address:	⌐ ⌐
HTTP password:	⌐ (EDA80B0BC2997E66D48DEF2 A9F665932) ⌐

Figure 10.1   Web authentication fields

in the person document in figure 10.1. Note that once the password is entered, it is encrypted so that it can't be read by other users, even if they have access to the NAB.

Fortunately, Lotus has included a Registration database in Domino Action that automates the process of creating these Web user documents in the NAB, so you do not have to create them manually. The Web user simply enters a user name and password in a form (as shown in figure 9.15). An agent in the Registration database runs when new documents are added, and the agent creates all the necessary data in the NAB. Within an hour or two of registering, the new Web user's account is automatically set up on your site.

10.2 Access Control Lists

Access Control Lists are the fundamental building blocks of Notes security. In the ACL you can specify the level of access for both anonymous and registered Internet users. The first thing you do when setting up the ACL for a Web database is decide how you want to handle anonymous users. For example, on your home page you certainly want to allow anonymous access; otherwise, no one could get onto your site to register!

Setting up anonymous database access rules is very simple:

1 Click on the database (e.g., your home page database) on your workspace.

2 Select the File|Database|Access Control menu.

3 Press the Add button to add a new user, and type in the user's name as Anonymous.

4 Use the Access menu to select the type of access; for a home page, that would be Reader, as shown in figure 10.2.

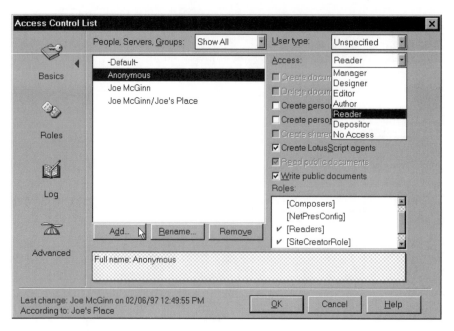

Figure 10.2 ACL for anonymous user access

If you do not create an Anonymous user in a Domino database, then the Default access for that database is used for Web users. For sites created using Domino SiteCreator, the default access will be assigned according to the options you selected when configuring the site. Here is a brief explanation of each security level you can select, starting with the least access:

- *No Access* The specified users cannot access the database at all.

- *Depositor* Users can create documents only; they cannot see any documents, even if they have created them. This is useful for customer surveys or feedback databases where the user fills out a form but does not have access to see documents in the database.

- *Reader* Users can read all documents, but they cannot create or edit documents.

- *Author* Users can read and create documents, and they can edit documents that they created. This is the most common access level used for interactive databases like discussion databases.

- *Editor* Users can read, create, and edit any documents. You will not normally give this access level to Web users. By default, this is the maximum access level allowed for Web users.

- *Designer*   Users can modify database design elements like forms and views. This level does not apply to Web users.
- *Manager*   A manager can basically do anything to the database, including editing ACLs. Again, this is not normally used for Web users, it is meant to apply to the "owner" of a database and perhaps one other person who has the authority to manage the database.

As an example, if you have a high security, confidential database you would set the Anonymous access and the Maximum Internet browser access to No Access, and carefully authorize individual users as readers and authors. For a slightly lower security (i.e., not confidential) project, you could set Anonymous to Readers. For a low security database, you might set Anonymous to Authors.

You can set the Maximum Internet browser access level for a database by clicking on the Advanced options, as shown in figure 10.3. This option allows you to specify the maximum level of access that will be given to any Internet user, regardless of the access rights assigned to the particular user. Normally, you would not change this from the default setting of Editor.

Using ACLs you should be able to accomplish most of your security needs.

10.3 Securing views, forms, and fields

If you need a finer level of control over database security, you can apply Access Control Lists to views and forms. For example, to secure a particular view, open it in design mode (Design|Views, double-click on the view) and select the Design|View Properties menu. If you click on the security tab (the tab with a picture of a key on it), you will see a dialog that shows all the users in that database's Access Control List. By default the All

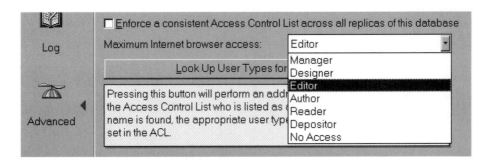

Figure 10.3   Setting maximum Internet access

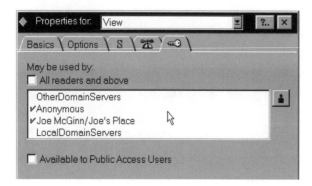

Figure 10.4   Customizing access to a view

Tip

There may be situations where you want to create a form for anonymous access that anyone can use without having a username recorded. To do this, select the Anonymous form checkbox on the form design properties, and remove all fields that calculate to the user's name.

readers and above option is selected, but if you deselect it, you can then specify which users you want to have access to the view, as shown in figure 10.4.

Similarly, you can edit a form and select Design|Form Properties. In the form properties window you can control who can read documents created using the form, and who can create new documents using the form, as shown in figure 10.5.

There are also security options at the field level. By selecting the option Must have at least editor access to use in the Security options for a field (figure 10.6) you can create a field that authors cannot edit. This can be useful, for example, if you have an area of a form that is only editable by a different user, such as a supervisor. This is the equivalent of the phrase *do not write in this area*, which often is seen on some areas of business forms.

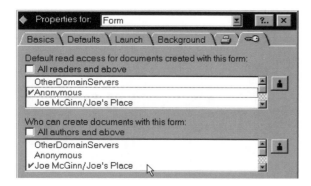

Figure 10.5   Customizing access to a form

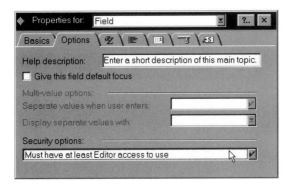

Figure 10.6   Customizing access to a field

10.4 Advanced security: secure sockets layer

The SSL is an Internet standard security protocol that provides a relatively high level of data security. When using SSL, Domino can encrypt data as they pass over the Internet between the Domino server and the Web browser client. This offers three main benefits for the Notes user transmitting sensitive data over the Internet:

- *Privacy*   The HTTP data are encrypted when they are moving over the Internet, so you can be assured that unauthorized users cannot get at your data, even if they physically intercept (which is not difficult to do on a public network like the Internet).

- *Message validation*   An encoded message authentication code accompanies transmitted data, so that if anyone tampers with your data you can detect it.

- *Server authentication*   The server's digital signature is also sent with data, so that the client can verify that the server's identity is authentic.

SSL uses the standardized RSA cryptosystem, which means that the server uses two mathematically related keys—a private key and a public key—to encrypt data. The client and the server both have a *certificate*, which is verified in real time during the transaction by a Certificate Authority. The CA can be in your company, a private Certificate Authority, or a public commercial CA like VeriSign. The CA issues certificates to both the client and the server. (VeriSign calls these certificates Digital IDs.) The certificate contains the public key and a certificate name, and when an SSL transaction is begun, the CA verifies the client's and server's identities. (If the verification fails, the transaction is stopped and you are notified.) Figure 10.7 summarizes this security process.

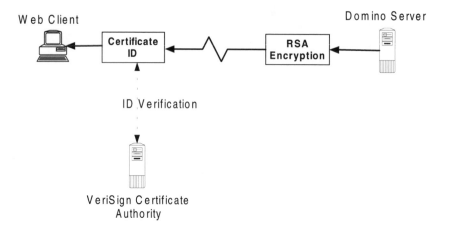

Figure 10.7 Domino security

If you're going to use SSL to communicate with Web browsers, you should probably use VeriSign since most Web browsers support VeriSign certificates (or Digital IDs). When accessing an SSL Web site, you use a slightly different syntax than the normal Web site addresses, putting `https://` figure at the beginning of the address. (For example, you'd use `https://www.lotus.com` instead of the normal `http://www.lotus.com`.) The Web client must have a certificate in common with the server.

10.5 Notes client versus Domino Web browser security

Most Notes security features work identically with both Notes clients and Web browser clients, but there are a few subtle differences.

- *User identification and authentication*   Notes clients users must have a Notes ID file, which provides a slightly higher level of security. Web users are authenticated by user names and passwords in the Public Address Book. A Web client needs only this user name and password to access Domino, but a Notes client can't access the Notes server without an ID file, even if a Notes user name and password has been compromised.

- *Access Control Lists*   ACLs work almost identically for Notes clients and Internet Web browser clients, except that for Internet clients you have one extra level of protection—the Maximum Internet browser access setting in the Advanced section of your Access Control List. This option allows you to set the maximum access that any Web user will ever be granted to a database, regardless of other ACL settings. For example, if you have a database that you never want updated by a Web browser client, you can set the maximum access to Reader.

- *Encryption* For Notes clients there are many options: you can encrypt specific databases, mail messages, specific documents, and network transactions. For Web browsers, SSL-encrypted public/private key transactions are your only option for secure data transmission.

- *Server access lists are used in Notes to restrict activities at the server* This option is not applicable to Web browsers. (That is, Web browsers cannot access server features and settings directly.)

- *Electronic signatures* Available only for the Notes client; they cannot yet be used with Web browsers.

10.6 Summary

In this chapter you've learned how to manage Web user names and HTTP (i.e., Web browser) passwords in your public address book, and how the Domino Action template automates the Internet user registration process. We've covered the various settings for handling anonymous Web users, how to set the maximum access level that Web users are allowed, and how to use ACLs to restrict access to databases, views, forms, and individual fields.

You've been introduced to the SSL for encrypting Internet data, and we've looked at the differences between Notes client security and Domino Web browser security options.

In the next chapter we'll investigate some advanced techniques for Web user interface development using Notes and Domino.

C H A P T E R   1 1

Web user interface development

In the last few chapters, you've created a Web site using Domino Action, linked it to a Notes database, and learned about the basic features of using Domino to publish a dynamic Web site. In this chapter, we'll take a closer look at advanced features of Domino and Notes that allow you to create more sophisticated Web sites. You'll learn how to:

- Use Notes forms to gather information from a Web user with forms.
- Create customized response items (i.e., the response page that Domino presents to the Web user after submitting a form).
- Create a custom submit button for your form so that you can take programmatic actions when the user has finished filling in a form.
- Effectively use Default Value and Input Validation formulas from the Web, including customized error messages for input validation failures.
- Change the user experience based on roles, for example, presenting a different user interface depending on whether a Notes client or a Web browser is accessing your application.
- Use HTML pass-through to access HTML features that don't have equivalent functions in Notes.
- Use the special $$ fields that Notes provides to get at special Web browser-only features and create advanced Web user interfaces, including:
  - Using $$ViewBody to display a view in a form.
  - Using view templates to combine the features of forms, views, and navigators.
  - Using navigator templates to add the features of forms to a navigator.
- Set up your databases for full text searching, including multidatabase full Web site searching.

11.1 Basic form-based input

Getting input from an Internet user is extremely easy because you have full access to both Notes forms and the databases in which Notes documents are stored. You don't have to learn complex scripting languages and use programming languages to save data to a database format, as you do with other Internet programming tools. You simply create the Notes form using the interactive form design tool, and launch the form with a Compose command. It will work almost identically for both Notes clients and Web browser clients.

As an example, we'll use the Office Locations database you created in chapter 10, and add a response form that allows the Web user to send comments or questions to any of your company's offices. The comments will be attached to the office location documents, so that you can identify the office to which the comments are addressed.

To begin, first open the Office Locations database.

1 Select Design|Forms, and double-click on the Main Topic form to load it in design mode.

2 Select the View|Action Pane menu.

3 Select Create|Action.

4 Under Title enter Send Feedback to this Office. Under Button Icon select an appropriate graphic, and then close the action properties window.

5 In the programming pane, enter the following formula:

```
@PostedCommand([Compose];"Response")
```

6 Save and close the Main Topic form.

Before trying this form in your Web browser, let's add a keyword field to allow the user to easily select the type of response he or she is entering.

1 Select Design|Forms, and double click on the Response form to load it in design mode.

2 Click your mouse above the Body field, then select the Create|Field menu.

3 Under Name enter Response Type. Under Type select Keywords.

4 In the choices box, enter the following items:

```
General Feedback
Question
Sales Inquiry
```

This field will help you determine how to handle any given feedback item.

5 Click on the Keyword options tab. (It's the one between the Basics and Options tabs.)

6 Under interface select Checkbox, and under columns select 3. This will cause all three items to appear on one line as checkbox items.

7 Save and close the Response form.

To test the form, make sure your Domino server is running, and then start your Web browser and point it at the Domino server (http://127.0.0.1/). Select the Click Here to Find Out Nearest Office on a Map link on your About the Company page, and then select an active state hotspot on the map. Note that your office information document now has an additional action bar item, as shown in figure 11.1.

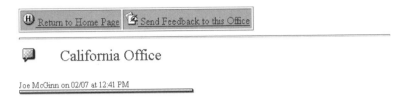

Figure 11.1   New action bar item

Press the Send Feedback to this Office button and you'll see your new response form in the Web browser, complete with the keyword radio buttons you added to the form, as shown in figure 11.2.

When you are finished entering data in the form, press the Submit button. This is one slight difference of forms presented through a Web browser; they always have a Sub-

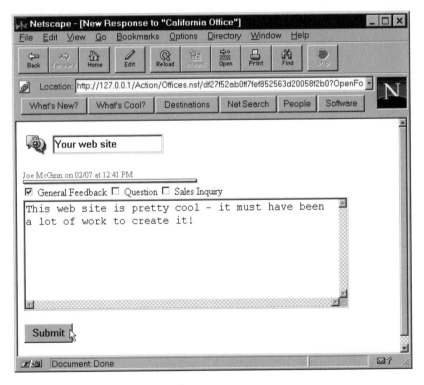

Figure 11.2   Feedback response form

mit button automatically appended to them so that it's easy for Web users to finish with the form and save the document they've entered. Note that the new data are automatically converted to a regular Notes document by Domino, as you can see in figure 11.3. No programming is needed to save form-based data to a Notes database; it's all handled automatically when the Web user presses the Submit button.

11.2 Creating a customized response with $$Return

When you pressed the Submit button to finish entering data in a form in your Web browser, you probably noticed that Domino displayed a plain page with the text *Form processed* on it. The only way to get out of this page in your Web browser is to press the Back button, which is probably not what you want the user to do, since that will return him or her to the data entry screen he or she just finished, which could be confusing.

You can add a customized $$Return field to your form that contains HTML code to present the Web browser with a more user friendly response page, such as a link back to your home page and a personalized message. You create a computed field named $$Return on the form, and use the @Return formula to indicate the values to be displayed.

1 Open the Office Locations database and click on Design|Forms. (The database will open to the Country Map navigator as specified in the database launch options, so you'll have to select View|Show|Design to see the design menus first.)

2 Double-click on the Response form to open it up in design mode.

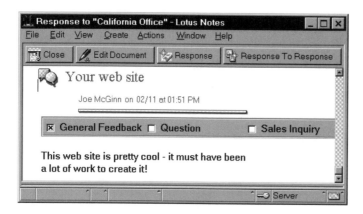

Figure 11.3 Feedback response document in Notes

3 Click the mouse to the right of the ResponseType field, and hit the enter key to create a new, blank line on the form.

4 Select the Create|Field menu.

5 Name the field $$Return, and set the type to Text and Computed. You must make this field Computed or it will not work.

6 Click on the hide/when tab (it's the one with a key on it, second from the right end) and select all the checkboxes except for Hide paragraph if formula is true. This makes the field hidden so that it isn't visible to the user.

Tip

You can go directly to the design menus of any database by clicking on the database (on your Notes workspace) with the right mouse button and selecting Go To Design from the context menu that pops up.

7 Close the field properties window, and enter the following formula in the programming pane:

```
who:=@If(@Left(From; " ") = ""; From; @Left(From;" "));
@Return("<h2> Thank you, " + who + "</h2><br><h4> <a href=/action/
HomePage.nsf?Open>Return to Home Page</a>")
```

The `who` variable holds the user's name (first name if one has been entered, the whole user name otherwise). The `@Return` function specifies the HTML code to execute after the user presses Submit. In this case it displays a personalized thank you message and a link back to your home page.

8 Close and save the response form.

Now, go and enter another response item through your Web browser, and then press the Submit button. This time you will see the more user friendly screen show in figure 11.4 instead of the plain Form processed page.

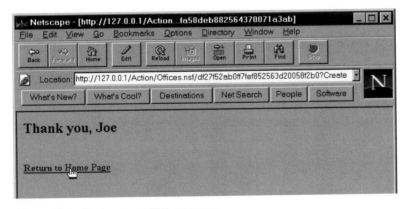

Figure 11.4 Customized HTML response

11.3 Creating a customized submit button

As you've seen, Domino automatically adds a Submit button to the bottom forms so that Web users can save documents when they are finished entering them. You can change the position and text of this button by simply adding a new button to any form. Generally Domino does not support buttons on forms (i.e., outside of the Action Bar), but a customized Submit button is the one exception to this rule. You can have only one Submit button per form, and any additional buttons you put on a form will be ignored by Domino. In this section I'll show you how to add a customized Submit button to the customer feedback response form you added to the Office Locations database.

1　Open the Office Locations database and click on Design|Forms.

2　Double click on the Response form to open it up in design mode.

3　Click the cursor to the right of the Body field, and press Enter to create a blank line at the end of the form.

4　Select the Create|HotSpot|Button menu.

5　Under Button Label enter the text you want to appear on the submit button (e.g., Send Feedback or Send Feedback to *your company name*).

6　Do not enter any formula—if you do Domino will just ignore it.

7　Save and close the Response form.

When the user accesses this form in a Web browser, he or she will see the customized Submit button shown in figure 11.5. The button functions exactly like the original Submit button, including support for a customized response you've created using the $$Return field.

11.4 Default values and input validation

Default values, computed for display fields, and input validation are all supported in Domino. Default values and computed fields work identically in Domino and Web browsers as they do in the native Notes client, using formulas to set the value. For example, in the Response form (in Office Locations), if you click on the From field you will see the default value formula @UserName. Just as in a Notes database, this formula stores the Web user's user name on the form so that you know who created the response. If you scroll down and click on the tmpFrom field (computed for display), you'll see the value formula @Name([CN];From), which displays the user's name in a more friendly format.

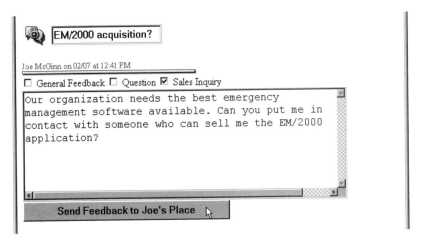

Figure 11.5 Customized Submit button

Input validation works slightly differently in Domino. In the Notes client, a dialog box is displayed with an error message, and then the cursor is put in the field having the error so that the user can correct it. With Domino and a Web browser, the error message is displayed on a separate Web page; it's a good idea to include a specific error message so that the user knows what to correct when he or she goes back to the form.

As an example, let's add a field to the feedback form to capture the user's Internet email address.

1 Open the Office Locations database and click on Design|Forms.

2 Double click on the Response form to open it up in design mode.

3 Click the cursor to the right of the ResponseType field, and press Enter to create a blank line on the form.

4 Select the Create|Field menu. Name the field InetEmail, and leave the field type as Text, Editable.

5 In the programming pane, select the Input Translation formula and enter the following formula:

```
@Trim(InetEmail)
```

This will remove any extra blanks the user might have entered.

6 Then select the Input Validation field, and enter the following formula to ensure that the user enters a valid Internet email address:

```
domain := @RightBack(InetEmail; ".");
```

```
@If(
    @Trim(InetEmail) = "" |
    !@Contains(InetEmail; "@") |
    @Length(domain) < 2 | @Length(domain) > 3 |
    (@Length(domain) = 3 & @Member(@LowerCase(domain);
"com":"edu":"org":"net":"gov":"mil":"int") = 0) |
    @Trim(@Left(InetEmail; "@")) = "";
    @Failure("<h2>A valid Internet email address is required. \"" + InetEmail
+ "\" is not valid. Please go back to the form to enter or correct the email
address."); @Success)
```

7 Click to the left of the InetMail field, and enter `Internet Email Address:` to identify the field.

8 Close and save the Response form.

Now try entering a new response through your Web browser. If the user enters an invalid email address, he or she cannot save the form, and will get the `@Failure` message as shown in figure 11.6.

11.5 *Changing the user experience based on client type*

You can make forms that detect whether the application is being accessed via the full Notes clients or a Web client, and change the user interface based on the type of client. You use the `@UserRoles` function to determine which type of client the user has. For example, let's say you want to add a Please Respond By date field to your feedback form, so that you can respond quickly to urgent requests.

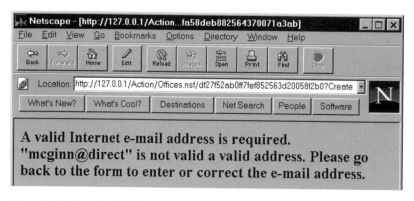

Figure 11.6 Input validation error message

In Notes 4.5, client date/time fields have been made much more user friendly with the addition of popup dialogs that allow the user to select the date or time with a click of the mouse. You enable this feature by putting the date field in a layout region, after which Notes automatically adds the new user interface features. But layout regions are not yet supported in Domino and the region will just be ignored, so the Web user won't see the new field at all.

The solution is to use computed subforms based on the client type—one subform with a layout region for Notes clients, and another plain date field for Web clients. You'll use the @UserRoles function to determine at runtime which subform to include.

1   Open the Office Locations database and select the Create|Design|Subform menu.

2   Select the Design|Subform Properties menu and enter Notes Client Date under Name, then close the subform properties window.

3   Select the Create|Layout Region|New Layout Region menu.

4   Select the Create|Field menu, then double-click on the field to open the field properties window.

5   Under Name enter RespondBy, and under type select Time. Under the Show menu on this screen select Date.

6   Close the field properties window. Select Default Value in the programming pane, and enter the following formula:

```
@Adjust(@Now;0;0;7;0;0;0)
```

The @Adjust formula will enter a default value one week from the day the message is entered. The user can edit the date if the message is urgent.

7   Click on the layout region, then select the Create|Layout Region|Text menu.

8   Move the text to the top left corner of the layout region, then double-click on it to open the properties window. Under text enter Please Respond By:, and close the properties window.

9   Move the RespondBy field up near the text, and then shrink the layout region so that it doesn't take up so much space, as shown in figure 11.7.

10   Double-click on the layout region, and deselect the Show border option. Close the layout properties window.

11   Save and close the new subform.

Now, we'll create a subform for Web clients. This form will be simpler, with no layout region and just one date field on it.

1   Open the Office Locations database and select the Create|Design|Subform menu.

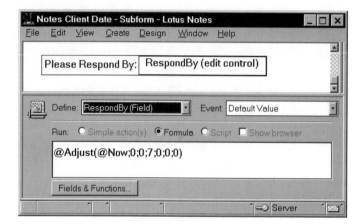

Figure 11.7   Notes Client subform

2   Select the Design|Subform Properties menu and enter `Web Client Date` under Name, then close the subform properties window.

3   Select the Create|Field menu.

4   Under Name enter `RespondBy`, and under type select Time. Under the Show menu select Date.

5   Close the properties window, and enter the following Default Value formula:

```
@Adjust(@Now;0;0;7;0;0;0)
```

6   Click your mouse to the left of the RespondBy field and enter the text `Please Respond By:` as a prompt.

7   Save and close the Web Client Date subform.

Finally, using the `@UserRoles` function we'll programmatically determine which subform gets pulled into the Response form.

1   Select Design|Forms, and double click on the Response form.

2   Click your mouse to the left of the $$Return field (i.e., below the InetEmail field) and select the Create|Insert Subform menu.

3   Do not select a subform; click on the option Insert Subform based on formula as shown in figure 11.8, then click on the OK button.

4   In the programming pane, enter the following formula:

```
IsWebClient:=@IsMember("$$WebClient";@UserRoles);
@If(IsWebClient;"Web Client Date";"Notes Client Date")
```

5   Save and close the response form.

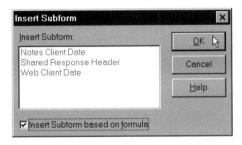

Figure 11.8   Insert subform based on formula

The user will now get a different user interface, depending on the client type. If using the full Notes client, he or she will get the advanced date interface shown in figure 11.9. If accessing the application from a Web browser, he or she will get a simple date field, as shown in figure 11.10.

11.6 Advanced formatting: using HTML

As you've seen, Domino allows you to put HTML codes on your Notes documents that Domino passes through to be interpreted by your Web browser. HTML codes can be

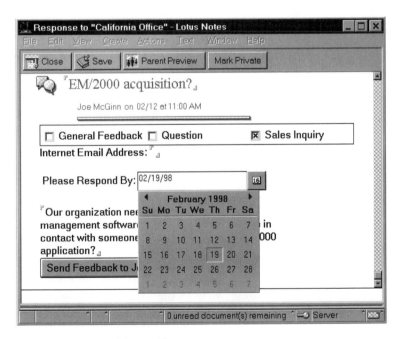

Figure 11.9   Notes Client subform

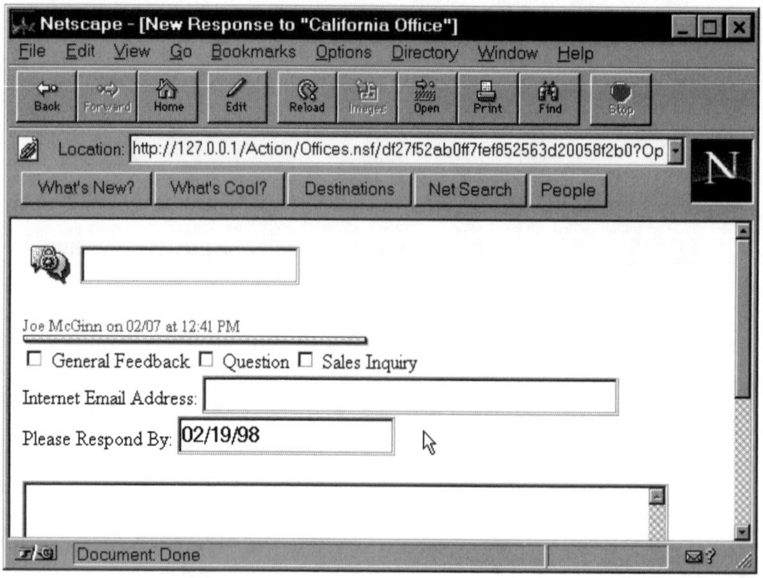

Figure 11.10   Web Client subform

included in documents, forms, fields, and view columns. This allows you to explicitly access HTML features that don't have Notes equivalents. The easiest place to experiment with HTML codes is on your Web site home page that you generated using Domino Action SiteCreator. By accessing the page via your Web browser, you can edit the page just by pressing the Edit/Approve This Page button and then republishing the page.

When you edit your home page, you'll see an area titled *Web page content: Text or [HTML]*. Simply put your HTML code into this area, surrounded by square brackets. For example, the following code is a hypertext link that opens the Office Locations database in the Action subdirectory:

```
[<a href=/Action/Offices.nsf?Open>Click Here to
Find Our Nearest Office on a Map</a>]
```

Another common requirement is for formatted text. The following code displays ordinary text with some bold, italic, and teletype font text and four different HTML heading sizes, using the <hN> codes (see figure 11.11):

Tip

If you don't see the Edit/Approve button it's probably because you haven't logged in to the Web site yet, and anonymous users don't get the contributor buttons. Press the Log In button, enter your user name and password, and then you will see the contributor buttons.

Some regular text with a paragraph break here

with a test of some **bold** text, *italics* and the `teletype monospace font.`

Heading 1 Text

Heading 2 Text

Heading 3 Text

Heading 4 Text

Figure 11.11   HTML text formatting and headings

```
[<a>Some regular text with a paragraph break here<p> with a test of some
<b>bold</b> text, <i>italics</i> and the <tt> teletype monospace font</tt>.</
a>]
[<h1>Heading 1 Text</a>]
[<h2>Heading 2 Text</a>]
[<h3>Heading 3 Text</a>]
[<h4>Heading 4 Text</a>]
```

As you can see, an HTML attribute is selected by placing the tag inside the < > characters, and the tag is ended by repeating it with a leading slash character. The following list shows some common HTML codes that you may find useful:

- `<h1>`–`<h6>`   Section headings; h1 is the largest h6 the smallest.
- `<a>`   Text.
- `<p>`   New paragraph.
- `<br>`   Line break.
- `<B>`   Bold text.
- `<I>`   Italic text.
- `<tt>`   Teletype monospace font.
- `<a href>`   Hypertext link.

A complete definition of the HTML specification is available at:

`http://www.w3.org/pub/WWW/MarkUp/html-spec/html-spec.html`

Perhaps somewhat more interesting than just formatting text (which, after all, is probably easier to do interactively in a Notes form or document) is the ability to attach

HTML attributes to editable fields on a form. To do this, you enter the HTML attributes in the Help description option for a field, as shown in figure 11.12. In this example the maximum data entry size of the field is set to 80 characters, and the maximum display size to 40 characters.

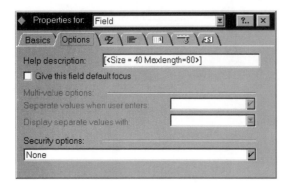

Figure 11.12   HTML maximum field size

There is a range of HTML options available, each applicable to certain field types:

- Rich text fields.
  - You can set the maximum number of rows and columns in a rich text field using [<ROWS=10 COLS=60>].
  - You can also set rich text fields to virtual wrapping style using [<WRAP=VIR-TUAL>]. This means that text wraps at the end of lines without the user pressing Enter.
- Keyword fields. Set the maximum number of visible choices using [<SIZE=5>].

11.7 Advanced Web user interfaces part 1: $$ fields

Earlier in this chapter, you learned how to use the $$Return field to creating a customized response when a Web user submits a new document to be saved. There are a number of other extremely useful $$ fields for creating advanced Web user interfaces, some of them for features that are not even yet available in the Notes 4.5 client.

The $$ fields of particular usefulness are:

- $$ViewBody displays the named view on the form. Only one $$ViewBody field is allowed per form.

- $$ViewList displays the list of views in the database, in the font specified in the field options.

- $$NavigatorBody is incredibly useful; it allows you to display one or more navigators on a form. The navigator can be anywhere on a form—in tables, collapsed sections, and so on.

- $$QueryOpenAgent allows you to run a specified agent before a document is sent to the Web browser by Domino, and $$QuerySaveAgent allows you to run an agent before a document is saved. These are equivalent to the Queryopen and Querysave form events in the Notes client (i.e., which are not available to Web browsers). I'll show you how to use $$QueryOpenAgent and $$QuerySaveAgent in chapter 12.

As an example, let's take a look at how $$ViewBody can be used to simulate the useful one-to-many database relation often used in relational (i.e., SQL) databases. In the office locations database you include phone numbers and addresses of your offices. But, what if you also want to include general contact information (i.e., phone numbers, pager numbers, email addresses, etc.) for a number of individuals in your company? You could include all this information in rich text fields on the office documents, but this would entail a lot of duplication if you have several offices and would be very difficult to maintain as numbers, names, and other contact information changes.

A better solution is to store the people and their contact information as documents in a separate form, and then use a relation to include the list of contacts in the office form itself. The names and numbers can then be maintained as a central database, and the changes will be automatically pulled into each office location form via the database relation. First, create a form to store simple contact information:

1 Open the Office Locations database in design mode.

2 Single click on the Main Topic form. Select the Edit|Copy menu, then Edit|Paste to create a copy of the form.

3 Double click on the Copy of Main Topic form to load it in design mode.

4 Select the Design|Form properties menu and rename the form `Person`.

5 Double click on the Subject field, and rename it `Name`. Click on the options tab and enter `Enter the person's name.` into the Help description field. Close the field properties window.

6 In the programming pane for the Name field, select the Input Translation event and enter the following formula:

```
@Trim(Name)
```

7 Delete the Category field.

8 Click the mouse above the Body field, and then use the Create|Field menu to create the following fields:

- `Title`: type Text, Editable.
- `PhoneNumber`: type Text, Editable.
- `FaxNumber`: type Text, Editable.
- `PagerNumber`: type Text, Editable.
- `EmailAddress`: type Text, Editable.
- `OfficeLocation`: type Text, Editable.

9 Click the cursor to the left of each field, and enter some prompt text as shown in figure 11.13.

10 Save and close the Person form.

Use the Create|Person menu to add several people to the database for testing purposes. After you've added these documents, create a Person view to display them.

1 Select the Create|View menu.

2 Name the view People, and click on the Shared checkbox option.

3 Under Selection conditions click on the Add Condition button.

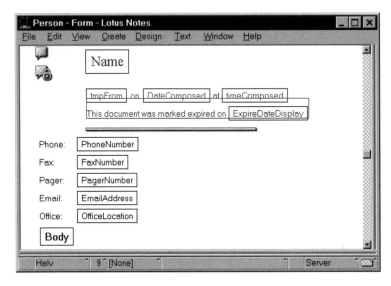

Figure 11.13   Person form

4 Under Condition select By Form Used, then select the Person form. Select OK, the OK again on the create view window to create the view.

5 Click on Design|Views, and double-click on the People view.

6 Delete the Date and Topic and By columns by clicking on the column header and selecting Edit|Delete (or just press the delete key).

7 Select the Create|Append New Column menu. In the programming pane click on Field, then select the Name field.

8 Double-click on the new column header and enter Name as the title, then close the Properties window.

9 Repeat steps seven and eight for each of the following fields:

```
Title
PhoneNumber
PagerNumber
EmailAddress
OfficeLocation
```

10 You should delete the action bar items from the view unless you want them to show up on the document in the Web browser. Select the View|Action pane menu and delete the Navigator, New Main Topic, Response, and Response to Response actions.

11 Close and save the view. In the Notes client the view should look something like figure 11.14.

Now you can add the $$ViewBody field to the Main Topic form:

1 Select Design|Forms and double click on the Main Topic form.

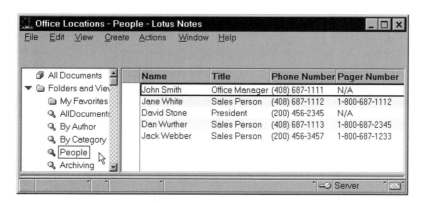

Figure 11.14 People view in Notes

2 Click to the right of the Body field and press the Enter key to make a new empty line at the bottom of the form.

3 Select the Create|Field menu, and name the field $$ViewBody. Set the type of the field to Text, Computed For Display.

4 Close the field properties window and enter the following formula in the programming pane (the Value event should be selected):

```
"People"
```

5 Save and close the Main Topic form.

Make sure your Domino server is running, then start your Web browser and go to your home page. Select About the Company, then click on the hypertext link to the map of your office locations. Click on an active state, and you will now see the People view included directly on the Main Topic office location form, as shown in figure 11.15. Note that it is a live, hypertext view, not just a display of names. You can click on a name to get the full document for it. And even more importantly, the view is automatically updated as you edit contact information or add new names using the Person form.

The one thing you don't get with an inform view like this is the default Web browser navigation pane for views that allows you to go through multiple pages of a view. Since views can have many documents, Domino shows only twenty-five

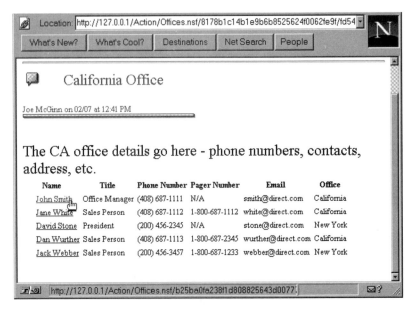

Figure 11.15   Live $$ViewBody field in Netscape

documents displayed in this kind of view. Fortunately, it provides a way to construct such a navigation pane using the $$NavigatorBody field.

First, create the graphical navigator for moving through multiple pages of a view:

1 Open your graphics program and load the VIEWNAV.PCX graphics file from the *Inside LotusScript* CD, then copy the image to the clipboard.

2 Open the Office Locations database, and select the Create|Design|Navigator menu.

3 Select the Design|Navigator Properties menu. Under Name enter View Navigator, then close the properties window.

4 Select the Create|Graphic Background menu. The graphic image you captured in step 2 will appear as the navigator background.

5 Select the Create|Hotspot Rectangle menu, and draw a box around the word *Previous* and its icon.

6 In the programming pane select Formula, and enter the following code:

```
@DbCommand("Domino";"ViewPreviousPage")
```

7 Use the Create|Hotspot menu to create similar hotspots around each of the words on the navigator, entering the following formulas for each one:

Next: `@DbCommand("Domino";"ViewNextPage")`
Expand: `@Command([ViewExpandAll])`
Collapse: `@Command([ViewCollapseAll])`
Search: `@Command([ViewShowSearchBar])`

8 Save and close the navigator. You can use this navigator in any Web database where you need a navigation bar to use with a $$ViewBody field on a form.

Now we'll add the navigator to the Main Topic form using the $$NavigatorBody field.

1 Select Design|Forms and double click on the Main Topic form.

2 Click to the right of the Body field and press the Enter key to make a new empty line at the bottom of the form.

Tip

Unlike views, you can have any number of navigators on a form. It's a good idea to put the view navigator on twice—once above the $$ViewBody field and once below it. That way a user has the navigator available even if he or she has scrolled to the bottom of the form.

1 In the Main Topic form, select the $$ViewNavigator field using the mouse.

2 Make a copy of it using the Edit|Copy menu.

3 Click to the right of the $View-Body field and press the Enter key, then select the Edit|Paste) menu.

4 The new field will be named $$NavigatorBody_1, which is the default format for multiple navigators within a form. (If you wanted to add more navigators they would be named $$NavigatorBody_2, etc.)

5 Save and close the form.

3 Select the Create|Field menu, and name the field $$NavigatorBody. Set the type of the field to Text, Computed For Display.

4 Close the field properties window and enter the following formula in the programming pane (the Value event should be selected):

```
"View Navigator"
```

5 Save and close the Main Topic form.

Try viewing an office location form through your Web browser. You will now have two functional view navigators on the form, including a working search page, as shown in figure 11.16.

11.8 Advanced Web user interfaces part 2: view templates

The $$ fields used in the previous example add a lot of power to Web form user interface development. It would takes weeks of advanced development to implement the form in

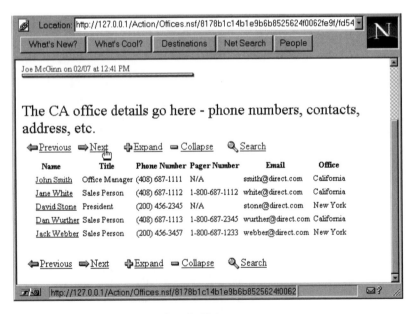

Figure 11.16   Navigators on a form in Netscape

figure 11.16 using Netscape's or Microsoft's Internet development tools. Lotus has added another feature to Domino that is perhaps even more powerful—view templates.

Using a view template, you can create a customized form to be used as the default user interface for accessing views in a Web browser. As an example, we'll create a discussion database for the Web, and create a view template that provides a user friendly and attractive way of accessing the database's views from a Web browser.

1 Create a new database by selecting File|Database|New.

2 Under Title enter `Office Locations`.

3 Under File Name enter `WebDisc.nsf`.

4 Click on the directory icon beside the file name.

5 Select the Action subdirectory (i.e., the directory that contains your Web site), and press OK.

6 Select the Discussion (R4) template.

7 Deselect the option Inherit future design changes.

8 Click on OK to save and open the new Customers database.

Now you'll create the view template form:

1 Select the Create|Design|Form menu.

2 Select the Design|Form Properties menu and enter $$ViewTemplateDefault as the Form name. Close the Form Properties window.

3 Create a table to align the items on the form. Select the Create|Table menu, and enter 4 rows by 2 columns for the size of the table. (You cannot use tabs and spaces to align form items in a Web browser.)

4 Click your mouse in the left hand column of the table, and select the Table|Table Properties menu.

5 Click on the layout tab, and deselect the option Fit table width to window. Under Cell width enter `1.6 inches`.

6 Click on the second column (i.e., right-hand side) of the table, and in the table properties window enter `8 inches`. Close the Table Properties window.

Now you have the form layout ready to begin adding the components that make up a template form.

1 Load your company logo or graphic into a graphics program and copy it to the clipboard.

2 Click your mouse in the top-left table cell and select the Edit|Paste menu.

3 Click the top-right cell and enter the text `Discussion:` in a large font, then select the Create Field menu.

4 Name the field `ViewTitle:`, type Text, Computed for Display. Click on the paragraph formatting tab and center the paragraph.

5 Close the field properties window and enter the following formula under the event in the programming pane:

```
@ViewTitle
```

6 Click to the right of the view title field and press Enter, then select the Create|Field menu.

7 Name the field $$NavigatorBody, type Text, Computed for Display. Enter the following formula in the Value event:

```
"View Navigator"
```

8 Load the SPLITTER.PCX "separator" graphic from the *Inside LotusScript* CD into a graphics program. Copy the graphic to the clipboard and click on the table cell below the one with the $$NavigatorBody field. Select the Edit|Past menu, and center the paragraph properties.

9 Click on the third cell from the top on the left-hand column. Enter the text `Select a View:` and press the Enter key.

10 Select the Create|Field menu. Name the field $$ViewList, type Text, Editable.

11 Click on the cell to the right of the `$$ViewList` cell and select the Create|Field menu. Name the field $$ViewBody, type Text, Editable.

Note: A $$ViewTemplateDefault form requires a $$ViewBody field somewhere on the form, but it ignores the value in that field (i.e., since all views are displayed in it, not just one specific view) so you do not have to enter any formula to initialize the value of this field when it's on a view template form.

12 Select the $$NavigatorBody field with your mouse and select the Edit|Copy menu.

13 Click on the bottom-right cell on the table and select the Edit|Paste menu.

14 Use your mouse to select the entire table, the select the Table|Table Properties menu.

15 Under the Borders tab press the Set All to 0 button. This will make your table invisible, but it will still align the objects inside of it.

16 Save and close the $$ViewTemplateDefault form.

Before you test this database, you must copy the View Navigator from the Office Locations database.

1 Open the Office Locations database to the design pane, and select Design|Navigators.

2 Single click on the navigator titled *View Navigator* and then select the Edit|Copy menu.

3 Close the Office Locations database and open the Web Discussion database.

4 Click on Design|Navigators, then select the Edit|Paste menu.

Make sure your Domino server is running, and open the All Documents view in the Web Discussion database using the following URL:

```
http://127.0.0.1/Action/Webdisc.nsf/($All)
```

Enter a few test documents using the New Main Topic view. You can select the view with the view list on the left side of the screen, and the documents in that view will show up on the right as shown in figure 11.17.

11.9 *Advanced Web user interfaces part 3: navigator templates*

You can also create templates for navigators by naming a form $$NavigatorTemplateDefault to associate it with all navigators, or $$NavigatorTemplate for navigatorname to associate it with a specific navigator. These kinds of forms require a $$NavigatorBody field to indicate where in the form you want the navigator inserted. As an example, I'll show you how to add Notes form features—such as an action bar—to the Country Map graphical navigator in the Office Locations database:

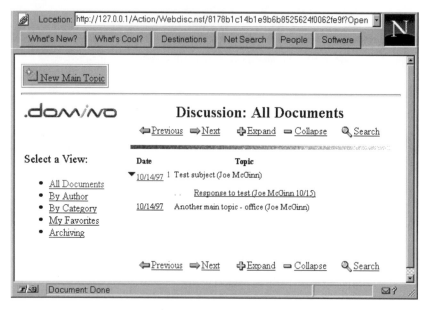

Figure 11.17 $$ViewTemplateDefault form in Netscape

1 Open the Office Locations database.

2 Select the Create|Design|Form menu.

3 Select the Design|Form Properties menu, and enter $$NavigatorTemplateDefault as the form name. Close the form properties window.

4 Select the Create|Field menu.

5 Under Name enter $$NavigatorBody. Set the field type to Text, Computed for Display, and close the properties window.

6 Enter the following text in the programming pane for the $$NavigatorBody field.

```
"Country Map"
```

Now you'll add an action bar item to the form that will allow the user to return to your Web site home page. This result will be a combination of form features—in this case, an action bar item—with a navigator.

1 Select the Create|Action menu. Under Title enter Return to Home Page. Under Button Icon select an appropriate icon, such as the letter H.

2 Close the action properties window, and enter the following formula into the programming pane:

```
@Command([FileOpenDatabase];"":"Action\\HomePage.nsf")
```

3 Save and close the $$NavigatorTemplateDefault form.

Start your Web browser and go to the Office Locations database. You will see that the Country Map navigator has an action bar, as shown in figure 11.18.

11.10 Setting up text searching

Setting up text searching within a view is very simple. As you've seen in a couple examples earlier in this chapter, you just use the following formula:

```
@Command([ViewShowSearchBar])
```

The formula can be attached to an action bar, or to a hotspot in a view template. When the user clicks on the button he or she sees a search form as shown in figure 11.19. When the search is submitted, Domino displays a hypertext list of the matching documents.

Domino Web sites often consist of many databases. The sites created by Domino Action SiteCreator consist of a separate Notes database for each section. Fortunately, Lotus included a powerful new Search Site template with Notes 4.5 that allows you to construct multidatabase search indices. As an example, we'll create a search that works across the Office Locations (Offices.nsf) and Web Discussion (WebDisc.nsf) databases:

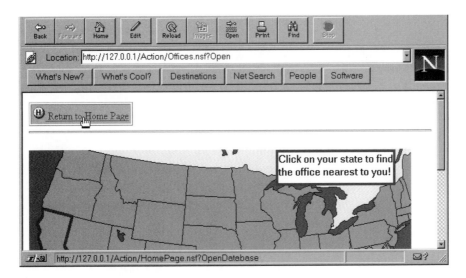

Figure 11.18   Navigator with an action bar

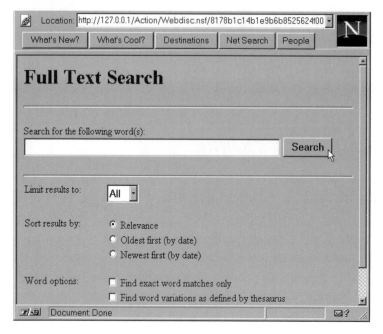

Figure 11.19 Search form in Netscape

1 From the Notes workspace, select the File|Database|New menu.

2 Under Title enter `Search Site`.

3 Under File name enter `Search.nsf`.

4 Select the Search Site template and press OK to open the new database.

You create a configuration in the Search Site database for each database you want to be included in the search path.

1 Select the Create|Search Scope Configuration menu.

2 Under Scope select Database.

3 Under Server enter the name of your server.

4 Under Filename enter `Action\Offices.nsf`.

5 Save and close the scope configuration document.

6 Repeat steps 1–5 for the Action\WebDisc.nsf database.

7 Close the Search Site database.

To activate the multidatabase search you have to set a few options. For both the Office Locations and Web Discussion databases go into the database options (click on the icon on the Notes workspace and select File|Database|Properties). Click on the Design tab, and select the option Include in multidatabase indexing, as shown in figure 11.20.

Now you just have to generate the actual index. Open the database properties for the Search Site database, then press the Create Index button. Set the Update frequency to tell the server how often you want the index updated. If you have created an index for large database, you should probably select Daily as the Update frequency. You do not have to create indexes in the Office Locations and Web Site databases.

To run a search from your Web site, create a hypertext link to the search database that opens the simple Web search form. For example:

```
[<a href=/Search.nsf/Web+Search+Simple/?OpenForm>Click Here to Search</a>]
```

When users clicks on the link they'll see the search form in their Web browsers, as shown in figure 11.21.

11.11 Summary

In this chapter, you've learned a complete range of ways to create Web user interfaces for Web sites. We've covered how to use forms to input data from the user and save them to a Notes database, and how to customize the response screen and the submit button. You've learned how to change the user experience based on the type of client (i.e., Web browser or Notes client). You've been introduced to HTML pass-through and formatting.

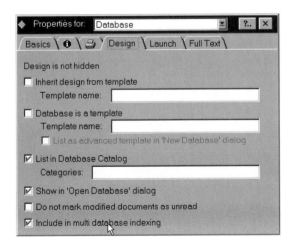

Figure 11.20 Multidatabase indexing option

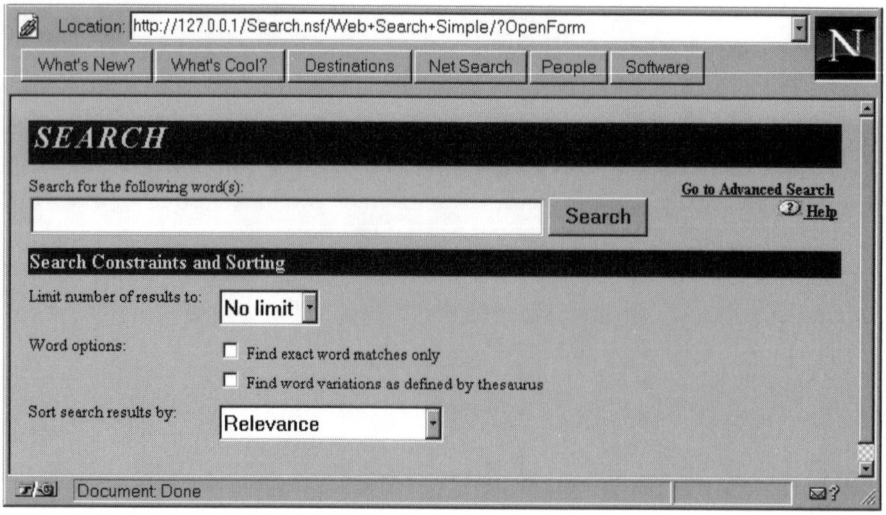

Figure 11.21 Web simple search form

In the advanced user interface section, you learned how to include views and navigators directly in forms, and how to create default forms that replace the standard Domino user interface for views and navigators. Finally, you've learned how to set up text searching including searching across multiple Notes databases from a Web browser.

Now that you know how to create powerful and flexible user interfaces, in the next chapter you'll learn how to add intelligence to your Internet applications with Lotus-Script agents that run on the server.

C H A P T E R   1 2

Internet LotusScript and agents

One of the most powerful and useful tools in Notes is LotusScript. This full featured programming language allows you to do any kind of processing you need. LotusScript code can be attached to form events, or it can be included in agents that run on the server, either on a scheduled basis or triggered by certain events. (For example, you can have an server agent that is triggered whenever documents are added to a database.)

One of the limitations of running your Notes applications over the Internet on a Web browser is that the browser does not have the ability to run LotusScript. The software that interprets and runs LotusScript programs is included in the Notes client and the Notes server, but Web browsers written by third parties (i.e., Netscape, Microsoft, etc.) do not have this software so they cannot run LotusScript. Fortunately, Lotus has provided some workarounds and features in Domino that allow you to access the Lotus-Script interpreter on the Domino server from a Notes application running on a Web browser. And of course, you can still use all of the server-based LotusScript capabilities with Domino such as running a scheduled or triggered LotusScript agent.

In this chapter, you will learn:

- How to use the Domino features that allow you to run an agent to do dynamic pre- and post-processing of a Notes document. This is equivalent to attaching code to the Queryopen and Querysave events in a Notes form.

- How to use the DocumentContext property to access CGI variables and the current Notes document from a LotusScript agent.

- How to generate HTML code and URL references from a LotusScript agent.

- How to debug Internet agents.

- How Notes security applies to agents.

- From a number of practical LotusScript agent examples:

  - An agent that generates sequential document numbers over the Internet. For the first time, it is possible to generate sequential numbers over a WAN.

  - I'll show you how to create an agent that is triggered on the server when new documents are added to a database, and how to send email notifications in this agent.

  - I'll show you how to run a server-based agent manually from a button, how to search for documents and present a list of hypertext links to the Web browser, and how to access a CGI variable.

12.1 Running agents to dynamically process Web documents

Domino includes features that allow you to run a LotusScript agent as a document is opened or saved. This is equivalent to attaching code to the Queryopen and Querysave events in the native Notes client. You can't use these events directly in a Web browser, but by using the new Domino features, you can accomplish the same results.

The features are accessed by including a field on a form called either $$QueryOpen-Agent or $$QuerySaveAgent. As the name implies, the $$QueryOpenAgent specifies an agent that Domino is to run before a Notes document is presented to the Web browser. The most common use for such an agent would be to do some complex calculations that can't be done using simple formulas. The $$QuerySaveAgent specifies an agent to be run when the document is saved (i.e., just after the user has pressed the Submit button but before Domino has actually saved the document to disk). Later in this chapter I'll show you how to use $$QuerySaveAgent to generate sequential document numbers on the Internet.

You make these fields Computed for Display, and include a Value formula that evaluates to the name of an agent. (The simplest way is to simply include the name of the agent in quotes.) Just as when using the Queryopen and Querysave events in the native Notes client, you can update field values on the form via a Domino agent. The agent itself will always have the following properties:

- The Shared Agent option must be selected.
- The option When should this agent run? must be set to Manually From Agent List.
- The option Which document(s) should it act on? must be set to All Documents In Database (even though you are only processing the current document).

In the next section, I'll show you how to access the document being processed via the DocumentContext property.

12.2 The DocumentContext property

Notes 4.5 includes a new property in the LotusScript NotesSession class. The property is called DocumentContext, and it returns a document that contains the fields of a document being opened or saved, as well as all CGI variables that are applicable to the session. (For a list of supported CGI variables, see the section "CGI variables supported in Domino" in the Domino user's manual.)

To access this property, you use the code in listing 12.1. You should always put this code at the beginning of your Domino agents.

Listing 12.1 Accessing the current document in an agent

```
Dim session As New NotesSession
Dim doc As NotesDocument
Set doc = session.DocumentContext
```

Once this code is executed, you can access the document normally. For example, if there is a From field on the form containing the author's name you can read it into a variable using the following LotusScript code:

```
Name$ = doc.From(0)
```

You can also modify fields on the form, both for $$QueryOpenAgent and $$QuerySaveAgent agents. For example, the following code puts the text `Hello World` into a text field called `Message`.

```
doc.Message = "Hello World"
```

Remember, you have to set the `doc` variable to the `DocumentContext` property before you can access the document's fields.

12.3 Generating HTML code from an agent

Another Domino feature added to LotusScript in Notes 4.5 is the ability to generate an HTML page as the output of an agent. The feature is accessed very easily, via the `Print` statement. For example, the following statement produces a Web browser page:

```
Print "<H2> Hello world></H2"
```

You can include any valid HTML text in the output. As a more useful example, the following code produces a hypertext link back to your home page:

```
Print  "<a href=/action/HomePage.nsf?Open>Return to Home Page</a>"
```

You can have more than one `Print` statement in an agent, and they will be appended to the HTML page that is output. For example, you could put the following two statements at the end of an agent to present the user with a personalized thank you as well as a hypertext link:

```
Print   "<h1> Thanks for the new message, " + doc.From(0) + "</h1>"
Print   "<a href=/action/HomePage.nsf?Open>Return to Home Page</a>"
```

Remember that if you include a `Print` statement in a $$QuerySaveAgent it will basically replace any output you may have included in a $$Return field. `Print` statements in a $$QueryOpenAgent are ignored completely, since this agent is run just before a form is displayed to the user.

12.4 Debugging Internet agents

Debugging agents run through a Web browser and Domino is not quite as easy as debugging native Notes client agents. Because the agent is actually triggered by the Web browser, you do not have access to the interactive Notes LotusScript debugger. The only alternative is to fall back to the old-fashioned debugging technique of `Print` statements. By using the `Print` statement wisely, you can debug Domino agents fairly easily.

The first line in your agents should always be an `On Error` statement, as follows:

Tip

The Messagebox statement in LotusScript normally sends output to a window on the user's screen. You can use the Messagebox statement in a Domino agent, but the output will be displayed on your server console instead of a window on your screen.

```
On Error Goto Error_Handler
```

There are a number of reasons for this. First, the default Domino error reporting does not display a detailed error message nor a line number, so debugging is difficult. Second, it is not very user friendly to let your users see Domino error messages. Last, and this is the most critical reason, there is a bug in Domino that can cause all subsequent attempts to run a $$QuerySaveAgent agent to hang on form submission. This means that the user will get a permanent Waiting for reply ... message in the Web browser and the new document cannot be saved, a situation that will persist until you manually stop and then restart the HTTP service on your Domino server. But, as long as you include an error handler in the agent, you will not encounter these problems.

The error handling code in listing 12.2 should be put at the end of the agent. When your script encounters an error, an HTML page will be generated for your browser that includes both the text of the error message and the line number where the error occurred.

Listing 12.2   LotusScript error handler for Domino agents

```
    On Error Goto Error_Handler
    REM … Code for your agent …
1   Exit Sub
2   Error_Handler:
3   Print "<a>Error on line number " + Format$(Erl()) + ": " + Error$ + "</a>"
4   Exit Sub
```

Listing Notes:

1 This line prevents your LotusScript routine from falling into the error handler when it completes successfully without an error.

2 This label is where control of the script will jump when any error occurs. If there are errors that you expect as part of the normal operation of your agent, you can trap for them gracefully here and continue program execution using the resume statement without printing the error message:

```
If Err = expected_error_number Then
    REM … processing to correct or handle the error condition
    Resume Next
End If
```

3 Prints the error message and line number as an HTML page.

4 Terminates the agent and the error handler. At this point the generated HTML page is displayed in the user's Web browser.

You can also use `Print` statements to simulate certain other capabilities of the interactive debugger, such as tracing the value of a variable you suspect has become corrupted. For example, if you have a counter variable called `j%` that you suspect is being

---

Tip

There are three options for the `Resume` statement:
`Resume Next`: Resumes at the line following the one that caused the error.
`Resume 0`: Resumes at the line that caused the error.
`Resume Label`: Resumes at the specified label.

---

corrupted at some point in an agent, you could put several Print lines throughout the agent to determine exactly at which point it is losing its value:

```
Print "<a>Debugging point 1, j% = " + Format$(j%) + "</a>"
Print "<a>Debugging point 2, j% = " + Format$(j%) + "</a>"
Print "<a>Debugging point 3, j% = " + Format$(j%) + "</a>"
```

If you run the agent and find that j% is corrupted at debugging point 2, you would then add more detailed lines between points 1 and 2:

```
Print "<a>Debugging point 1.1, j% = " + Format$(j%) + "</a>"
Print "<a>Debugging point 1.2, j% = " + Format$(j%) + "</a>"
Print "<a>Debugging point 1.3, j% = " + Format$(j%) + "</a>"
```

It may seem a bit of a laborious process, but within a few runs of the agent it will enable you to locate the problem exactly in your script.

12.5 Agent security

It's important to understand what access rights your agents have when run on a Domino server. An agent is subject to the ACL rights assigned to databases, just like a user. There are three different possibilities to consider:

- Agents that are triggered on the server. Triggered agents (e.g., run when new documents are added to a database) have the same access rights as the agent's owner.

- Agents run or triggered by a Web browser (i.e., either run manually from a button or via $$QueryOpenAgent or $$QuerySaveAgent) have the access rights of the person running the Web browser, as long as the agent is accessing only the current document or documents in the current database.

- Agents run via a Web browser that access other, external database have the access rights of the agents' owner while they are working with the external database.

12.6 Example 1: generating sequential numbers on the Internet

Generating sequential document numbers has long been one of the biggest challenges for Notes developers. Sequential numbers are almost always part of the requirements for database programs, even more so for groupware applications like Notes programs, because Notes is often used to implement various kinds of tracking applications (such as the customer service application you created in the tutorial). In the customer service program the service representative running the Notes program can give the number to a customer, who can then call back later to check on the status of the request.

Until Notes 4.x was released, sequential numbers had to be generated using formulas, which was problematic at best. It was difficult to set up a workable and flexible scheme for multiple users, and almost impossible to guarantee that the generated numbers were unique. In the section "Generating sequential numbers" in chapter 4, I presented LotusScript code that solves these problems and provides a very flexible document number generator. (See also chapter 17 for a more detailed description.) Record locking is used to guarantee unique numbers, and prefix/suffix codes can be attached to the number.

Even with this flexible LotusScript solution, there is one remaining requirement without a completely satisfying solution. This is the need to generate these numbers over a WAN. My LotusScript solution works by updating the last used number for any given document in a centralized database. This means that a user must be physically connected to the network to generate a number. (If he or she weren't connected, the record locking wouldn't work, so there would be duplicate numbers). The connection can be over a LAN or a modem, but a modem connection is often impractical because you usually have only one or two modem connections on your server which are normally used by many users for replication; you don't want these connections tied up for long periods of time by people working interactively over the modem. And if your organization is spread out geographically, then working online via modem can also be prohibitively expensive. I presented a partial solution to this problem that uses an agent to generate numbers on the server for remotely entered documents. This may work in some cases, but sometimes it won't, because the user needs to see the generated number as soon as he or she has saved the document, and can't wait until the document has been replicated to the server to find out the number.

The need to generate sequential numbers over a WAN could be called the *Holy Grail* of Notes programming—programmers have been looking for a solution to this problem for years. Finally, with Domino and the $$QuerySaveAgent feature, it is possible to generate sequential numbers over the Internet for users at any geographical location, without the need to incur long-distance phone charges or to tie up your server's modem connection. The agent in this section supports all the features of the LotusScript number generator and works over the Web.

First, you need to create a copy of the document numbers database in the Action directory where your Domino Web site is stored. (If you haven't yet gone through the tutorial in this book, you can go through the section "Document numbers database"in chapter 4 to create it before you continue, or you can copy it from the *Inside Lotus-Script* CD.)

1 On your Notes workspace, click on the Document Numbers database you created in the tutorial. You can also find a copy of this database on the *Inside LotusScript* CD.

2 Select the File|Database|New Copy menu.

3 Under title enter `Internet Document Numbers`. Leave the file name as Doc-Nums.nsf.

4 Click on the directory icon next to the file name and select the Action subdirectory (or whatever directory you put your Domino Web site in).

5 Under the Copy Options select Database design only.

6 Press OK to save the new copy.

You do not need to make any changes to the Document Numbers database; it will work as is. Now you'll add fields to the Response form in the Office Locations database to enable sequential number generation:

1 Open the Office Locations database in design mode.

2 Select Design|Forms and double click on the Response form to open it in design mode.

3 Scroll down and click to the left of the tmpFrom field, and press Enter to create a blank line on the form. Click on the blank line and select the Create|Field menu to create the following three fields:
   - `Prefix`   type Text, Editable
   - `DocumentNumber`   type Number, Editable
   - `Suffix`   type Text, Editable

4 Close the field properties window. Click to the left of the Prefix field and type the text `Document Number:` as a prompt.

5 Select the Prefix, DocumentNumber, and Suffix fields with the mouse, and then select the Text|Text Properties window.

6 Click on the hide/when tab (the second tab from the right) and select the options Previewed for editing and Opened for editing. This will hide the field at data entry time, since you don't want the user to enter a value in this field. Close the text properties window.

7 Scroll down in the form and click your mouse to the right of the hidden $$Return field, then select the Create Field menu.

8 Under Name enter $$QuerySaveAgent, and make the field type Text, Computed.

9 Close the field properties window, and enter the following formula in the Value event in the programming pane:

"Generate Document Number"

This is the name of the agent you will create next.

10 Save and close the Response form.

The final step is to create the Generate Document Number agent that will run on your server whenever a Response document is saved in this database:

1 Select the Create|Agent menu item.

2 Under Name enter Generate Document Number.

3 Select the Shared Agent option checkbox.

4 Under the question When should this agent run? select Manually From Agent List.

5 Under the question Which document(s) should it act on? select All documents in database.

6 Under the question What should this agent do? select the Script option.

7 Select the Initialize event, and then enter the LotusScript code in listing 12.3. For a more detailed explanation of some parts of this code, see listing 17.2.

8 Save and close the agent.

Listing 12.3   Generating document numbers over the Internet

```
1   On Error Goto Error_Handler
    Dim session As New NotesSession
    Dim ServerDoc As NotesDocument
    Set ServerDoc = session.DocumentContext

    Dim db As NotesDatabase
    Dim numbers_db As New NotesDatabase("","")
    Dim view As NotesView
    Dim doc As NotesDocument
    Dim Item As notesitem

    Dim PrefixCode
    Dim SuffixCode
    Dim NextDocumentNumber As Long
    Dim Database_Path As String
    Dim New_Document_Number As String, DB_Name As String

    Set db = session.CurrentDatabase
2   DB_Name = Left$(db.FilePath, Instr(1, db.FilePath, db.Filename, 1)-1) +
    "DocNums.NSF"
    REM Open the document numbers database
3   If ( Not (numbers_db.Open(db.Server, DB_Name))) Then
```

Listing 12.3   Generating document numbers over the Internet (continued)

```
      REM Exit if not found
      Print "<a>Database '" + DB_Name + "'not found</a>"
      Exit Sub
   End If

4  Start_Lock:
5  Set ServerDoc = session.DocumentContext

   REM Only generate the number if the field is blank
   Set item = ServerDoc.GetFirstItem( "DocumentNumber" )
   If Len(item.Text) = 0 Then

   REM Get the Document Number for this database
      Set view = numbers_db.GetView("($All)")
      Set doc = view.GetDocumentByKey(db.Title)
6     If doc Is Nothing Then
         REM No LastUsedNumber document exists for this database, so create
   one
         Set doc = New NotesDocument(numbers_db)
         doc.Form = "Document Number"
         doc.DatabaseTitle = db.Title
         doc.LastUsedNumber = 0
         Call doc.Save (True,True)
      End If

7     PrefixCode = doc. Prefix(0)
      SuffixCode = doc.Suffix(0)
      NextDocumentNumber = Clng(doc.LastUsedNumber(0))
      NextDocumentNumber = NextDocumentNumber + 1
      doc.LastUsedNumber = NextDocumentNumber
      New_Document_Number = PrefixCode & Format$(NextDocumentNumber) &
   SuffixCode

   REM Save the incremented LastUsed value
8     flag = doc.Save(False, False)
      If flag = False Then
9        Goto Start_Lock
      End If

10    ServerDoc.Prefix = PrefixCode
      ServerDoc.DocumentNumber = NextDocumentNumber
      ServerDoc.Suffix = SuffixCode
   End If

11 Print  "<h2> Document number '" + New_Document_Number + "' saved.</
   h2><br><h4> <a href=/action/HomePage.nsf?Open>Return to Home Page</a>"

   Exit Sub
```

Listing 12.3 Generating document numbers over the Internet (continued)

```
12 Error_Handler:
13 Print "<a>Error on line number " + Format$(Erl()) + ": " + Error$ + "</a>"
   Exit Sub
```

Listing Notes:

1 You must use the `On Error` statement to go to an error handler in all agents that are run from the Internet. If you don't, you risk hanging the HTTP service on your Domino server, and users will no longer be able to save new documents.

2 This statement creates a file name for DocNums.nsf that is based on the current directory. This means that this agent will work on any Internet database, as long as there is a DocNums.nsf file in the same subdirectory as the database. The reason it's done this way is so that you do not have to modify this code for sites that are stored in different directory names; the code will always work. For a more detailed discussion of directories and referencing Notes databases, see chapter 3.

3 This line opens the Document Numbers database that contains the last used number and prefix/suffix codes. If this database is not found, the agent is exited with the `Exit Sub` command to prevent an error message. (You can remove the `Print` statement that follows from your production code—it is included here to aid your debugging if you have any difficulties getting this agent to work.)

4 The `Start_Lock` label indicates the beginning of the record locking loop that is used to guarantee that generated numbers are unique. Record locking is explained in more detail in listing notes 8 and 9.

5 This line sets the `ServerDoc NotesDocument` variable to the document about to be saved (i.e., the document entered by the Web user, just before Domino saves it to disk).

6 This line checks to see if there is an existing last used number stored in Doc-Nums.nsf for the current document/database. If not, the next several lines generate and initialize a document that starts at number 0.

7 These lines retrieve the last user number and prefix/suffix codes, increments the number and stores it in back into the last used number document, and combines the prefix, number, and suffix into the `New_Document_Number` variable.

8 This line saves the incremented last used value back into the Document Numbers database. This line is the key to record locking. Because the parameters of the save are set to `False, False` the save will not create a replication conflict if two users are generating and saving a document number at the same time. Instead, in this case, it returns a value of False to the flag variable of one of the users; the other user will have the document saved successfully.

9 If saving the last used number returned False, it means that another user got and saved the number just generated, so the Goto statement goes back to the beginning of this agent to generate the next available sequential number.

10 This line sets the Prefix, DocumentNumber and Suffix fields on the Office Locations Response form to the newly generated number.

11 The Print statement outputs an HTML page that displays the generated number and includes a link back to your home page.

12 This label is where the On Error statement (see listing note 1) jumps if your script encounters an error.

13 This Print statement generates an HTML page that displays the line number of the error and the text of the error message. If there are any errors that you expect could normally occur in your script, you should trap for them before this Print statement by checking the value of the Err predefined variable (i.e., Err will contain the error number of the latest error).

Now that you are finished creating the agent, go to a main document in the Office Locations database in your Web browser. (Remember, there is a link to this database on your About the Company page; select a state on the map to display a main document.) Click on the Send Feedback to This Office button and fill out the form normally in your Web browser. When you submit the document to be saved by Domino, the agent you entered above displays the generated document number and a link to your home page, as shown in figure 12.1.

12.7 Example 2: a server triggered agent to send email notifications

Another way to use agents in Domino applications is to have agents on the server that are triggered by various conditions, such as when new documents are added to a database. In this example, we'll add an agent to send an email notification whenever a user submits a feedback document to the Office Locations database.

1 Open the Office Locations database.

2 Select the Create|Agent menu item.

3 Under Name enter `Email Notification`.

4 Select the Shared Agent option checkbox.

5 Under the question When should this agent run? select the option If documents have been created or modified.

6 Under the question What should this agent do? select the Script option.

7 Select the Initialize event, and then enter the LotusScript code in listing 12.4.

8 Save and close the agent.

Listing 12.4   Agent to send email notification

```
    REM Get the current database
    Dim db As NotesDatabase
    Set s = New NotesSession
    Set db = s.CurrentDatabase

    REM Get the collection of new documents
    Dim coll As NotesDocumentCollection
1   Set coll = db.UnprocessedDocuments

    REM variables used to generate the email
    Dim newdoc As NotesDocument
    Dim rtitem As NotesRichTextItem
    Dim i As Integer

    Set db = session.CurrentDatabase
2   For i = 1 To coll.Count
       Set doc = coll.GetNthDocument( i )
3      If doc.Form = "Response" Then
```

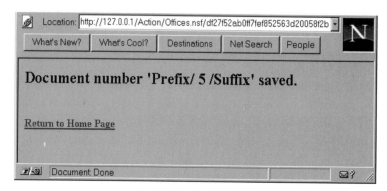

Figure 12.1   Sequential number generated on the net

Listing 12.4   Agent to send email notification (continued)

```
      Set newdoc = New NotesDocument(db)
      Set rtitem = New NotesRichTextItem (newdoc, "Body")
      Call rtitem.AppendText("There is a customer feedback for you. Double
 click on the link below to see it:")
      Call rtitem.AddNewLine(1)
      Call rtitem.AddNewLine(1)
4     Call rtitem.AppendDocLink (doc, doc.Subject(0))
      newdoc.Subject = "New Feedback: " + doc.Subject(0)
5     newdoc.SendTo = "Joe McGinn/Joe's Place"
6     Call newdoc.Send (False)

    End If   'this is a Response document
 Next

 Exit Sub
```

Listing Notes:

1 Gets the collection of documents specified in the agent (i.e., in this case all new and modified documents in the database).

2 Cycles through the new documents one at a time.

3 Checks to see if the document was created with the Response form, and skips the email notification if it wasn't.

4 Appends a document link to the new document into the email notification. The user who receives the email can double-click on it to go to the new feedback document.

5 Specifies the email address of the recipient for email notification. You might want to add code here to direct the email differently depending on which office was selected for feedback.

6 Sends the email.

Whenever new feedback is entered into the Office Locations database, an email notification will be sent for it.

12.8 Example 3: a customized search engine

In the native Notes client you can attach LotusScript code to action bar items and buttons on forms. You can't attach LotusScript code directly to a form being run from a Web browser, but you can accomplish the same thing indirectly by running a server-based agent when a Web user presses a button. In this section I'll show you how to create a customized search engine agent that allows a Web user to search through the feedback database for all documents that he or she authored.

This agent also demonstrates two other useful features:

- The more sophisticated uses of generating HTML using the `Print` statement, such as setting the background color and generating a list of hypertext links to documents.
- The use of a CGI variable, to get the name of the user.

1 Open the Office Locations database.

2 Select the Create|Agent menu item.

3 Under Name enter `Author Search`.

4 Select the Shared Agent option checkbox.

5 Under the question When should this agent run? select the option Manually from agent list.

6 Under the question Which document(s) should it act on? select the option All documents in database.

7 Under the question What should this agent do? select the Script option.

8 Select the Initialize event, and then enter the LotusScript code in listing 12.5.

9 Save and close the agent.

Listing 12.5 Agent to search for documents a Web user authored

```
On Error Goto Error_Handler

' Get the document context, so that we can retrieve the user's name
' from a CGI variable
Dim session As New NotesSession
Dim doc As NotesDocument
1  Set doc = session.DocumentContext

' Print the HTML page header
2  Print {<html><body text="000000" bgcolor="f7f7f7">}

' Search the current database for Response documents authored by the
' current user.
Dim db As NotesDatabase, collection As NotesDocumentCollection
Dim Search_String as String
Set db = sess.CurrentDatabase
3  Search_String = "@Contains(From; """ + doc.remote_user(0) + """) & Form =
""Response"""
```

Listing 12.5   Agent to search for documents a Web user authored (continued)

```
4   Set collection = db.Search(Search_String, Nothing, 0)

    ' Loop over the collection of matching documents.
    Dim MatchDoc As NotesDocument
5   Print "<font size=5><b>There are " & Str$(collection.Count) & " documents
    authored by " + doc.remote_user(0) + ".</b></font><br>"

6   For i% = 1 To collection.Count
        Set MatchDoc = collection.GetNthDocument(i%)

        'Print the hypertext link to the document
7       Print {<br><a href="/Action/Offices.nsf/($All)/} & MatchDoc.UniversalID
    _ & {?OpenDocument">} & MatchDoc.Form(0) & "</a><br>   "

8       Forall item In MatchDoc.Items
            If Ucase(item.Name) = "SUBJECT" Then
9               Print "   <b>" & item.Name & "</b>: " & item.Text
            End If
        End Forall
    Next
    Exit Sub

    Error_Handler:
    Print "<a>Error on line number " + Format$(Erl()) + ": " + Error$ + "</a>"
    Exit Sub
```

Listing Notes:

1 Sets the doc variable to DocumentContext. This will enable you to retrieve the user's name from a CGI variable.

2 This Print statement sets the background color for the page and the foreground color for text.

3 This line constructs the search criteria, getting the user's name from the CGI variable doc.remote_user(0). The extra double quotes are how you tell LotusScript to insert a double-quote character into the string, which you have to do here. For example, if the user name is Joe McGinn then the Search_String variable will evaluate to:

@Contains(From; "Joe McGinn") & Form = "Response"

4 The database Search method requires either a date/time parameter to limit the search or the keyword Nothing. Here you use the latter so that all documents

Tip

You can create hypertext links to edit documents as well, simply by changing `?OpenDocument` in line 7 to: `?EditDocument`.

Tip

Normally you can run an agent from a button using the simpler `@Command([ToolsRunMacro]; "Author Search")` command. But for this agent the user must be logged in, since the user's name is used as the search criteria in the agent (i.e., the user name is retrieved from a CGI variable). So, instead of the `ToolsRunMacro` command, you use the more flexible OpenURL command. The `@Subset(@DbName; 1)` part gets the current server, and the `&Login=1` part at the end ensures that the user is logged in before the agent is run. Of course, if the user is already logged in he or she does not have to log in again.

matching the search criteria will be retrieved. The search returns the results as a Notes document collection.

5　Displays the number of matches on the HTML output page.

6　Loops through all the documents returned by the search.

7　Creates the hypertext link to each retrieved document.

8　Loops through each field in the retrieved document.

9　Prints the Subject field.

Now that you've created the agent, you need to create a button to run it.

1　Select Design|Forms and double-click on the Main Topic form.

2　Select the View|Action Pane menu, then select Create|Action.

3　Under Title enter `View Your Feedback Documents` and select an icon under Button Icon. Close the action properties window.

4　Insert the following formula into the programming pane that runs the agent:

```
@URLOpen( @Subset(@DbName; 1) + "/Action/
Offices.nsf/Author+Search?OpenAgent&Login=1")
```

5　Close and save the form.

Make sure Domino is running, and use your Web browser to go to an Office Location document. When you click on the View Your Feedback Documents button, you will get back a page containing hypertext links to all the Response documents you authored, as show in figure 12.2.

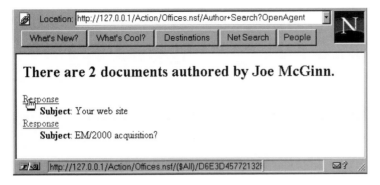

Figure 12.2   Documents you authored agent results

12.9 Summary

In this chapter you've learned how to add intelligence to your Web applications by adding LotusScript agents to it (and if you haven't realized it yet, you've also written your first true client/server software!).

We've covered how to run agents to process forms using the $$QueryOpenAgent and $$QuerySaveAgent features to simulate the Notes client Queryopen and Querysave events. You've learned how to use the DocumentContext property to access and modify fields on a Domino form.

We have looked at how to generate HTML data and hypertext links from Lotus-Script, how to use the `Print` and `Messagebox` statements to debug Internet agents, and how Notes security applies to agents.

Last but not least, you have implemented several practical examples of Internet agents. The first one enables you to generate sequential document numbers on the Web and demonstrates the use of the $$QuerySaveAgent feature. In example 2, I showed you how to run a triggered agent on the server when documents are added to a database, and how to send email notifications. The third agent showed you how to use LotusScript to create a customized search engine that uses CGI variables and generates a list of hypertext links to the search results, and how to run an agent from a button.

A programmer's toolbox

Part 4 of this book explores LotusScript and formula solutions to common Notes programming requirements. In chapter 13, I'll show you how to access the Notes formula user interface functions (e.g., @Prompt and @Command) from LotusScript. You will learn how to pass parameters back and forth between formulas and LotusScript code modules so that you can combine them to solve problems that neither can solve by themselves.

In chapter 14, I'll show you how to use the new programming features of Notes 4.5. Chapter 15 contains a complete library of LotusScript list-processing functions for Notes 4.5.

Chapter 16 shows how to simulate various relational database capabilities in Notes. You'll find out how to add a server-based sequential number generator to any Notes 4 application in chapter 17. This includes an exploration of record locking, which guarantees that the sequential numbers are unique within a LAN. Various solutions for generating numbers over WANs are also presented.

In chapter 18, you'll find some useful LotusScript agents, as well as tips on how to debug agents that are running in the background on your server. The agents include a LotusScript search engine that can search through all Notes databases in a subdirectory.

In chapter 19, I'll present several tips and tricks that are useful in many situations, including dynamic checkboxes and radio buttons, and instructions on how to store user-specific options in a database.

Last, in chapter 20, we'll look at what you can expect in future versions of Lotus Notes.

C H A P T E R   1 3

LotusScript user interface programming

13.1 They said it couldn't be done!

Like many programmers, I'm a bit of a perfectionist. I like to make my users happy. One of my frustrations with certain Notes 4 programming tasks was telling users "Sorry, it can't be done." This is what I was told about accessing the Notes user interface from LotusScript, and as far as I could tell from LotusScript statements and object classes this was the case.

By accessing the user interface I mean things as simple as displaying a menu of choices to the user, or displaying a particular document on the screen. You can use commands like @Prompt, @Picklist, and @Command to do these things from a formula, but there are no equivalent commands in LotusScript. LotusScript can run a limited set of formula commands using the Evaluate statement, but unfortunately the user interface commands are not included.

In this chapter I will present a practical workaround for this problem. The solution lies in using agents to combine LotusScript code and formulas, and using environment variables to pass parameters between the two. This allows you to combine the best of both worlds by combining LotusScript and formula code.

13.2 Make a menu selection

Tip

Environment variables are the Notes equivalent of global variables. They are stored in the Notes INI file, so they persist even after your database and Notes have been closed. Because of this, they should always be initialized before you use them.

One of the most basic requirements for any computer program is the ability to display a menu to allow a user to make a selection from a number of choices. In a formula this can be done using the @Prompt command. But there's no way to do it in LotusScript. The formula code in listing 13.1 shows how to present a menu selection in a formula, and store the result in an environment variable. We will use agents to pass this parameter over to LotusScript code for processing.

First, you need to create a test development database to use throughout this chapter:

1 Select File|Database|New and under Title enter LotusScript Testing.

2 Select the Discussion (R4) template, or any other template with which you are comfortable working.

3 Deselect the option Inherit future design changes. This is a new test development database, so you don't want your new design overwritten.

4 Press OK to save the new database.

Now create the first agent in your development database. This agent contains the formula code to display a menu.

1 Select the Create|Agent menu.

2 Under Name enter `Color Selection Part 1`.

3 Select the Shared Agent check box option.

4 Under the question When should this agent run? select the option Manually From Actions Menu.

5 Under the question Which document(s) should it act on? select the option Run once(`@Commands` may be used).

6 Under the question What should this agent do? select the Formula option.

Enter the code in listing 13.1 into the formula window.

Listing 13.1   Presenting a menu selection part 1

```
1  @Environment("Choice";"");
2  Choice:=@Prompt([OkCancelList]; "Select a Color";"Select your favorite
   color.";"";"Blue":"Green":"Red":"Purple");
3  @Environment("Choice";Choice)
```

Listing Notes:

1 It's a good idea to set your environment variable to an empty string. If the user presses Cancel, this string will remain empty. This gives you a way to test for the Cancel condition later in your LotusScript code.

2 The `@Prompt` function is the easiest way to display a menu.

3 Stores the selection made by the user into an environment variable called `Choice`.

4 Save and close the agent.

The agent should look like the screen in figure 13.1.

Now you will create a second agent that reads the result of the menu selection in a LotusScript function:

1 Select the Create|Agent menu item.

2 Under Name enter `Color Selection Part 2`.

3 Select the Shared Agent option.

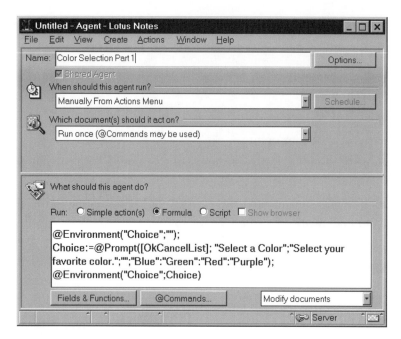

Figure 13.1   Color selection agent

4   Under the question When should this agent run? select the option Manually From Actions Menu.

5   Under the question Which document(s) should it act on? select the option Run once(@Commands may be used).

6   Under the question What should this agent do? select the Script option.

7   Select the Initialize event, and then enter the LotusScript code in listing 13.2.

8   Save and close the new agent.

Listing 13.2   Presenting a menu selection part 2

```
1  Dim session As New NotesSession
   Dim Choice As String
2  Choice = session.GetEnvironmentString("Choice", False)
3  If Choice = "" Then Exit Sub
4  Messagebox Choice
```

Listing Notes:

1 The session variable is what you use to get and set environment variables in Lotus-Script.

2 Retrieves the selection made by the user in the agent from listing 13.1. The `False` parameter tells Notes to retrieve a user-defined environment variable. If you set this to `True`, then `GetEnvironmentString` can be used to retrieve Notes system variables from the NOTES.INI file.

3 Checks to see if the user selected Cancel, and exits the script without further processing if he or she did.

4 Displays the user's selection in a message box.

The final step is to combine the two agents you have created to run them as a single program. Fortunately, Notes makes this part a lot easier than it sounds. Use these instructions any time you want to create a button that runs two (or more) agents.

1 Open a form or view in design mode, and select the View|Action menu to display the action pane.

2 Create a new action button by selecting the Create|Action menu.

3 Under Title enter Choose Color, and select a Button Icon. Close the action properties window.

4 In the programming pane select Simple actions(s).

5 Press the Add Action button.

6 Under Action select Run Agent.

7 Under Agent select Color Selection Part 1 and press OK.

8 Press the Add Action button a second time.

9 Under Action select Run Agent.

10 Under Agent select Color Selection Part 2 and press OK.

11 Save and exit the form or view.

This button will now run the combined formula/LotusScript agent as a single function. When you press it, it will display the menu, and after you make a selection, it will be immediately displayed by the LotusScript code in part 2 of the agent. You can create a three (or more) part agent if, for example, you need to access a user

> **Tip**
>
> You should always document the names of environment variables that you use, and what they are for. This way you can reuse temporary variables, and can also avoid accidentally overwriting permanent ones. It's probably also a good idea to prefix your environment variable names with something unique, like the name of your organization or product. For example, for a sales application you could use `Sales_Choice`.

interface function between two blocks of LotusScript code. For this case agents 1 and 3 would be LotusScript, and agent 2 would be the formula code that displays the menu.

13.3 Search for and display a document

Let's take this technique and apply it in a more practical context. A common requirement is the need to display a document on the Notes user interface. Many users want a simple search mechanism for a specific purpose that is simpler and quicker to use than the generic Notes Search Bar.

For example, if you have a DocumentNumber field used for tracking purposes, the users may want to enter a number and search just in that column of a view. The Notes built-in full-text find command may not work, because many numbers are embedded in the data in other fields, so the search will return many documents. LotusScript has powerful searching capabilities, but many programmers have been frustrated to find that there is no built-in way to display the results of your search. (*Note:* this has changed in Notes 4.5—see the tip for Notes 4.5 users at the end of this section.) By combining a LotusScript agent and a formula agent, the result of the search can be displayed on the user interface.

1 First, edit the form that you want to search for, add a field named DocumentNumber to it with the Create|Field command, and make the field type Number.

2 Save and close the form, and add or edit a few documents to create some DocumentNumber values.

   Now you can create the two agents to search for and display a document:

1 Select the Create|Agent menu item.

2 Under Name enter Display Document Part 1.

3 Select the Shared Agent option.

4 Under the question When should this agent run? select the option Manually From Actions Menu.

5 Under the question Which document(s) should it act on? select the option Run once (@Commands may be used).

6 Under the question What should this agent do? select the Script option.

7 Select the Initialize event, and then enter the LotusScript code in listing 13.3.

Listing 13.3   Display document by UNID Part 1

```
    Dim session As New NotesSession
    Dim workspace As New NotesUIWorkspace
    Dim doc As NotesDocument
    Dim db As NotesDatabase
    Dim unid As String
    Dim document_to_find As String
    Dim collection As NotesDocumentCollection

    document_to_find = Inputbox$("Enter the document # you want to find:",
    "Find a Call")

    If document_to_find = "" Then
1     Call session.SetEnvironmentVar("UNID","")
    Exit Sub
    End If

    Set db = session.CurrentDatabase
2   Set collection = db.Search( "DocumentNumber="+ document_to_find, Nothing,
    0)
    If collection.Count = 0 Then
3   Messagebox "Document number " + document_to_find + " not found."
    Call session.SetEnvironmentVar("UNID","")
    Exit Sub
    End If
4   Set doc = collection.GetFirstDocument
5   unid = doc.UniversalID
6   Call session.SetEnvironmentVar("UNID",unid)
```

Listing Notes:

1 If the user did not enter any data, this code sets the UNID environment variable to the empty string and exits the subroutine, so that Part 2 of the agent won't display an error message.

Tip

The code here shows the syntax for searching a numeric field. If you want to search a text field (e.g., Subject) you need to add quotation marks around the search parameter as follows:

```
Set collection = db.Search( "Subject=" + Chr$(34) + document_to_find + Chr$(34),
dateTime, 0)
```

The Chr$(34) adds a double-quote character.

---

2 Uses the NotesDatabase Search method to search the database. Because DocumentNumbers are unique, the search will return a document collection with only one document in it.

3 If the document the user is looking for is not found, an error message is displayed.

4 Retrieves the NotesDocument from the document collection retrieved by the Search method.

5 Gets the document's UniversalID.

6 Sets the UNID environment variable to the UniversalID of the retrieved document. Part 2 of the agent needs the UniversalID value to display the document.

Now create the second agent to display the retrieved document on the screen.

1 Select the Create|Agent menu item.

2 Under Name enter Display Document Part 2.

3 Select the Shared Agent option.

4 Under the question When should this agent run? select the option Manually From Actions Menu.

5 Under the question Which document(s) should it act on? select the option Run once (@Commands may be used).

6 Under the question What should this agent do? select Formula.

7 In the programming pane enter the code in listing 13.4.

Listing 13.4   Display document by UNID Part 2

```
1  @Command([OpenView];"($All)");
2  @Command([OpenDocument]; "0"; @Environment("UNID"))
```

Listing Notes:

1 The view needs to contain the document you are searching for or you will get an error. This line ensures that the All Documents view is open so that the document you are searching for can always be found.

2 Opens the specified document on the user interface. The 0 option opens the document in read mode. Specifying 1 will open the document in edit mode.

Notes 4.5 has a new and very useful LotusScript feature for converting a document directly into an editable NotesUIDocument, which means you do not need a two-part agent to display a document. (It also allows you to display a document from anywhere, whether it's a view containing the document or not.) You can display any document on the user interface with the following line of code, where doc is a NotesDocument (the first parameter specifies the edit mode) and workspace is a NotesUIWorkspace variable.

```
Call workspace.EditDocument (False, doc)
```

In the LotusScript code in listing 13.3, simply remove the code for setting environment variables and add the above line at the end of the subroutine. Because no formula agent is required, you do not have to make the LotusScript code an agent; you can attach it directly to a button or action bar item.

Last, you need to create a button to run the agents. Open a view in design mode, and create a new Action bar button. Use the simple actions option to combine two Run Agent commands for Display Document Part 1 and Display Document Part 2 (i.e., as you did for the color selection agents earlier in this chapter). When you press this button, it will ask you for a document number, search for the document, and then display that document on the screen.

13.4 Creating summary reports

There are sometimes situations where you want to create a new document in LotusScript, and then display it on the screen. For example, you might want to programmatically collect various pieces of information, include them in a summary report, and then display the report in edit mode so that the user can add additional comments. Creating a new document is easy, as shown in the code in listing 13.5. The code creates a link to all selected documents, adds some text information for them, and then opens the document on the screen in edit mode.

Tip

As you are probably aware, the NotesDatabase Search method can return multiple documents. This book also includes LotusScript code that searches for multiple documents (i.e., a document collection) and displays the results on the screen:

1 For Notes 4.5 users, see the section "Search and display multiple documents" in chapter 14.

2 For Notes 4.0 and 4.1 users, see the section "Search and display multiple documents agent" in chapter 18.

Tip

For searching across a complete multidatabase application, see the section "Search all databases in a subdirectory" in chapter 18.

First, you need to have a form named Summary Report with a text field called Subject on it, in the current database. If you're working off a test Discussion database template, just use cut-and-paste to copy the Summary Report form from the Main Topic form:

1 Select Design|Forms, and singe-click on the Main Topic form.

2 Select the Edit|Copy menu, then select the Edit|Paste menu.

3 Double-click on the Copy of Main Topic form.

4 Select the Design|Form Properties menu and rename the form Summary Report.

5 Save and close the form.

Now create the first agent that will create the report document.

1 Select the Create|Agent menu item.

2 Select the Shared Agent property.

3 Under Name enter Summary Report Part 1.

4 Under the question When should this agent run? select the option Manually From Actions Menu.

5 Under the question Which document(s) should it act on? choose the option Selected documents.

6 Under the question What should this agent do? select the Script option.

7 Select the Initialize event, and then enter the LotusScript code in listing 13.5.

Listing 13.5 Create summary report Part 1

```
Dim db As NotesDatabase
Dim session As New NotesSession
Dim workspace As New NotesUIWorkspace
Dim unid As String
Dim reportitem As Variant
Dim collection As NotesDocumentCollection
Dim newdoc As NotesDocument
Dim doc As NotesDocument

    Set db = session.CurrentDatabase
1   Set newdoc = New NotesDocument (db)
2   newdoc.Form = "Summary Report"
3   newdoc.Subject = "Selected subject documents"
4   Call newdoc.CreateRichTextItem("Body")
    Set reportitem = newdoc.GetFirstItem("Body")
5   Set collection = db.UnProcessedDocuments
```

Listing 13.5 Create summary report Part 1 (continued)

```
     For j =1 To collection.Count
        Set doc = collection.GetNthDocument(j)
6          Call reportitem.AppendDocLink (doc, doc.Subject(0))
7          Call reportitem.AppendText(" " + doc.Subject(0))
           Call reportitem.AddNewLine(1)
     Next
8    Call reportitem.AppendText(" ")
9    Call newdoc.Save(True,False)
     unid = newdoc.UniversalID
10   Call session.SetEnvironmentVar("UNID",unid)
11   Call workspace.ViewRefresh
```

Listing Notes:

1 Creates the new report document in the current database.

2 Specifies `Summary Report` as the form to use for the new document.

3 Enters data into the new document's Subject field.

4 Creates a rich text Body field on the report.

5 Sets a NotesDocumentCollection variable to the documents currently selected in the view.

6 Creates a document link to each of the selected documents.

7 Appends the Subject text for each selected document.

8 Due to a bug in Notes, you cannot leave a `NewLine` character as the last line in a rich text field, or the field will not be displayed correctly in edit mode (it will lose the end-marker for the field). As long as you add some text after the last `NewLine`, as done here, it will work fine.

9 Saves the new summary report.

10 Saves the new document's `Universal ID` into the `UNID` environment variable.

11 Refreshes the current view so that the new document can be displayed by the Summary Report Part 2 agent.

Tip for Notes 4.5 Users

You can use the new Notes 4.5 feature to display the document directly, without the need for the second agent. Just add the following line of code to the end of the agent:

```
Call workspace.EditDocument(True, newdoc)
```

If you don't have Notes 4.5, you need to create a second agent to display the new document.

1 Select the Create|Agent menu item.

2 Under Name enter `Summary Report Part 2`.

3 Select the Shared Agent option.

4 Under the question When should this agent run? select the option Manually From Actions Menu.

5 Under the question Which document(s) should it act on? select the option Run once (`@Commands` may be used).

6 Under the question What should this agent do? select Formula.

7 In the programming pane enter the code in listing 13.6.

Listing 13.6   Display document by UNID Part 2

```
1  @Command([OpenDocument]; "1"; @Environment("UNID"))
```

Listing Notes:

1 Displays the newly created document on the screen. Because it is a new report, the document is opened in Edit mode. To open in Read mode, specify 0 instead of 1.

Now combine the two agents into one function. In any view, create an Action bar button. Use the Simple Actions option to combine two Run Agent commands for `Summary Report Part 1` and `Summary Report Part 2`. When you press this button, a new report will be created, and then it will be opened on the screen in edit mode. A sample summary report is shown in figure 13.2

Tip

If you want to add advanced formatting features such as controlling fonts and colors of text added to a report, see the section "Manipulating Rich Text Fonts and Colors" in chapter 19.

13.5 Summary

You have learned how to use agents and environment variables to combine LotusScript and formula code into a unified function, and how to access the formula user interface functions from LotusScript. This technique can be used in almost any situation where

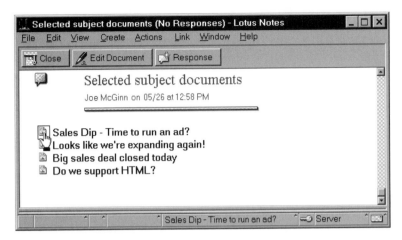

Figure 13.2   Summary report

you must to access formula functions from LotusScript (or vice versa). You have example code that shows you how to search for and display a document, and how to create and display a report document.

CHAPTER 14

New features in Notes 4.5

There are many valuable new features in Notes 4.5. They range from enhancements to the user interface to basic improvements to the Notes programming model (i.e., such as LotusScript libraries that allow "global" database code).

In this chapter you will learn:

- How to implement calendar views to display any date/time stamped documents on a calendar.

- How to use the new graphical date and time popup editors on date/time fields.

- How to use profile documents to conveniently store user-specific options for a database.

- How to implement global database variables and functions using LotusScript libraries.

- How to run an agent directly from LotusScript code, including examples that show how to pass parameters to formula functions from LotusScript.

- About the new graphical design features for text, tables, layout regions, and forms.

- How to use the new EditDocument method to search for and display multiple documents on the screen.

- How to use other new programming features like specifying a startup database, designating the default layout of the document preview form, and how to inherit the About Database and Using Database documents from a template to a database.

14.1 Calendar views

The new Calendar views in Notes 4.5 allow you to display any Notes data on a calendar. You can also use a new view event to determine what action to take when a user double-clicks on a calendar region.

A Calendar view always has the following format:

- The View Properties window's Style item must be set to Calendar.

- Column 1 of the view contains the start date. This can be a simple date or a date and time value.

- Column 2 contains the event's duration. If this is not applicable for the view you are creating, you have to create a dummy column that displays the value 0 (zero). Column 2 must be hidden.

Tip

If you have completed the Internet Programming part of this book, feel free to use the Office Locations view you created there—calendar views are fully compatible with Domino and Web browsers.

- The third (and subsequent) columns contain whatever text you want displayed in the calendar items. Remember that space is limited, so you should usually limit this to one graphical icon column and one text column.

As an example, I'll show you how to add a view to a Discussion database that displays main topics and responses on a calendar. First, you need to open or create a Discussion database.

1 Select the Create|View menu.

2 Enter `Calendar` as the view name, and select the Shared option.

3 Under Selection Conditions click on the Add Condition button. Under Condition select By Form Used, then select the Main Topic and Response forms. Press OK, then press OK again on the Create View screen.

4 Select Design|Views and double click on the Calendar view.

5 Double click on the Date column to load the properties window.

6 Click on the date/time tab and under Show select Date and time. Close the column properties window.

7 Click on the Topic field and select the Create|Insert New Column menu.

8 In the programming pane select Formula and enter 0 (zero) as the formula.

   Note: The second column represents an item's duration, such as you would have in a scheduling database. This doesn't apply to a discussion database, so you need a dummy column here that evaluates to 0.

9 Select Design|Column Properties and enter `Duration` as the title. Select the Hide Column option and close the properties window.

10 Click on the Topic column, then select the Create|Insert New Column menu. Select the Design|Column Properties menu and select the option Display values as icons. Close the properties window.

11 In the programming pane select formula and enter the following code:

```
@If(Form="Response"; 58;4)
```

   Note: If you want to change these values to display different icons, see the chart on page 241 of *Notes Application Developer's Guide*.

12 Drag the edge of the icon column to make it narrow—one character wide.

13 Select the Design|View Properties menu. Under Style select Calendar.

14 Save and close the view.

Your view should look something like figure 14.1.

Try selecting View, and you'll see that it displays in the default two-week mode, and that it shows your offices and responses with the appropriate icons. Now you should add action buttons to the view to allow the user to view it in other formats, such as one day, one month, and so on.

1 Select Design|Views and double-click on the Calendar view.

2 Select the View|Action Pane menu.

3 Delete the Navigator, New Main Topic, Response, and Response to Response actions, so that there will be room for several new action bar items.

4 Select the Create|Action menu.

5 Under Title enter Two Days. Select an appropriate Button Icon (see figure 14.2). Close the Action properties window.

6 In the programming pane enter the following formula:

```
@Command([CalendarFormat]; "2")
```

7 Repeat steps 4–6 to create the following action buttons and formulas:

One Week: `@Command([CalendarFormat]; "7")`

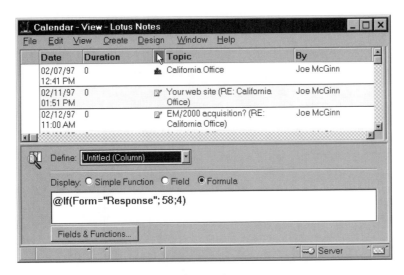

Figure 14.1 Calendar view in design mode

Two Weeks: `@Command([CalendarFormat]; "14")`

One Month: `@Command([CalendarFormat]; "30")`

Go To Today: `@Command([CalendarGoTo];@Date(@Now))`

8 Save and close the Calendar view.

Now when you use the view, you can choose the amount of time you want to see with these action items, as shown in figure 14.2.

Tip

If you have a scheduling type application, where you want to generate a new item at the date/time on which the user double-clicks, use the following code. First, edit the Main Topic form and add a date/time field called StartTime on it. You should probably also make this the field you show in the first column of the Calendar view, so that items show up in the view based on StartTime rather than the document creation time as in the previous example in this section. Then add the following code to the view's Regiondoubleclick event:

```
Set ws = New NotesUIWorkspace
Set UIdoc = ws.ComposeDocument("", "", "Main Topic")
Call UIdoc.FieldSetText("StartTime", source.CalendarDateTime)
```

The final piece of programming you normally implement on a calendar view is code that determines what happens when someone double-clicks in a blank region. In a Discussion database like this one, you might simply display a message that tells the user there is no item available for the date they clicked, as follows:

1 Select Design|Views and double click on the Calendar view.

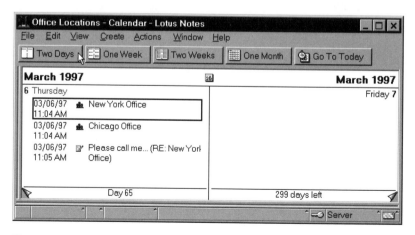

Figure 14.2 Calendar view

2 In the programming pane under Define select Calendar (View). (It's just above the View Selection item in the drop down list.)

3 Enter the following LotusScript code:

```
Messagebox "There is no document available for " + source.CalendarDateTime
```

`source.CalendarDateTime` is automatically filled in by Notes to the date and time where the user clicks on the calendar view.

14.2 Date and time popup fields

Two of the nicest new features in Notes 4.5 are the new popup GUI date and time editors. Now your users can enter dates and times without worrying about the format in which they must type information on the keyboard. The only limitation of these new features is that they work only on date, time, or time range fields; they don't work on fields that display both the date and time in one field.

To enable these features, you simply put the fields on a layout region. First, open up a form where you want to add the date/time controls:

1 Select the Create|Layout Region|New Layout Region menu.

2 Double-click on the region to display its properties window. Select the 3D style option and the Snap to grid option. Close the layout properties window.

3 Select the Create|Field menu, and double-click on the new field.

4 Under Name enter Date, Type Time, and under Show select Date. Close the field properties window.

5 Select the Create|Field menu, and double click on the new field.

6 Under Name enter Time, Type Time, and under Show select Time. Close the field properties window.

7 Select the Create|Field menu one more time, and double click on the new field.

8 Under Name enter TimeRange, Type Time, and under Show select Time. Select the Allow multivalues option to indicate that the field contains a date range.

9 For a time range field you also have to click on the Options tab and select Blank Line under both Separate values when user enters and Display separate values with. Close the field properties window.

10 Use the mouse to line up the fields on the form, and use the Create|Layout Region|Text menu to add text prompts to the fields.

11 Save and close the Main Topic form.

Now try creating a new Main Topic document, and you'll see the GUI date/time editors as shown in figure 14.3 (the date editor) and figure 14.4 (the time range editor).

14.3 Using profile documents

Tip

For users who don't have Notes 4.5, you can find out how to implement profile document functionality manually in the section "Storing User Specific Options" in chapter 19.

Profile documents are a special kind of document added in Notes 4.5. They are used to store user-specific options and preferences. The documents are hidden, so they don't show up in the views in a database. In this section I'll show you how to add a feature that allows users to maintain a tagline that is automatically appended to their messages in a discussion database.

First, open or create a discussion database:

1 Select the Create|Design|Form menu.

2 Select the Design|Form Properties menu and name the form User Options. Close the properties window.

3 Select the Create|Field menu. Under Name enter Tagline.

4 Save and close the form.

There are two ways to edit a profile form. If the form has multiple fields on it, you can edit it directly using the following formula command:

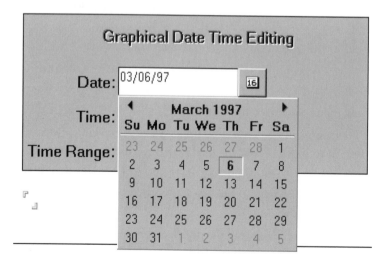

Figure 14.3   GUI date editor

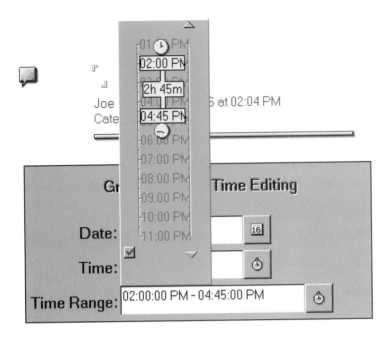

Figure 14.4 GUI time range editor

```
@Command([EditProfile];"User Options";@UserName)
```

The first time a user executes the commands a new profile document will be created for him or her. If the user executes it again, he or she will be taken into the existing document to edit it. There can be only one profile document per user for each profile form in your database. You can attach the command above to an action button on a view, or you can put it in a Run Once type of agent and run the agent from the Actions menu.

If you have only one option on the form, though, as in the example in this section, it's probably simpler for the user to edit and set the item directly by attaching the code in listing 14.1 to a button or agent. This code displays an input box (with a default value of the user's previous entry) and stores the result directly into the profile document using the @SetProfileField command.

Listing 14.1 Editing a profile variable directly

```
1  temp:=@Prompt([OKCANCELEDIT]; "Enter Tagline";"Enter the tagline to be
   attached to your messages.";@GetProfileField("User
   Options";"Tagline";@Username));
2  @SetProfileField("User Options"; "Tagline"; temp; @UserName)
```

Listing Notes:

1 Displays an edit box where the user can enter a tagline. The `@GetProfileField` command, the last parameter in the `@Prompt` call, sets the default value of the edit box to whatever value the user previously entered as the tagline. The result of the `@Prompt` input box is stored in the `temp` variable.

2 Saves the `temp` variable into the `Tagline` field of the `User Options` profile document.

The final step is to simply add a default value formula to the Body field of the Main Topic and Response forms so that the Tagline value is pulled in for all new documents:

1 Select Design|Forms and double-click on the Main Topic form.

2 Click on the Body field and enter the following formula as its default value.

```
@GetProfileField("User Options";"Tagline";@Username)
```

3 Save and close the Main Topic form.

4 Repeat steps 1–3 for the Response and Response to Response forms.

A tagline that the user can easily edit will now be automatically inserted into the Body field of all new messages.

14.4 LotusScript libraries

One of the biggest improvements for programmer in Notes 4.5 is LotusScript libraries. They allow you to create global variables and functions that can be accessed from anywhere in a database. If you've ever had to repeat the same code several times in one database, you know how difficult it can be to maintain. By using LotusScript, libraries you can centralize such code in one place, which makes it much easier to update and maintain.

For example, one commonly needed function is code to send automatic email notification. This is very often done in workflow applications where users need to be informed that a document needs their attention. The email usually includes a subject, text message, and a document link to the relevant document. I'll show you how to implement this function as a global subroutine that can be accessed throughout a database.

First, open a database that needs email notification. (A Discussion database will do.)

1 Select the Create|Design|Script Library function.

2 Select the Edit|Properties menu and enter `Email Notification` as the Title. Close the properties window.

3 Paste the code in listing 14.2 into the code window.

4 Save and close the new script library.

Listing 14.2 Subroutine to send email notification

```
    Sub EmailNotify (Subject As String, Message As String, Users As String, doc
    as NotesDocument)
    Dim session As New NotesSession
    Dim db As NotesDatabase
1   Set db = session.CurrentDatabase
    Dim newdoc As NotesDocument
    Dim rtitem As NotesRichTextItem

2   Set newdoc = New NotesDocument(db)
3   Set rtitem = New NotesRichTextItem (newdoc, "Body")
4   Call rtitem.AppendText(Message)
    Call rtitem.AddNewLine(1)
    Call rtitem.AddNewLine(1)
5   Call rtitem.AppendDocLink (doc, Subject)
    newdoc.Subject = Subject
6   newdoc.SendTo = Users
7   Call newdoc.Send (False)
    End Sub
```

Listing Notes:

1 Gets access to the current database.

2 Creates a new document for the current database. The mail document must be created in a database so it's convenient to use the current database. But the document will not be saved in the current database; it will be mailed instead.

3 Creates a rich text item on the mail message. This is needed so that you can append a Notes document link to the message

4 Appends the text of the message to the email.

5 Appends a Notes document link to the relevant document.

6 Specifies by whom the mail will be received.

7 Sends the mail.

Now you just have to call the function. The most common place to call it from is a form's Querysave event, so that you can notify a user that a document needing attention has been created or edited.

1 Select Design|Form and double-click on the Main Topic form (or any other form to which you want to add email notification).

2 Under the Event menu select (Declarations), and enter the following line of code:

```
Use "Email Notification"
```

This is how you "link" to the LotusScript library. You must include the Use statement in any form or module where you want to access the global functions.

3 Select the Querysave event and under Run select the Script option.

4 Enter the code in listing 14.3.

5 Save and close the form.

Tip

There may be cases where you want to allow the user to specify to whom the email notification is sent. This is very easy to do by adding a Names field to the form as follows:

1 Select the Create|Field menu.

2 Name the field EmailNotification. Under Type select Names, Editable.

3 Under Choices select Use Address dialog for choices. This will bring up the same user interface used to address Notes email messages.

4 If you want to allow notification of multiple individuals, select the Allow multivalues option. Close the properties window.

5 Click to the left of the EmailNotification field and enter EmailNotification: as a prompt.

6 Click on the form and select the Querysave event.

7 Change the calls to EmailNotify as follows:

```
Dim temp As String
temp = source.FieldGetText("EmailNotification")
EmailNotify "New Document", "A new document has been added that requires your
attention. Please double click on the document link below.", temp, Source.Document
```

8 Save and close the form.

Listing 14.3   Calling email notification subroutine

```
1  If Source.Isnewdoc Then
2  EmailNotify "New Document", "A new document has been added that requires
   your attention. Please double click on the document link below.", "Joe
   McGinn/Joe's Place", Source.Document
   Else
   EmailNotify "Edited Document", "A document has been edited that requires
   your attention. Please double click on the document link below.", "Joe
   McGinn/Joe's Place", Source.Document
   End If
```

Listing Notes:

1 Checks to see if it's a new document being saved.

2 Calls the `EmailNotify` subroutine. `Source.Document` refers to the current document (i.e., `Source` is the NotesUIDocument that is automatically passed to the Querysave event). In this case the document is mailed to `Joe McGinn/Joe's Place`. You'll have to change this to a valid name for your Notes server, of course.

The user can now select any names from the Name and Address Book to receive email notification of new or edited documents.

You should use a LotusScript library anytime you have a function or subroutine that needs to be accessed from several places in a database.

If you really need to store a variable globally you have two options, environment variables and profile documents. Environment variables are useful when the code is running on the client and the data you want to save are small and simple. If the code is to be run on a server you should use profile documents since they are tied to particular users, so they can work on server-run code.

14.5 Running an agent

The NotesAgent class in Notes 4.5 has a new method called Run that allows you to run an agent from Lotus-Script. The Run method is somewhat limited, however, because the user cannot interact with an agent run in this way. (You can't run an agent from LotusScript to access the formula `@Commands` for user interface functions.) If you want to freely mix LotusScript with formulas, including user interface commands, you have to use the workarounds presented in chapter 13.

Despite this limitation, the new `Run` method is still extremely useful. You can think of it as a less crippled version of the LotusScript `Evaluate` statement that runs a formula (but which is limited to formulas that can be evaluated to a constant string at compile time). For the first time, now, you can pass parameters to a formula agent and read

Tip

It's important to understand the scope of variables declared in LotusScript libraries. While you can use libraries to share Lotus-Script code over an entire database, you generally can't use libraries to create global Lotus-Script variables. When you declare a variable in a library and then access it, the variable has the same scope as a locally declared variable. For example, if you have a `Use` statement for a library in a form then the library's global variables will only be available as long as the form is opened—just as if you had declared the variables in the form's declarations event. If you use a library at a database level—in the database PostOpen event, for example—it will remain available until the database is closed, but only to other database level events. If you have another `Use` statement at the form or view level, it will create a new, separate copy of the variables.

the results back into LotusScript. For example, one common complaint about Lotus-Script is that handling and manipulating lists directly is much more difficult than it is using formulas. I'll show you how to use the Run method to write a LotusScript function that takes advantage of the list-processing capabilities of formulas. In a second example, I'll show you how to access a handy formula date manipulation function.

Note: The technique shown here passes parameters to formulas by using environment variables, and is therefore appropriate for running on only a Notes client. You cannot use this technique on an agent that runs on the server, because the environment variables would be saved to the server's Notes.INI file, which could cause conflicts and errors if two users are running the agent at the same time.

14.6 Example 1: a LotusScript list processing function

Tip

For a complete library of Lotus-Script list processing functions, see chapter 15.

The function we'll write is called ExtractFromList, and it takes two parameters—a text list, and the number of the item you want to extract from the list. The function returns the extracted item as a string. The list can be a string you've constructed in LotusScript code, or it can be from a multivalue field list. I'll show you how to use both of these techniques in the example here.

First, open or create a test Discussion database.

1 Select Design|Forms and double-click on the Main Topic form.

2 Select the Create|Action menu.

3 Under Title enter `Display a Category`, and select an appropriate Button Icon. Close the action properties window.

4 Under Run select Script, then enter the code in listing 14.4 into the code window.

Listing 14.4 ExtractFromList LotusScript function

```
    Function ExtractFromList (ListToProcess As String, item_number) As String
        Dim session As New NotesSession
        Dim db As NotesDatabase
        Dim theAgent As NotesAgent

        Set db = session.CurrentDatabase
1       Set theAgent = db.GetAgent("Select Item From List")
```

Listing 14.4   ExtractFromList LotusScript function

```
2     Call session.SetEnvironmentVar("PARAM_List",ListToProcess)
3     Call session.SetEnvironmentVar("PARAM_ItemNumber",
Format$(item_number))

4     Call theAgent.Run
5     ExtractFromList = session.GetEnvironmentString("PARAM_Return", False)
End Function
```

Listing Notes:

1 Sets a `NotesAgent` variable to the `Select Item From List` agent in the current database. (You haven't created this agent yet, we'll do that in a minute. It will be a formula agent that does the actual list processing.)

2 Stores the text list to be processed into the `PARAM_List` environment variables. Environment variables are the only way to communicate between LotusScript and formulas, so you use them to pass parameters back and forth between the two. The `NotesSession` variable has two methods—`SetEnvironmentVar` and `GetEnvironmentString`—for setting and retrieving environment variables.

3 Stores the number of the item to extract from the list.

4 Uses the new `Run` method to run the agent.

5 Retrieves the extracted list item from the `PARAM_Return` environment variable and returns it as the return value for this LotusScript function.

Now you can add the code to call this function to the Display a Category action button's click event.

1 Under Event select the Click event.

2 Enter the code in listing 14.5 into the Click subroutine.

3 Save and close the Main Topic form.

Listing 14.5   Calling the ExtractFromList function

```
Dim workspace As New NotesUIWorkspace
Dim UIdoc As NotesUIDocument
Dim item_number As Integer

Set UIdoc = workspace.CurrentDocument
item_number  = Inputbox("Enter the item number to extract from the Catego-
ries field")
1   Messagebox ExtractFromList(UIdoc.FieldGetText("Categories"),item_number)
```

Listing 14.5   Calling the ExtractFromList function (continued)

```
2   Messagebox ExtractFromList("Blue, Red, Green", 2)
```

Listing Notes:

1 Calls the ExtractFromList function with the contents of the form's Categories field and extracts the item number specified by the user. The result is displayed in a Messagebox.

2 Extracts the second item (Red) from a normal LotusScript text string.

Last, you need to create the Select Item From List formula agent that physically processes these lists:

1 Select the Create|Agent menu.

2 Under Name enter Select Item From List.

3 Select the Shared option.

4 Under the question When should this agent run? select the option Manually From Actions Menu. (You must select this option or the agent will not run via the Lotus-Script Run method.)

5 Under the question Which document(s) should it act on? select the option Run once (@commands may be used).

6 Under the question What should this agent do? select Formula.

7 Enter the formula code in listing 14.6.

8 Save and close the new agent.

Listing 14.6   "Select Item From List" formula agent

```
1   item_number:=@TextToNumber(@Environment("PARAM_ItemNumber"));
2   item_list:=@Explode(@Environment("PARAM_List"));
3   list_item:=@Subset(@Subset(item_list;item_number);-1);
4   @Environment("PARAM_Return";list_item)
```

Listing Notes:

1 Retrieves the item number to be extracted from the list from the PARAM_ItemNumber environment variable.

2 Retrieves the list to be processed from its environment variable. Note that the @Explode command is needed to convert the text string into a true list that can be used in the list processing functions.

3 Extracts the item from the list. This requires two `@Subset` commands. The inner one retrieves the left `item_number` items from the list, and the outer one retrieves the rightmost element from this sub list by specifying `-1` as the item number to extract.

4 Stores the extracted item into the `PARAM_Return` environment variable.

Now try adding a new Main Topic document to the database. Fill in three or four items into the Categories field, then press the Display a Category action button. The item number you enter at the input box is extracted from the list and displayed in a message box. It's followed by a message box displaying the item extracted from the plain text string list (i.e., extracting "Red" from "Blue, Red, Green").

14.7 Example 2: a LotusScript date/time processing function

The technique in the previous section is very useful, but there are situations where it is easier to simply write the entire source code for a function in LotusScript. For example, the handy `@Adjust` formula is used to adjust a time forward or backward by any number of years, months, days, hours, minutes, or seconds. LotusScript doesn't have an adjust command, but it does have similar functions in the NotesDateTime class.

We'll create a LotusScript AdjustDate function that has the same functionality as `@Adjust`. The function accepts one `NotesDateTime` parameter, and six numeric parameters, one each for years, months, days, hours, minutes, and seconds. Use positive numbers to adjust the date into the future, negative numbers to adjust it into the past.

First, open or create a test Discussion database:

1 Select Design|Forms and double click on the Main Topic form.

2 Select the Create|Action menu.

3 Under Title enter `Adjust Date`, and select an appropriate Button Icon. Close the action properties window.

4 Under Run select Script, then enter the code in listing 14.7 into the code window.

Listing 14.7 AdjustDate LotusScript function

```
        Function AdjustDate(Original As NotesDateTime, Years, Months, Days,
      Hours, Minutes, Seconds) As NotesDateTime
1           Call Original.Adjustyear(Years)
            Call Original.Adjustmonth(Months)
            Call Original.Adjustday(Days)
            Call Original.Adjusthour(Hours)
            Call Original.Adjustminute(Minutes)
            Call Original.Adjustsecond(Seconds)
            Set AdjustDate = Original
      End Function
```

Listing Notes:

1 The NotesDateTime class methods are used to do the actual calculations.

Now you need to add the code to call this function to the action buttons click event:

1 Under Event select the Click event.

2 Enter the code in listing 14.8 into the Click subroutine.

3 Save and close the Main Topic form.

Listing 14.8 Calling the AdjustDate function

```
1   Dim temp As New NotesDateTime (Now)
    Dim days As Integer
    CurrentDate$ = temp.Localtime
2   days = Inputbox("How many days ahead to you want to adjust the time?")
3   Call AdjustDate(temp,0,0,days,0,0,0)
4   Messagebox "Now: " + CurrentDate$ + ". Adjusted by " + Format$(days) + "
    days: " + temp.localtime,  ,"AdjustDate"
```

Listing Notes:

1 Sets a NotesDateTime variable to the current date and time.

2 Asks the user by how many days he or she wants to adjust the current date. Enter a positive number to adjust into the future, or a negative number to adjust into the past.

3 Calls the AdjustDate LotusScript function

4 Displays the results of the adjusted date in a message box, as shown in figure 14.5.

Figure 14.5   Adjusted date/time

This example shows that you should always carefully check the LotusScript class libraries before turning to @functions. The native LotusScript code is faster, and can be used in places where environment variables don't work well (i.e., running on the background on a server). Like the list processing functions, in practice you should put the LotusScript functions for manipulating dates and times into a LotusScript library.

14.8 Graphical design update

Notes 4.5 includes a few new features that give you more options for designing the graphical appearance of your forms. Figure 14.6 shows a number of new features available for formatting tables and text.

The first new feature is the 3D table border style. On the main table properties window, there is a new option that allows you to select from three table border styles—Standard, Extruded (as seen here), and Embossed. As you can see by the text in the lefthand column, the new 3D styles are also available as a text property. Finally, you can set the background color of each cell in the table in the new Colors tab on the table properties window.

There is also a useful and long-awaited new feature

Tip

If you use the graphics background feature, you should put all your fields on tables or layout regions. Otherwise, the fields will be difficult or impossible to read on the graphics background. As you can see in figure 14.8, fields on tables and layout regions look fine but the Body rich text field is very difficult to see even in a large font.

in layout regions. Fields in layout regions now have a white background color, rather than sharing the same background color as the layout region, as in previous versions of Notes. As a result, you can create the "standard" Microsoft Windows look and feel for forms that present white fields with a 3D border on a gray background, as shown in figure 14.7.

Table Heading	
Extruded Text	data entry field
Embossed Text	

Figure 14.6   New table features

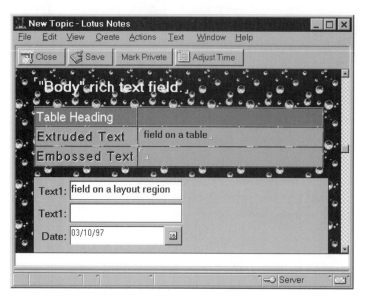

Figure 14.8 Form with a background graphic

Another new feature in Notes 4.5 is the ability to paste a graphics background into a form (figure 4.8). You do this by pressing the Paste Graphic button on the Background tab of the form properties window (i.e., with the form in design mode). You can paste a large graphic that is a complete background for a form, or a small texture bitmap. Notes will automatically fill the entire form with the background image.

Figure 14.7 New layout features

14.9 Search and display multiple documents

A subtle but extremely useful new feature in Notes 4.5 is the ability to display any document directly from LotusScript. The EditDocument method of the NotesUIWorkspace class now accepts a NotesDocument variable as a parameter as follows:

```
Dim workspace As New NotesUIWorkspace
Dim doc as NotesDocument
'…set value of doc
workspace.EditDocument False, doc
```

By itself, this is a very useful feature for which Notes programmers have long asked. But it can be taken further than just displaying a document. By combining this feature with a NotesNewsLetter, it is now possible to display a document collection by displaying a form that has document links to all of the documents in the collection.

In the section "Search and display a document" of chapter 13, I showed you how to write a customized search function that finds a document via LotusScript and then displays it on the user interface. The new Notes 4.5 EditDocument feature allows you to implement a custom search function that displays an index to multiple documents. It works by creating a newsletter document, but instead of mailing the newsletter, it is displayed (i.e., without being sent or saved) by using the new feature of the NotesUIWorkspace class that allows you to display any document directly from LotusScript.

First, open or create a test discussion database. Before creating the search agent, you should create a form in which to display the search results.

1 Select the Create|Design|Form menu to create a new form.

2 Select the Design|Form Properties menu, and name the form `Results`. Close the properties window.

3 Use the Create|Field menu to create a field named `SearchFor`, type Text, Editable.

4 Type the text `Searching for:` as a prompt to the left of the SearchFor field. To be consistent with the Notes newsletter format, you should set the text properties for this text to the color light blue, size 10, style Bold.

5 Use the Create|Field menu to create a field named Body, type Rich Text, Editable.

6 Select the Create|Action menu. Under Title enter `Close`, and select a button icon. Close the properties window and enter the following formula code for the action:

```
@PostedCommand([FileCloseWindow])
```

7 Save and close the Results form.

Now you can create an agent that searches for multiple documents. If you prefer, you can attach the code in listing 14.9 directly to a button instead of putting it in an agent.

1 Select the Create|Agent menu item.

2 Under Name enter `Display Documents`.

3 Select the Shared Agent option.

4 Under the question When should this agent run? select the option Manually From Actions Menu.

5 Under the question Which document(s) should it act on? select the option Run once(@Commands may be used).

6 Under the question What should this agent do? select the Script option.

7 Select the Initialize event, and then enter the LotusScript code in listing 14.9.

Listing 14.9   Display multiple documents

```
Dim session As New NotesSession
Dim workspace As New NotesUIWorkspace
Dim doc As NotesDocument
Dim db As NotesDatabase
Dim collection as NotesDocumentCollection
Dim newsletter As NotesNewsletter
Dim text_to_find As String

text_to_find = Inputbox$("Enter the text you want to find:", "Find Docu-
ments")

Set db = session.CurrentDatabase
```

```
1   Set collection = db.ftsearch(text_to_find, 0)

2   Set newsletter = New NotesNewsletter( collection )
    newsletter.DoSubject = True
    newsletter.SubjectItemName = "Subject"
3   Set doc = newsletter.FormatMsgWithDoclinks( db )
4   doc.Form = "Results"
    doc.SearchFor = text_to_find
5   workspace.EditDocument False, doc, True
```

Tip

For complete instructions and source code to search all databases in a subdirectory, see the section "Search all databases in a subdirectory" in chapter 18.

Listing Notes:

1 Conducts a full text search based on the text the user entered.

2 Creates a newsletter based on the collection of documents returned by the search.

3 Creates the document links to the documents in the collection.

4 Specifies the form in which to display the newsletter document.

5 Displays the document using the new `EditDocument` method. The last parameter (`True`) tells Notes not to allow the document to be edited.

When you run this agent (i.e., select the Actions|Display Documents menu), you will be prompted for search text, and the results of the search will be displayed as a document with links to all matching documents, as shown in figure 14.9.

14.10 Other new features

There are a few other useful new programming features in Notes 4.5 that I'll introduce in this section:

- Attaching code to database-level events.
- Specifying a startup database to be opened by default when Notes is started.
- Specifying the default location of the document preview pane.
- Telling Notes to include the database help About and Using documents (and the database icon) when a template updates a database.

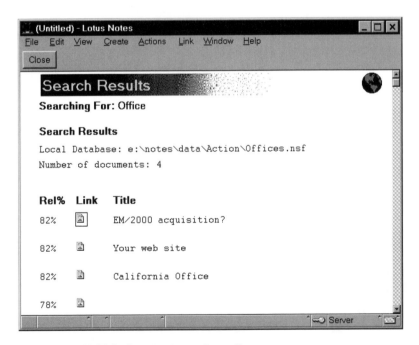

Figure 14.9   Multiple document search results

In Notes 4.5 you can attach LotusScript or formula code to database-level events such as document deletions. You access database events through the new Database Script object located under Other in the Notes Design pane. For an example of how to use them, see the section "Referential integrity" in chapter 16.

Another useful new feature is that you can specify a Notes database to open automatically when Notes starts up. This can be useful if you have users who are not highly trained in general Notes usage, and you have a user interface database that is the starting point for your application. To specify the default database on any workstation select the File|Tools|User Preferences menu. Then click on the Startup database button and select the default database. (All databases on the user's workspace tabs will appear in the menu.)

You can specify the default location of the document preview pane for any database. In the Database Properties screen click on the Launch tab and press the Preview Pane Default button. From the dialog windows shown in figure 14.10 you can choose the position of the preview pane and also specify if you want the pane maximized by default.

An important new feature for application developers is the ability to allow the Other design elements—Using Database document, About Database document, and the database Icon—to be inherited when a template updates a database design. The About screen is a useful place to store information like your application version number so that when answering support calls you can ask the user what version they are using. By default, these items are all set to not inherit the design. To change this default, select Design|Other, single click on the design element, and select the File|Document Properties menu. Click on the Design tab and deselect the option Do not allow design refresh/replace to modify.

14.11 Summary

In this chapter you've learned about all the important new Notes 4.5 features for programmers and application designers. You've learned how to create the calendar views, and how to enable the new GUI date and time popup editors.

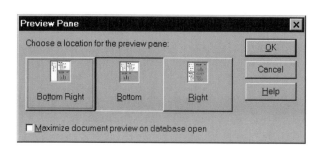

Figure 14.10   Preview pane default menu

We've covered the important new areas of using profile documents to store user options and using LotusScript libraries to write global functions for a database.

You've learned how to use the valuable new Run method of the NotesAgent class to interface LotusScript functions with formula commands for manipulating lists and date/time values. These techniques can be used to dynamically access any nonuser interface formula command.

You've used the new EditDocument method to search for and display multiple documents on the screen.

Last, we've looked at the new graphical design features in Notes 4.5 and various other new features such as specifying a startup database.

C H A P T E R   1 5

LotusScript list processing in Notes 4.5

In the previous chapter I presented a LotusScript function that interfaces to a formula command for list processing. This chapter provides the code for a complete library of LotusScript list processing functions. All functions in this chapter must use the new Notes 4.5 `Run` method of the NotesAgent command to interface to formula language @ functions, so they will only work for Notes 4.5. LotusScript functions are provided for the following formula @ commands:

- `@Subset` extracts a given number of items from a list.
- `@Elements` counts the number of items in a list.
- `@IsMember` searches a list for an item.
- `@Member` finds the position of an item in a list.
- `@Replace` replaces a set of words in a list with new words.
- `@Unique` removes duplicate entries from a list.

In addition to the list processing functions themselves, the formula agents called by the LotusScript functions here make use of the following commands:

- `@TextToNumber` is used to convert numeric LotusScript arguments to numbers. (Because environment variables are used to pass parameters back and forth between formulas and LotusScript, all parameters are physically passed as strings.)
- `@Explode` is used to convert a text string of items into a list.
- When necessary, `@Text` and `@Implode` are used to convert formula results back into strings to be passed back to LotusScript.

Each of the functions consists of two parts, a LotusScript function for use by your application and a formula that does the actual list processing. The functions should be placed in a LotusScript library which you then link to from any module by putting the following line of code in the `(Declarations)` section:

```
Use "List Processing Library"
```

All the functions and agents here are included in a LotusScript library called "List Processing Library" in `Chap15.NSF` on the *Inside LotusScript CD*. To use them in your application, copy the code library to your database (i.e., by selecting the library and using the Edit|Copy and Edit|Paste menus). Then copy all the agents whose names start with *LSList* to your database. You can also find the text of all code listings in the `CodeList.NSF` database on the CD.

Note: Because environment variables are used to pass parameters from LotusScript to formulas, the technique in this chapter is not suitable for agents running on the server. It is intended for client agents and processing of front end documents.

15.1 List processing functions

If you want to create these functions manually by typing them in and creating the agents, each of the formula agents must be created as follows:

1 Select the Create|Agent menu.

2 Under Name enter the name exactly as it appears in the agent code listing (e.g., `LSList Extract Item From List`).

3 Select the Shared option.

4 Under the question When should this agent run? select the option Manually From Actions Menu. (You must select this option or the agent will not run via the Lotus-Script Run method.)

5 Under the question Which document(s) should it act on? select the option Run once (`@commands` may be used).

6 Under the question What should this agent do? select Formula.

7 Enter the formula code from the appropriate agent code listing in this chapter.

8 Save and close the new agent.

15.2 ExtractFromList function

`ExtractFromList (ListToProcess as String, item_number)` accepts a string of items and an `item_number`, and returns the specified item as a string.

Listing 15.1 ExtractFromList LotusScript function

```
Function ExtractFromList (ListToProcess As String, item_number) As String
    Dim session As New NotesSession
    Dim db As NotesDatabase
    Dim theAgent As NotesAgent

    Set db = session.CurrentDatabase
1   Set theAgent = db.GetAgent("LSList Extract Item From List")

2   Call session.SetEnvironmentVar("PARAM_List",ListToProcess)
    Call session.SetEnvironmentVar("PARAM_ItemNumber",
    Format$(item_number))
3   Call theAgent.Run

4   ExtractFromList = session.GetEnvironmentString("PARAM_Return", False)
    End Function
```

Listing Notes:

1 References the named agent with a `NotesAgent` variable.

2 The `SetEnvironmentVar` method of the `session` NotesSession variable is used to pass parameters to the formula agent.

3 Calls the formula agent using the NotesAgent `Run` method.

4 Retrieves the agent result using the `GetEnvironmentString` method and returns the result as the value of the current function.

Listing 15.2 "LSList Extract Item From List" formula agent

```
1  item_number:=@TextToNumber(@Environment("PARAM_ItemNumber"));
2  item_list:=@Explode(@Environment("PARAM_List"));
   list_item:=@Subset(@Subset(item_list;item_number);-1);
   @Environment("PARAM_Return";list_item)
```

Listing Notes:

1 The `@TextToNumber` function must be used on numeric arguments.

2 The `@Explode` function is used to convert a LotusScript string of items into a true list.

Example function call:

`ExtractFromList("Red, Green, Blue", 2)` returns the string `Green`.

15.3 SubSet function

`SubSet (ListToProcess as String, number)` accepts a string of items and the number of items to extract from the list. A negative number extracts items from the right side of the list. The resulting list is returned as a string.

Listing 15.3 Subset LotusScript function

```
Function Subset (ListToProcess As String, number) As String
    Dim session As New NotesSession
    Dim db As NotesDatabase
    Dim theAgent As NotesAgent

    Set db = session.CurrentDatabase
    Set theAgent = db.GetAgent("LSList Subset")
```

Listing 15.3   Subset LotusScript function (continued)

```
    Call session.SetEnvironmentVar("PARAM_List",ListToProcess)
    Call session.SetEnvironmentVar("PARAM_Number",Format$(number))

    Call theAgent.Run

    Subset = session.GetEnvironmentString("PARAM_Return", False)
End Function
```

Listing 15.4   LSList Subset formula agent

```
    number:=@TextToNumber(@Environment("PARAM_Number"));
    item_list:=@Explode(@Environment("PARAM_List"));
    list:=@Subset(item_list;number);
1   @Environment("PARAM_Return";@Implode(list))
```

Listing Notes:

1 Because the result of the @Subset command is a list, the @Implode function must
   be used to pass the result back to LotusScript as a string.

   Example function call:

Subset("Red, Green, Blue",2) returns the string Red Green.

15.4 *Elements function*

Elements (ListToProcess as String) accepts a string of items and returns the number of items as an integer.

Listing 15.5   Elements LotusScript function

```
    Function Elements (ListToProcess As String) As Integer
        Dim session As New NotesSession
        Dim db As NotesDatabase
        Dim theAgent As NotesAgent

        Set db = session.CurrentDatabase
        Set theAgent = db.GetAgent("LSList Elements")

        Call session.SetEnvironmentVar("PARAM_List",ListToProcess)

        Call theAgent.Run
```

Listing 15.5 Elements LotusScript function (continued)

```
1      Elements = Cint(session.GetEnvironmentString("PARAM_Return", False))
    End Function
```

Listing Notes:

1 The `Cint` LotusScript function is used to convert the result of the `@Elements` function back into an integer (i.e., so that it matches the data type of the `Elements` function).

Listing 15.6 "LSList Elements" formula agent

```
item_list:=@Explode(@Environment("PARAM_List"));
result:=@Elements(item_list);
@Environment("PARAM_Return";@Text(result))
```

Example function call:

```
Elements("Red, Green, Blue")
```
returns the integer `3`.

15.5 IsMember function

`IsMember (ListToProcess as String, item as String)` accepts a string of items and an item, and returns `True` (1) if the item is in the list; otherwise, returns `False` (0). *Note:* `item` can also be a list, in which case `True` is returned if all of the items in it are found in the `ListToProces`.

Listing 15.7 IsMember LotusScript function

```
Function IsMember (ListToProcess As String, item As String) As Integer
    Dim session As New NotesSession
    Dim db As NotesDatabase
    Dim theAgent As NotesAgent

    Set db = session.CurrentDatabase
    Set theAgent = db.GetAgent("LSList IsMember")

    Call session.SetEnvironmentVar("PARAM_List",ListToProcess)
    Call session.SetEnvironmentVar("PARAM_Item",item)

    Call theAgent.Run
```

Listing 15.7 IsMember LotusScript function (continued)

```
        IsMember = Cint(session.GetEnvironmentString("PARAM_Return", False))
    End Function
```

Listing 15.8 "LSList IsMember" formula agent

```
1  item:=@Explode(@Environment("PARAM_Item"));
   item_list:=@Explode(@Environment("PARAM_List"));
   result:=@IsMember(item;item_list);
   @Environment("PARAM_Return";@Text(result))
```

Listing Notes:

1 In this function both parameters are passed through the @Explode function, since
   item can optionally be a list as well.

   Example function calls:

```
IsMember("Red, Green, Blue", "Blue") returns TRUE (1).
IsMember("Red, Green, Blue", "Yellow") returns FALSE (0).
IsMember("Red, Green, Blue", "Green, Red") returns TRUE (1).
IsMember("Red, Green, Blue", "Green, Yellow") returns FALSE (0).
```

15.6 MemberPosition function

MemberPosition (ListToProcess as String, item as String) accepts a string of
items and an item, and returns the position of item in the list. Returns 0 (zero) if the
item is not in the list.

Listing 15.9 MemberPosition LotusScript function

```
Function MemberPosition (ListToProcess As String, item As String) As
Integer
    Dim session As New NotesSession
    Dim db As NotesDatabase
    Dim theAgent As NotesAgent

    Set db = session.CurrentDatabase
    Set theAgent = db.GetAgent("LSList MemberPosition")

    Call session.SetEnvironmentVar("PARAM_List",ListToProcess)
    Call session.SetEnvironmentVar("PARAM_Item",item)
```

Listing 15.9   MemberPosition LotusScript function (continued)

```
    Call theAgent.Run

        MemberPosition = Cint(session.GetEnvironmentString("PARAM_Return",
    False))
    End Function
```

Listing 15.10   "LSList MemberPosition" formula agent

```
    item:=@Explode(@Environment("PARAM_Item"));
    item_list:=@Explode(@Environment("PARAM_List"));
    result:=@Member(item;item_list);
    @Environment("PARAM_Return";@Text(result))
```

Example function calls:

```
MemberPosition("Red, Green, Blue","Green") returns the integer 2.
MemberPosition("Red, Green, Blue","Yellow") returns the integer 0.
```

15.7 Replace function

Replace (ListToProcess as String, FromList as String, ToList as String) accepts a string of items to process, and two strings with the replace strings. All items in FromList found in ListToProcess are replaced with the corresponding item in Tolist.

Listing 15.11   Replace LotusScript function

```
    Function Replace (ListToProcess As String, FromList As String, ToList As
    String) As String
        Dim session As New NotesSession
        Dim db As NotesDatabase
        Dim theAgent As NotesAgent

        Set db = session.CurrentDatabase
        Set theAgent = db.GetAgent("LSList Replace")

        Call session.SetEnvironmentVar("PARAM_List",ListToProcess)
        Call session.SetEnvironmentVar("PARAM_FromList",FromList)
        Call session.SetEnvironmentVar("PARAM_ToList",ToList)

        Call theAgent.Run

        Replace = session.GetEnvironmentString("PARAM_Return", False)
```

Listing 15.11 Replace LotusScript function (continued)

```
End Function
```

Listing 15.12 "LSList Replace" formula agent

```
item_list:=@Explode(@Environment("PARAM_List"));
to_list:=@Explode(@Environment("PARAM_ToList"));
from_list:=@Explode(@Environment("PARAM_FromList"));
list:=@Replace(item_list;from_list;to_list);
@Environment("PARAM_Return";@Implode(list))
```

Example function call:

`Replace("Red, Green, Blue, Blue","Green, Blue","Yellow, Purple")` returns the string `"Red Yellow Purple Purple"` (i.e., each instance of Green is changed to Yellow, each instance of Blue to Purple).

15.8 Unique function

`Unique (ListToProcess as String)` accepts a string of items and returns a string of items with all duplicates removed.

Listing 15.13 Unique LotusScript function

```
Function Unique (ListToProcess As String) As String
    Dim session As New NotesSession
    Dim db As NotesDatabase
    Dim theAgent As NotesAgent

    Set db = session.CurrentDatabase
    Set theAgent = db.GetAgent("LSList Unique")

    Call session.SetEnvironmentVar("PARAM_List",ListToProcess)

    Call theAgent.Run

    Unique = session.GetEnvironmentString("PARAM_Return", False)
End Function
```

Listing 15.14 "LSList Unique" formula agent

```
item_list:=@Explode(@Environment("PARAM_List"));
list:=@Unique(item_list);
@Environment("PARAM_Return";@Implode(list))
```

Example function call:

```
Unique("Red, Green, Blue, Blue, Red, Green, Green") returns the string "Red
Green Blue".
```

15.9 Summary

In this chapter I've presented a complete library of LotusScript list processing functions. The functions work by calling the equivalent formula @commands and using environment variables to pass the results back and forth. You can use the techniques in this chapter to interface to any formula command except for commands that interact with the user interface.

C H A P T E R   1 6

Database relations

Lotus Notes is not a relational database management system (RDBMS). It does not feature the commit/rollback commands and other features necessary to maintain complete referential integrity and disaster recovery (e.g., guaranteeing referential integrity even after a client or server computer crash). If you need these features, then you need an RDBMS such as Oracle, DB/2, or Structured Query Language (SQL) Server. If needed, you can interface Notes to the data in these systems with the addition of third-party tools like Notes Pump which transfer data back and forth between Notes and RDBMSs in real time.

Having said that, many programmers using Notes have at one time or another programmed with a relational database and are familiar with the advantages of organizing data by way of its relationships. The one-to-many relationship, for example, accurately models much of the data we encounter in the real world. One site or company will have many phone contacts. One customer service problem report has many phone calls, and so on.

In this chapter I'll show you how these standard database relations can be simulated in Notes. You will learn:

- How to avoid file name conflicts when implementing relationships in multidatabase applications.

- How to implement the one-to-many relationship, both within one database and between multiple databases.

- How to implement many-to-many relationships.

- How to implement referential integrity code in LotusScript.

16.1 Avoiding filename conflicts

Most Notes applications consist of more than one database file. To implement reliable interdatabase relations, it is necessary to have a reliable method of referring to external databases programmatically. You need a way to do this that has the following characteristics:

- *Reliability* The system cannot depend on hard-coded database filenames, which can cause conflicts with other applications that might use the same name.

- *Flexibility* Server names, for example, also cannot be hard-coded (i.e., all Notes database references require a server name in addition to a database filename), since you often won't know the server name at development time.

- *User Friendly*   The system you use cannot depend on a high level of end user maintenance, as is the case with simple schemes based on user-editable environment variables.

This is such an important areas that I've devoted an entire chapter to it. If you haven't already read chapter 3, I recommend that you do so before trying to implement database relations. I'll summarize the results from chapter 3 in this section, but I won't go into the rationalizations for each of the decisions.

First, your database files should be stored in a subdirectory under the Notes DATA directory, on both the server and the clients. If your application includes templates (NTF files), you'll have to store the templates in the DATA directory, but application databases (NSF files) should always be stored in a subdirectory. Because your application will always have its own directory, you won't run into filename conflicts with other Notes programs, so you can hard code the filenames (but not the subdirectory name).

You can access the *current subdirectory* and the *current server* in both of the Notes programming languages, so these items never need to be hard coded. Listing 16.1 shows how to reference an external database name in the formula language.

Listing 16.1   Referencing a database in a formula

```
    SubDir:=@LeftBack(@Subset(@DbName;-1);"\\");
1   DB_Name:=@If(SubDir="";"";SubDir+"\\") + "Dblog.nsf";
2   @Command([FileOpenDatabase];@Subset(@DbName;1):DB_Name);
```

Listing Notes:

1 This statement creates a new database name using the subdirectory of the current database.

2 If this example is run in a database in the S_Live directory, DB_Name is set to Notes\Data\S_Live\Dblog.nsf. If it is running in the Sales_Training directory, then DB_Name evaluates to Notes\Data\S_Training\Dblog.nsf. Note that you still have to specify the current server with @Subset(@DbName;1), so that it will work on both connected and remote systems.

Listing 16.2 shows how to reference an external database in LotusScript.

Listing 16.2   Referencing a database in LotusScript

```
Dim session As New NotesSession
Dim db As NotesDatabase
Dim DB_Name As String
```

```
1   Set db = session.CurrentDatabase
2   DB_Name = Left$(db.FilePath, Instr(1, db.FilePath, db.Filename, 1)-1) +
    "Dblog.NSF"
    REM Open the Dblog.NSF database
    Dim log_db As New NotesDatabase("","")
3   If ( Not (log_db.Open(db.Server, DB_Name))) Then
        Exit Sub
    End If
```

Listing Notes:

1 Gets the current database, which is where the database filename, filepath, and server name of the current database are stored.

2 The `Left$` statement removes the filename from the right side of the filepath, and then appends the name of the database to reference. For example, if the current database is `C:\NOTES\DATA\S_TRAIN\Sales.NSF`, the result will be:

`C:\NOTES \DATA\S_TRAIN\Dblog.NSF`.

3 As with the formula code, note that you still have to specify the current server with `db.Server`.

As long as you use this code and always store your application in a subdirectory, your relationships will always work. Because it is always based on the current subdirectory and server, it will work on both servers and remote (i.e., unconnected) clients. There is another benefit too; you can have multiple versions of your application installed in different subdirectories on one Notes server or client. This means, for example, that you can install separate training and test versions of your application, and your users can create fully functional backup versions on a regular basis.

Tip

If you just want to create simple one-to-one relationships, you may find the section "Creating document links in a new document" in chapter 19 useful.

16.2 *One-to-many relations*

One way to create one-to-many relationships in Notes is to use the built-in Notes parent/child document relationship. This is a one-to-many relationship, and has the advantages of being easy to implement and maintain. If you start with a template like Discussion, the forms, fields, and views for creating and managing the relationship are already done. You just have to do two things: create the main parent forms/fields for the "one" side of the relation, and create the response documents for the "many" side.

Response documents can easily inherit fields from their parents (i.e., just by naming the field in the default value formula on the response). When using the response document, users can select the Parent Preview button to see the parent document on the same form as the related response. The only programming you may want to do is to display values from the response document on the parent form, so that users can see a summary of related documents without having to actually open each response document or look in a view. Such values should be Computed for Display fields that compute their values dynamically so that the most current information is always available on the parent. I don't recommend trying to programmatically alter editable fields on the parent document from the response. It's difficult to implement reliably and causes difficulties in setting up security. (That is, you don't necessarily want authors of response documents to be able to edit parent documents that may have been authored by someone else.)

The following example shows how to dynamically display the Subject fields from response documents on a parent document. First, you should create or open a test Discussion database. The you need to create a view as follows:

1 Select the Create|View menu.

2 Enter `Response Documents` as the view name.

3 Select the Shared option.

4 Under the Selection Conditions press the Add Condition button.

5 Under condition select By Form Used, and select the Response form. Press OK, then press OK again on the Create View screen.

6 Select Design|Views and double click on the Response Documents view.

7 Delete the Date, By, and Topic columns.

8 Select the Create|Insert New Column menu.

9 In the programming pane select Formula, and enter the following formula:

```
@Text($REF)
```

This formula is the key to how this technique works. $REF is a special field on all response documents that contains the universal ID of the parent document. So this view is really a list of response documents indexed by the UNID of the parent, which makes it possible to create a formula on the parent form (shown later in this section) that queries and pulls in the related response documents.

10 Select the Design|Column Properties menu.

11 Under title enter `Parent ID`, then click on the Sorting tab. Select the Ascending option and then close the properties window.

12 Select the Create|Append Column menu.

13 In the programming pane select the Field option and click on the Subject field.

14 Select the Design|View Properties window. Click on the propeller beanie tab and under Discard index select After each use.

15 Save and close the view.

Now you can add the code to the parent form that displays the values from related response documents:

1 Select Design|Forms and double click on the Main Topic form.

2 Click to the right of the Body field and press return to create an empty line on the form.

3 Type the text `Related Documents` on the form and press return again.

4 Select the Create|Field menu.

5 Name the field `RelatedSubjects`, and set the field type to Text, Computed for Display.

6 Select the Allow multivalues option.

7 Click on the Options tab and under "Display separate values with" select New Line. You might also want to click on the hide/when tab and hide the field when "Previewed for editing" and "Opened for editing".

8 Close the properties window and enter the following code into the Value event for the RelatedSubjects field:

```
temp:=@DbLookup("":"NoCache";"":"";"Response Documents";@Text(@DocumentU-
niqueID);2);
@If(@IsError(temp);"";temp)
```

The @DBLookup result must be stored in a variable and tested with the @IsError function. Otherwise, you would get an error when you opened a Main Topic document that doesn't yet have any responses.

9 Save and close the Main Topic form.

Now try adding a main document and several responses for it. The responses will show up in the field on the parent as shown in figure 16.1.

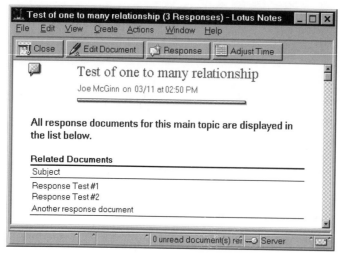

Figure 16.1 Parent document showing responses

16.3 One-to-many relations across databases

There are situations where you want to create relationships between documents in different databases. If the data to which you are relating have their own purpose, to be used independently of the parent document, as is often the case. For example, you might have a contacts database based on the Name and Address Book template that you want to link to a discussion or customer support database. This is not too hard to do, as long as you use the coding guidelines outlined in the section "Avoiding filename conflicts" in this chapter.

There are a few steps you have to take to implement this kind of interdatabase relationship:

1 On the *one* side of the relation (i.e., in this example that's the contact's database), you need a view that includes parent documents and their universal IDs. This view will be used as a menu to select the related contact from the discussion Main Topic form.

2 On the *many* side (the discussion database here), you create fields on the form that implement and manage the relation.

3 Optionally, on the *many* side (the discussion database) you can create categorized views that display discussion items by the relation (i.e., a list of contacts and the discussion items related to each of them).

First, create a test discussion database (i.e., the Discussion (R4) template) called TestDisc.NSF. Create a test contacts database (with the Personal Address Book template) called Contacts.NSF. The databases must be created in the same subdirectory. Now we'll create the view described in step 1 above:

1   Open the Contacts database.

2   Select the Create|View menu.

3   Enter Contacts as the view name.

4   Select the Shared option.

5   Under Selection Conditions enter the following formula:

```
SELECT Type = "Person" | Type = "Company"
```

6   Press OK on the Create View screen.

7   Select Design|Views and double-click on the Contacts view.

8   Click on the Name column, and enter the following formula:

```
@If(Type="Person";@Trim(@Subset(LastName;1))+@If(Firstname !="";",
"+@Trim(@Subset(FirstName;1));"");CompanyName)
```

9   Select the Create|Insert New Column menu.

10   In the programming pane select Formula, and enter the following formula:

```
@Text(@DocumentUniqueID)
```

11   Select the Design|Column Properties menu.

12   Under title enter Universal ID and select the Hide column property.

13   Click on the Sorting tab. Select the Ascending option and then close the properties window.

14   Select the Design|View Properties window. Click on the propeller beanie tab and under Discard index select After each use.

15   Save and close the view.

Enter a few test contacts (as either People or Companies) and close the Contacts database. Now we'll create fields in the Discussion database to link to a contact. First, open the Discussion database:

1   Select Design|Forms, and double-click on the Main Topic form.

2   Click to the right of the Categories field, and press Enter to create a new line on the form just below the Categories field.

3 Type `Contact:`, and then select Create Field. Name the new field `ContactName`, type Text, Editable. Close the field properties window.

4 Press Enter again, and then select Create|Field. Name this one `RelatedDocument`, type Text, Editable. Click on the hide/when tab and make it a hidden field by selecting all options. (You do not need to select the option Hide paragraph if formula is true.) Close the field properties window.

5 Press enter to get another blank line, and add a button with the Create|Hotspot|Button menu. Under Button Label enter `Select Contact`.

6 Click on the hide/when tab for the button and put checkmarks on the options Previewed for reading, Opened for reading, printed, and previewed for editing. Deselect the option Opened for editing. This will cause the Select Contact button to be displayed only when the document is in edit mode.

7 In the programming pane for the button select Formula, and enter the formula code from listing 16.3.

8 To the left of the ContactName fields, select the text `Contact:` with the mouse. Then select the Create|Hotspot|Action Hotspot menu. In the formula pane for this hotspot, enter the following code:

```
FIELD RelatedDocument:=RelatedDocument;
SubDir:=@LeftBack(@Subset(@DbName;-1);"\\");
DB_Name:=@If(SubDir="";"";SubDir+"\\") + " Contacts.NSF";
@Command([FileOpenDatabase];@Subset(@DbName;1):DB_Name;"Customers");
@Command([OpenDocument]; "0"; RelatedDocument);
@Command([OpenView]);
@Command([FileCloseWindow])
```

When the user clicks on this hotspot with the mouse, the code will open the related contact document.

9 Save and close the Main Topic form.

Listing 16.3   Code for select a contact button

```
  SubDir:=@LeftBack(@Subset(@DbName;-1);"\\");
1 DB_Name:=@If(SubDir="";"";SubDir+"\\") + "Contacts.NSF";
2 Choice:=@PickList([Custom];@Subset(@DbName;1):DB_Name; "Contacts";"Select
  A Contact";"Select the related contact.";1);
3 Chosen_Contact:=@Subset(Choice;1);
4 @If(Chosen_Contact ="";"";@Do(
5   @SetField("RelatedDocument"; @Text(Chosen_Contact));
6   @SetField("ContactName";@DbLookup("":"NoCache"; @Sub-
  set(@DbName;1):DB_Name; "Contacts"; Chosen_Contact;2))))
```

Listing Notes:

1 This code builds a pathname for `Contacts.NSF` using the subdirectory of the current database (i.e., in this case, `Contacts.NSF`).

2 The `@Picklist` command displays the `Contacts` view as a menu that the user can select a customer from. The choice the user makes is stored in the `Chosen_Contact` variable. The last parameter, in this case 1, indicates which column in the view is to be returned by `@Picklist`. You specify 1 here to retrieve the Universal ID column.

3 Ensures that only a single contact is selected.

4 If the `Chosen_Contact` variable is empty, it means the user pressed cancel so the function does nothing (indicated by the empty string `" "`). Otherwise, the `@Do` command executes the two `@Setfield` commands.

5 Sets the hidden `RelatedDocument` field to the Universal ID of the selected contact document. This hidden field is used by the `Contact:` hotspot to load and display a contact record.

6 Uses the contact document's Universal ID to look up the contact's name (i.e., the second column) from the `Contacts` view, and stores it in the `ContactName` field for display purposes.

Now try creating a discussion Main Topic document and linking it to a Contacts document. When you press the Select A Contact button, you'll see a menu with a list of all contacts, as shown in figure 16.2.

Once you select a contact, you will see its name on your form, and you can jump directly to it via the hotspot link shown in figure 16.3.

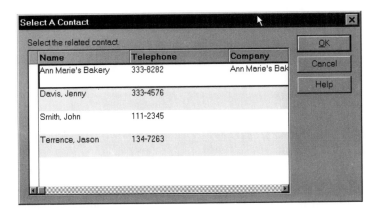

Figure 16.2 Select A Contact dialog

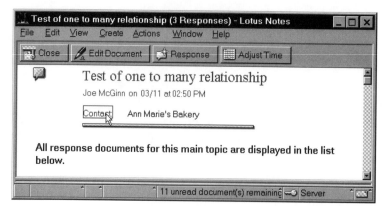

Figure 16.3   Contact hotspot

Last, you may want to create a categorized view in the discussion database that shows a listing of discussion items by contact:

1   Select Design|Views and single click on the By Author view.

2   Select the Edit|Copy menu followed by the Edit|Paste menu.

3   Double-click on the Copy of By Author view.

4   Select the Design|View Properties menu and rename the view By Contact. Close the properties window.

5   Click on the leftmost column of the view. In the programming pane select Field, then click on the ContactName field.

6   Click on the main view area to bring up the View Selection event.

7   Click on the Add Condition button. Select By Form Used and select the Main Topic form.

8   Press OK, then save and close the new view.

This view will show you contacts and the discussion database items that are related to them.

16.4 Many-to-many relations

A many-to-many relation in Notes is constructed the same way it is in a relational database—by combining two one-to-many relations. For example, in the previous section a one-to-many relation was created between contacts (the one side) and discussion items (the many side). To change this into a many-to-many relationship, you simply implement the reverse relationship of the previous section:

1　In the discussion database, create a view that includes parent documents and their universal IDs. This view will be used as a menu to select the related discussion item from the individual contact documents.

2　In the Contacts database create fields on the form that implement and manage the relation (i.e., a Select a Discussion Item button).

3　In the Contacts database create a categorized view that displays contacts by the related discussion field (i.e., a list of discussion items and the contacts related to each of them).

I'm not including the examples and code for this relation because it uses the same code and techniques as in the previous section; it is simply creating a one-to-many link in the opposite direction. Once you've implemented this, each contact can be related to many discussion items, and each discussion item can be related to many contacts—a many-to-many relationship.

16.5　*Referential integrity*

In this section I must reiterate the warning at the beginning of this chapter: Lotus Notes is not a relational database. If you require guaranteed 100 percent reliable referential integrity or disaster recovery for your , then you should use a relational database (i.e., Oracle, DB/2, SQL Server), not Notes.

Having said that, there are some new features in Notes 4.5 that allow you to implement some basic referential integrity features in Notes applications. The code in this section requires Notes 4.5; it will not work with earlier versions of Notes.

For example, one useful feature is to prevent documents from being deleted if they are currently related to another Notes document. In the section "One-to-many relations across databases," you implemented a relation between a discussion database and a Contacts (i.e., Personal Address Book template) database. Using the Notes 4.5 database-level programming events, you can use the following technique to ensure that no Contacts are deleted if they are currently referred to by a discussion document:

1　Open the Contacts database.

2　Select Design|Other and double click on the Database Script item. This is where you attach code to database-level events.

3 Under Event select `Querydocumentdelete`. This event is called before each document deletion, and provides a parameter called `Continue` that can be used to override the user's delete command.

4 Enter the code in listing 16.4.

5 Save and close the Database Script.

Listing 16.4 Querydocument delete check

```
Dim db As NotesDatabase, discussion_db As New NotesDatabase("","")
Dim collection As NotesDocumentCollection
Dim discussion_collection As NotesDocumentCollection
Dim DB_Name As String, j As Integer
Dim Contact As NotesDocument
Set db = Source.Database
1 DB_Name = Left$(db.FilePath, Instr(1, db.FilePath, db.Filename, 1)-1) +
"TestDisc.nsf"
2 If ( Not (discussion_db.Open(db.Server, DB_Name))) Then
  Messagebox "Warning: Discussion database:" + DB_Name + " not found."
  Exit Sub
End If

3 Set collection = Source.Documents
4 For j = 1 To collection.Count
  Set Contact = collection.GetNthDocument(j)
  If Contact.HasItem("LastName") Then
    temp$ = Contact.LastName(0)
  Elseif Contact.HasItem("CompanyName") Then
    temp$ = Contact.CompanyName(0)
  End If
5   Set discussion_collection = discussion_db.Search( "RelatedDocument=
"+Chr$(34)+ Contact.UniversalID + Chr$(34), Nothing, 0)
  If discussion_collection.count > 0 Then
    Messagebox "Warning: " + temp$ + " is referenced from another
database—delete operation cancelled."
6     Continue = False
    Exit For
   End If
Next
```

Listing Notes:

1 Constructs a database file name pointing to `TestDisc.NSF` in the current subdirectory.

2 Opens the discussion database.

3 Source is a NotesUIDatabase variable initialized by Notes and passed to the Querydocumentdelete event. The Documents collection refers to the collection of documents that the user has marked to delete.

4 This loop looks at each document being deleted.

5 Searches the discussion database, looking for the current Contact's Universal ID in the RelatedDocument field of TestDisc.NSF.

6 If any one of the contacts being deleted is found referenced in the discussion database a warning is printed and the delete operation is aborted by setting the Continue variable to False.

Now, try deleting some documents from the Contacts database. If you try to delete a contact that is related from the TestDisc.NSF database, a warning is displayed and the delete operation is canceled.

16.6 Summary

In this chapter you've learned how to implement relationships in Notes. We've covered how to avoid file name conflicts by storing your application in a subdirectory. I have showed you two ways to implement one-to-many relations—within a database using the Notes parent/child document relationship, and an interdatabase relationship.

You've learned how to implement a many-to-many relationship by combining two one-to-many relations, and how to implement basic referential integrity code for a Notes database.

C H A P T E R   1 7

Generating sequential numbers

17.1 Why are sequential numbers so important?

One of the most common requests from users are for forms that have automatically generated, sequential document numbers on them. Users often want certain prefix or suffix codes for the number generated. For example, *EasternSalesForce/ 23/ 1997*, where *23* is generated and incremented for each new document. Users may want a number generated for each document in an application, or they may want different sequences of numbers and prefix/suffix codes for different databases or forms. And most importantly, the numbers must be guaranteed to be unique for each document, at least within a LAN. (There should also be some mechanism for generating numbers over a WAN.)

Are users just being picky? Why worry so much over one little feature? The answer is that these numbers are extremely important because they are usually used for tracking purposes. For example, in a customer support application the customer is usually on the phone talking to a support person who is doing the data entry into the system. The person recording the problem will usually give the customer the generated document number as a reference number. That way, when the customer calls back later, he or she can provide the operators with the code they need to find the document for that customer's support incident.

There are several formula-based techniques for generating document numbers, having varying degrees of elegance (or lack of it), and all having significant drawbacks in one area or another. None of them can meet the full requirements. Fortunately, LotusScript provides all the pieces necessary for a professional quality document number generator. To summarize the features of the technique presented in this chapter:

- It generates sequential numbers for forms, databases, or applications.
- It allows optional prefix and suffix codes (e.g., `EasternSalesForce/ 23/ 1997`).
- It guarantees numbers to be unique on a LAN.
- It presents various solutions for generating sequential numbers over a WAN.
- It works for any number of forms, databases, and applications, and with any number of sets of document numbers being generated.
- It allows the user to see the generated number just by pressing Save; they do not have to exit the form.
- It sorts by document numbers.

17.2 Sequential number generator

Tip

You can find a completed copy of the `DocNums.NSF` database on the *Inside LotusScript* CD.

The principle behind the technique is that a centralized database of document numbers, which is stored on the server, maintains the numbers being generated. This database is titled Document Numbers and named Doc-Nums.NSF. It contains one document for every entity (i.e., form, database, application, etc.) for which you want to generate sequential document numbers. Each Document Numbers document contains a LastUsedNumber which maintains the last number that was generated for a database. It also contains the optional Suffix and Prefix codes. All of your users must have Editor access to the Document Numbers database, so that they can update the LastUsedNumber when they generate a new document. The following steps take you through the process of creating the Document Numbers database:

1 Create a new, empty database by selecting File|Database|New.

2 Under Title enter `Document Numbers`, and under File Name enter `DocNums.nsf`. (*Note:* If you like, you can title it something more descriptive, such as `Sales Document Numbers` for a sales database. It does not matter what the title of this database is, but the filename must be `DocNums.nsf` to work correctly with the code in this chapter.) You can locate this database in a subdirectory, as all references to it follow the "safe referencing" rules that were presented in chapter 3.

3 Do not select any template, and press OK to save and open the new database.

4 Create a new form by selecting the Create|Design|Form menu.

5 Select Design|Form|Properties. Under Name enter `Document Number`.

6 Create the following fields on the form using the Create|Field … menu selection.

- *DatabaseTitle*   Text, Editable.
- *LastUsedNumber*   Number, Editable. Set the default value for this field to "0" (including the quotes).
- *Prefix*   Text, Editable.
- *Suffix*   Text, Editable.

7 Save and close the form.

8 Click on Design|Views, and double-click on the `*($All)` view to open it in design mode. (*Note:* `($All)` is a special view name that appears as the All Documents view to the user.)

9 Create a new column in the view using Create|Append Column.

10 Select Field in the programming pane. Select the DatabaseTitle field. Select Design|Column Properties menu and give the column a title.

11 Optionally, you can also add columns to display the LastUsedNumber, Prefix and Suffix fields. Be sure to use the Create|Append Column menu so that the Database-Title column remains the leftmost one.

12 You must set the DatabaseTitle column to be sorted. To do this, first Click on the DatabaseTitle column. Select Design|Column Properties, and click on the Sorting tab. Under Sort select Ascending.

13 Save and close the view.

14 Close the Document Numbers database.

You do not need to create documents manually in this database. On the first usage (i.e., in the database where you are generating numbers), the LotusScript code in listing 19.1 will automatically create the necessary documents when a user generates the first number.

Go into the Access Control List of the Document Numbers database by selecting the File|Database|Access Control menu. Give all of your users Editor access to the Document Numbers database (or select Editor as the Default access). This does not affect the rest of your application security; you can give your users whatever access to forms, views and databases that they need.

Now, open the database in which you want to generate numbers. To enable number generation in a form, first you must add a few fields:

1 Open a form in design mode. (If it's a Discussion database, you can edit the Main Topic form.)

Tip

If you want to restrict some users from editing document number records directly:

1 Open the Document Number form in design mode. Click on the LastUsedNumber field and select the Design|Column Properties menu.
2 Click on the Hide/When tab (the one with a picture of a key on it).
3 Select the formula option Hide paragraph if formula is true, and insert the following code:

```
(@IsDocBeingEdited & @TextToNumber(@Subset(@UserAccess(@DbName);1)) < 5)
```

This will hide the field when an Editor-access user tries to edit the form directly. If you give your network administrator Designer or Manager access, they will still be able to edit it. (For example, they might want to reset the LastUsedNumber under certain circumstances.) You can add this formula to any of the fields on this form.

---

2 Make a blank empty line on the form (i.e., click on the form and press Enter).

3 Use the Create|Field menu to create three new fields on the same line, with the following field names and types:

- Prefix, type Text, Editable
- DocumentNumber, type Number, Editable
- Suffix, type Text, Editable

It's very important that you remember to make this DocumentNumber field of type Number. If you don't, then you will have difficulties sorting on this field in views.

Note: There are two reasons these fields are not combined into one text field. One, as mentioned above, is to allow sorting to work properly. (See the section "Sorting on document numbers" later in this chapter.) The second reason is to allow users to manually edit both the number and the prefix/suffix codes, which may be a requirement for some applications.

4 Click your mouse to the left of the Prefix field, and enter Document #: as a prompt.

5 Click on the form (i.e., not a field) so that the forms events show up in the programming pane.

6 Under Event select Querysave. Enter the code in listing 17.1. This is the code that actually generates the number. You want to place the code in the Querysave event so that the user doesn't have to close the form to see the new document number, which is handy for tracking applications. The document number will appear on the form as soon as the user presses the Save button.

7 Save and close the form.

Listing 17.1   Generating document numbers

```
Dim session As New NotesSession
Dim db As NotesDatabase
Dim numbers_db As New NotesDatabase("","")
Dim view As NotesView
Dim doc As NotesDocument

Dim workspace As New NotesUIWorkspace
Dim PrefixCode As String
Dim SufficCode As String
Dim NextDocumentNumber As Long
Dim Database_Path As String
Dim New_Document_Number As String, DB_Name As String

Set db = session.CurrentDatabase
```

Listing 17.1   Generating document numbers (continued)

```
1   DB_Name = Left$(db.FilePath, Instr(1, db.FilePath, db.Filename, 1)-1) +
    "DocNums.NSF"
2   Start_Lock:
    Set doc = source.Document

    REM Only generate the number if the field is blank
3   If doc.DocumentNumber(0) = "" Then
    REM Open the document numbers database
4     If ( Not (numbers_db.Open(db.Server, DB_Name))) Then
        REM If the numbers database does not exist (i.e., as would normally be
    the case on a laptop)
        REM then do nothing.
5         Exit Sub
      End If

    REM Get the document number for this database
      Set view = numbers_db.GetView("($All)")
6     Set doc = view.GetDocumentByKey(db.Title)
7     If doc Is Nothing Then
        REM No LastUsedNumber document exists for this database, so create one
        Set doc = New NotesDocument(numbers_db)
        doc.Form = "Document Number"
8         doc.DatabaseTitle = db.Title
        doc.LastUsedNumber = 0
9       Call doc.Save (True,True)

      End If

10      PrefixCode = doc.Prefix(0)
        SuffixCode = doc.Suffix(0)
11      NextDocumentNumber = CIng(doc.LastUsedNumber(0))
12      NextDocumentNumber = NextDocumentNumber + 1
13      doc.LastUsedNumber = NextDocumentNumber
14      New_Document_Number = PrefixCode & Format$( NextDocumentNumber) &
    SuffixCode

        REM Save the incremented LastUsed value
15      REM Messagebox "Got " & New_Document_Number & ": just before Save"
16      flag = doc.Save(False, False)
17      If flag = False Then
        REM This means another user edited the LastUsedNumber while we were
    trying to, so
        REM go back to the beginning of this function and try again.
18        REM Messagebox "Number " & New_Document_Number & "used by another
    user, press OK to get another number"
19        Goto Start_Lock
      End If
```

Listing 17.1 Generating document numbers (continued)

```
20      REM Messagebox "Number " & New_Document_Number & "acquired, press OK
   to save"

21      Call Source.FieldSetText("Prefix", PrefixCode)
22      Call Source.FieldSetText("DocumentNumber", Format$( NextDocumentNum-
   ber))
        Call Source.FieldSetText("Suffix", SuffixCode)
      End If
   End Sub
```

Listing Notes:

1 Uses the safe database referencing method from chapter 3 so that `DocNums.NSF` can be found, even if it is in a subdirectory.

2 The beginning of the document number generation process. There can be a record locking conflict if two users try to generate a number at exactly the same time. If this occurs, one user will get the number and the other user will return to this label to regenerate the next available document number. (See listing notes 16–19.)

3 Prevents the document number from being regenerated on subsequent edits when the document is saved. It would have been possible to check whether the document is new, but there is an advantage to checking for a blank value. If a number is not generated on a remote system (which it normally would not be—see listing notes 4–5), then a number can be generated simply by editing and saving a document once it's on the server.

4, 5 If the `DocNums.NSF` file is not found, no number is generated. This is how number generation is disabled on remote systems like laptops. As long as you don't replicate the `DocNums.NSF` database to any remote systems, they will not generate numbers. Once a remote document has been replicated to the server, simply open and save it to generate the number. Later in this chapter, I'll present an agent that runs on the server to generate such numbers automatically.

6 Retrieves the `DocNums.NSF` document for the current database. In this example, `db.Title` is used as the `DocNums.NSF` "key," so all forms in this database that use this code will generate one set of numbers. If you want to have a set of document numbers generated for a specific form, or for a complete application, you would specify the key you want to use here and in listing line 8. For example, if you wanted all of the databases in a Sales application to work off one set of document numbers, regardless of which database they are in, you would change lines 6 and 8.

Line 6 would be replace with `Set doc = view.GetDocumentByKey("Sales")` and line 8 with `doc.DatabaseTitle = "Sales"`

7 Determines whether or not a `DocNums.NSF` document exists for the current database. If not, it is created and saved. Once the document is saved, it is easy for a developer or user to go into the `DocNums.NSF` database and edit the optional `Suffix` and `Prefix` codes.

8 Sets the key by which this `DocNums.NSF` document will be retrieved. See listing note 6.

9 Saves the new `DocNums.NSF` document.

10 Gets the optional Prefix and Suffix codes from the `DocNums.NSF` document.

11 Gets the LastUsedNumber. This number is the last one that was generated for the current database.

12 Adds one to the LastUsedNumber to generate the new number to be used for the current document.

13 Puts the incremented number back into the `DocNums.NSF` document.

14 Combines the prefix, the newly generated document number, and the suffix into a variable called `New_Document_Number`.

15 Lines 15, 18, and 20 are commented out `Messagebox` statements. If you want to simulate a race condition (i.e., where to users try to generate a number at exactly the same time) to test the record locking, uncomment these lines and try generating document numbers on two workstations side-by-side. You will see that when two users try to generate a number at the same time, one of them will get the number and the other will generate a new one.

16 This line is the key to record locking, which is what guarantees that the document numbers will be unique. With the parameters of the `Save` method set to `False`, `False`, Notes returns an error if someone else has edited the DocNums.NSF document while the current script is running. In other words, if two users request a new document number by saving two new documents at the exact same time, they may both run this script at the same time. One of them will get the number on the first pass through. The other will get an error status returned on this line.

17 If the response to the document `Save` method is `False`, it means that another user got the number that was retrieved.

18 See note 15.

19 Since another user got this number, you use the `Goto` statement to jump back up to the `Start_Lock` label (see listing note 2), where the next available number will be retrieved. The `Goto` statement is sometimes criticized as a "bad" programming practice, and it can create bad code if abused. But, here is a case where it makes for clean, readable, easily maintainable code (just don't overuse it).

20 See note 15.

21 Enters the retrieved `Prefix` code into the `Prefix` field on the new document. Note that we're using the `NotesUIDocument FieldSetText` method, so that the changes appear immediately on the user interface.

22 Writes only the numeric part of the document to the numeric `DocumentNumber` field.

You now have a complete document number generation system. Save the form and try creating a few records with it. The first document will be numbered 1, the second 2, and so on. Open the Document Numbers database, and you will see that it now has a document in it for the database in which you are generating document numbers. Double-click on this document to edit it. Try adding a Prefix code and a Suffix code, and then create a few more documents to see how they work.

You should probably add a Document Number column to your views:

1 Select Design|Views, and double click on the (`$All`) view.

2 Select the Create|Insert New Column menu.

3 In the programming pane click on the Formula option, and enter the following code:

```
Prefix+@Text(DocumentNumber)+Suffix
```

4 Select the Design|Column Properties menu and name the column `Document Number`.

5 Save and close the view.

Now when you select the All Documents view, you will see the Document Number as the first column.

17.3 Sorting on sequential numbers

You will find that many users want to sort by document numbers. Unfortunately, you can't just do a sort on the text DocumentNumber column, because numbers don't sort correctly when sorted as text. This is an inherent property of text sorting, not a limitation of LotusNotes per se. For example, the documents in figure 17.1 are sorted correctly by text rules, but they are sorted incorrectly numerically.

This happens because the numbers are sorted as text would be: first all the numbers that start with 1, then all the numbers that start with 2, and so on.

The solution is to base a sorted column on the numeric DocumentNumber field, rather than the combined text field that shows all three columns. Because it is a numeric field, it will sort numbers correctly. You can still display DocumentNumber in a separate column if desired, as shown in figure 17.1, with a correct numeric sort. First, you need to add a new column to the All Documents view:

1 Select Design|Views, and double click on the (`$All`) view.

2 Select the Create|Insert New Column menu.

3 In the programming pane click on the Field option, and select the DocumentNumber field.

4 Select the Design|Column Properties menu and click on the Sorting tab.

5 Select the Ascending option, then select the "Click on column header to sort" Descending option. Users often want to sort these numbers in descending

Tip

You may want to add a search function using the code from the section "Search and display a document" in chapter 13—Lotus-Script user interface programming (listings 13.3 and 13.4). This will allow your users to quickly search for and display a given Document Number. If you do the search on the DocumentNumber column, then your users don't have to enter the Prefix and Suffix codes while searching; they can just enter the number of the document they want to retrieve.

Tip

You don't have to show the DocumentNumber column. You can select the Hide column property to hide it, and the view will still be sorted on the hidden column.

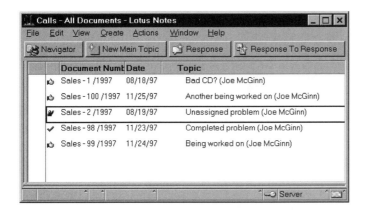

Figure 17.1   Sort by DocumentNumber column

order so that the most recent documents appear at the top of the view; you may want to make Descending the default sort order.

6 Save and close the view.

The document numbers are now sorted correctly, as shown in figure 17.2.

17.4 Generating sequential numbers over a wide area network

The code in listing 17.1 includes a feature that allows you one potential solution to the WAN number generation problem. The problem occurs if you have multiple servers over which you have replicated your application, in which case the record locking solution that ensures each generated number is unique will not work. The record locking code requires a direct connection to the document numbers database, so it really only works within a LAN. You can't generate one set of numbers across a WAN, but what you can do is have different prefix and suffix codes for different servers. To do this, create a separate copy of the DocNums.NSF database on each server. It must be a copy, created using the Files|Database|New Copy menu, *not* a replica. This is because as a copy, a separate set of Prefix and Suffix codes (and LastUsedNumbers) is stored on each server. For example, if you have two sales offices, one for the eastern half of the country and one for the western, you would use the prefix code to indicate from which office the document came. You could enter `WesternOffice` as the Prefix code on one server, and `EasternOffice` on the other, and you might get a sequence of numbers as follows:

```
WesternOffice - 1
```

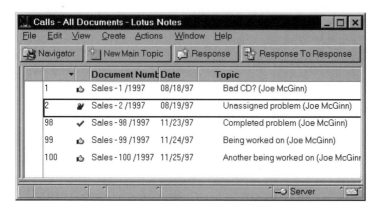

Figure 17.2   Sort by ActualDocumentNumber field

```
WesternOffice - 2
EasternOffice - 1
EasternOffice - 2
EasternOffice - 3
WesternOffice - 3
EasternOffice - 4
EasternOffice - 5
EasternOffice - 6
WesternOffice - 4
```

These numbers can fulfill their primary purpose as tracking numbers, and you can also categorize a view on this field to get a list of documents by sales office.

17.5 Another approach to wide area networks

There's another way to implement document number generation over a distributed network of users. It may or may not work for you, depending on your requirements. If all of your users need to see generated document numbers when they first save new documents, then you are probably better off using the method presented in the previous section. Sometimes, though, there are situations where your remote users don't need numbers immediately generated on their screens. In this section I will show you how to write an agent that you can run on the server (automatically, of course) when remote users replicate their new documents to the server.

For example, you might have a person who occasionally enters a remote document from his or her home computer or laptop. Make sure there are no copies or replicas of the Document numbers database on the laptop. When new documents are created, the DocumentNumber field remains blank and no number is generated. When the user replicates the new document to the server, the agent you create in this section is triggered, and it will generate the Document Number on the server, just as it would for a connected user. The next time the remote user replicates, they will see the generated document numbers on their computer as well.

1 Select the Create|Agent menu item.

2 Select the Shared Agent option.

3 Under Name enter `Generate Document Numbers`.

4 Under the question When should this agent run? select the option If Documents have been created or modified.

5 Click on the Schedule button and select the option to run the agent only on your server. You may need to contact your Notes network administrator if you don't have

permission to run agents on the server. (This is set up in the Agent Restrictions section of the server document in your public Name and Address Book.)

6 Under the question What should this agent do? select the Script option.

7 Select the Initialize event, and then enter the LotusScript code in listing 17.2. This code is identical to the code in listing 17.1, except that it must update the documents through the back end LotusScript classes since it runs on the server. The listing notes cover the differences in this server based code.

Listing 17.2   Generating document numbers on the server

```
     Dim session As New NotesSession
     Dim db As NotesDatabase
     Dim numbers_db As New NotesDatabase("","")
     Dim view As NotesView
     Dim doc As NotesDocument
1    Dim ServerDoc As NotesDocument

     Dim PrefixCode
     Dim SuffixCode
     Dim NextDocumentNumber As Long
     Dim Database_Path As String
     Dim New_Document_Number As String, DB_Name As String
     Dim collection As NotesDocumentCollection
     Dim Item As notesitem

     Set db = session.CurrentDatabase
     DB_Name = Left$(db.FilePath, Instr(1, db.FilePath, db.Filename, 1)-1) +
     "DocNums.NSF"
     REM Open the document numbers database
     If ( Not (numbers_db.Open(db.Server, DB_Name))) Then
        REM Exit if not found
        Exit Sub
     End If
2    Set collection = db.UnprocessedDocuments
     For i = 1 To collection.Count
3       Start_Lock:
4       Set ServerDoc = collection.GetNthDocument(i)
     REM Only generate the number if the field is blank
        If ServerDoc.HasItem( "ActualMessageNumber" ) Then
           Set item = ServerDoc.GetFirstItem( "DocumentNumber" )
           If Len(item.Text) = 0 Then
           REM Get the Document Number for this database
              Set view = numbers_db.GetView("($All)")
              Set doc = view.GetDocumentByKey(db.Title)
              If doc Is Nothing Then
```

Listing 17.2   Generating document numbers on the server (continued)

```
        REM No LastUsedNumber document exists for this database, so create
    one
            Set doc = New NotesDocument(numbers_db)
            doc.Form = "Document Number"
            doc.DatabaseTitle = db.Title
            doc.LastUsedNumber = 0
            Call doc.Save (True,True)
        End If

        PrefixCode = doc. Prefix(0)
        SuffixCode = doc.Suffix(0)
        NextDocumentNumber = Clng(doc.LastUsedNumber(0))
        NextDocumentNumber = NextDocumentNumber + 1
        doc.LastUsedNumber = NextDocumentNumber
        New_Document_Number = PrefixCode & Format$(NextDocumentNumber) &
    SuffixCode

    REM Save the incremented LastUsed value
        flag = doc.Save(False, False)
        If flag = False Then
           Goto Start_Lock
        End If
5       ServerDoc.Prefix = PrefixCode
        ServerDoc.DocumentNumber = NextDocumentNumber
        ServerDoc.Suffix = SuffixCode
6       flag = ServerDoc.Save(False, True)
        REM i.e., If someone else is editing it, create a response document
        REM for this saved document.
      End If
        End If
    Next
```

Listing Notes:

1 `ServerDoc` is a document record used to examine new documents that have arrived on the server.

2 The `UnprocessedDocuments` property sets the collection variable to the documents specified when the agent was created. (That is, under the question When should this agent run? you selected the option If Documents have been created or modified, so that's what ends up in this collection.)

3 The start of the record-locking loop is inside the collection loop, so that record locking applies to each record processed.

4 This line sets the `ServerDoc` variable to refer to the current document in the collection.

5 Stores the `Prefix/Suffix` and the newly generated `DocumentNumber` into the document, via the back end NotesDocument class.

6 Saves the document. (The second parameter of the `Save` method is set to `True`, so that a replication conflict document will be created if someone is currently editing this document.)

This agent will now automatically update all new documents with blank DocumentNumber fields, even if entered over a WAN.

17.6 Generating sequential numbers on the Internet

We've looked at two different methods for generating document numbers over a WAN, each with its own advantages and disadvantages. The first method—using prefix codes to separate the numbers generated on different servers—has the advantage that it displays the generated number immediately on any server, but the disadvantage that it does not generate one numeric sequence for all documents in the organization. The second method—using an agent to generate all numbers on one server—solves that problem, but at the cost of a delay for number display. (That is, remote users cannot see the generated number until after they have replicated their new documents to and from a central server.)

There is yet another way of solving this problem that has the advantages of both these methods, but the disadvantages of neither. The solution is to publish your database on the Web using Domino and generate the numbers using an agent that runs on the Domino server. This technique displays a number instantly, as soon as the document is saved. And because it's implemented over the Internet, users can create documents from any geographic location. For the complete source code and instructions on how to implement such an agent, see the section "Example 2: generating sequential numbers on the Internet" in chapter 12—Internet LotusScript and agents.

17.7 Record locking

Record locking can be a valuable technique in many situations. For example, a resource tracking application needs to update documents that indicate when a resource is used.

This is just the sort of situation where you don't want two users to claim a resource simultaneously, which would overbook it. The record locking technique described in listing 17.1 can be used in these situations. To recap, the key is to use the backend NotesDocument `Save` method to save the document, and to set the parameters to `False, False`:

```
flag = doc.Save(False, False)
```

If the return value is `False` it means another user has edited the record while the current script was running, and you must use a `Goto` to jump back to an early point in your subroutine.

```
If flag = False Then
    Goto Start_Lock
End If
```

Remember to allow for initialization of any needed variables when you jump back. It is a good idea to reopen any views you are using to access documents, so that you get the latest documents from disk, not old ones cached in memory. For example, in listing 17.1 this is done just before line 6:

```
Set view = numbers_db.GetView("($All)")
```

Tip

To be sure that view you are using for record locking contains the latest records, you need to enable the discard index feature for the view. To do this for any view:

1   Click on Design, Views, and double-click the view to open it in design mode.

2   Select the Design|View Properties menu.

3   Click the "propeller beanie" tab.

4   Under Discard Index, select After Each Use.

Now the view will always display the latest documents and changes.

17.8 Summary

You have learned how to build a professional quality server-based document number generator. It works for all users, connected and remote, and we've explored three different methods of supporting distributed document number generation over a WAN. You've learned how to sort views on these document numbers, and how to use record locking to make this kind of function foolproof.

C H A P T E R   1 8

LotusScript agents

In this chapter I'll present some tips on how to debug server-based agents, and a few LotusScript agents that may be useful to you. The agents presented in this chapter are:

- An agent that collates an expense report and emails it to someone.

- An agent that searches a database and presents the resulting documents to the user.

- A multidatabase application search agent that searches through all databases in the current subdirectory.

- A graphical front end that allows you to save searches, and an agent that runs scheduled queries in the background and emails the results to the query author.

18.1 Debugging server-based agents

Agents that run on the client are easy to debug because you can use `Messagebox` statements to display messages on the screen, and you also have access to the interactive LotusScript debugger. Agents that run on the server are a little trickier to debug as you have access to neither of the tools. You can, however, simulate a Messagebox function by sending email messages to yourself from within the server agent. Simply add the MailMessagebox function from listing 18.1 to your agent, and call it as you would do with Messagebox to display debugging messages:

```
MailMessagebox "1: Starting server agent."
' agent code…
MailMessagebox "2: At this point temp = " + temp
```

By sprinkling these calls throughout an agent, you are debugging you can quickly narrow down problems in a server-based agent. It's a good idea to include a unique number in each MailMessagebox, as shown above, so that you can match up your email messages to particular places in the agent.

Listing 18.1 MainMessagebox function

```
Sub MailMessagebox (temp As String)
   Dim session As New NotesSession
   Dim db As NotesDatabase
   Set db = session.CurrentDatabase
   Dim newdoc As NotesDocument
   Dim rtitem As NotesRichTextItem
1  Set newdoc = New NotesDocument(db)
   Set rtitem = New NotesRichTextItem (newdoc, "Body")
2  Call rtitem.AppendText(Format$(Now) + ": " + temp)
3  newdoc.Subject = Left$(temp,50)
```

Listing 18.1   MainMessagebox function (continued)

```
4    newdoc.SendTo = "Joe McGinn/Joe's Place"
5    Call newdoc.Send (False)
   End Sub
```

Listing Notes:

1 Creates a mail document.

2 Enters the current date/time and the text of the message into the Body field.

3 Enters the first part of the message as the mail `Subject`.

4 Addresses the mail. You'll have to change this line to include your Notes mail address.

5 Sends the mail.

One other technique that can really assist with debugging server agents is to include an error trapping routine as shown in listing 18.2. This way, all errors get reported to you by email, along with an error message and a line number. The error handler makes use of the MailMessagebox statement to send the error message to you.

Listing 18.2   LotusScript error handler for server agents

```
   On Error Goto Error_Handler
   REM … Code for your agent …
1  Exit Sub
2  Error_Handler:
3  MailMessagebox "Error on line number " + Format$(Erl()) + ": " + Error$
4  Exit Sub
```

Listing Notes:

1 Prevents your LotusScript routine from falling into the error handler when it completes successfully without an error.

2 This label is where control of the script will jump when any error occurs. If there are errors that you expect as part of the normal operation of your agent, you can trap for them gracefully here and continue program execution using the `Resume` statement without printing the error message:

```
If Err = expected_error_number Then
    REM … processing to correct or handle the error condition
    Resume Next
End If
```

3 Emails the error message and line number to you.

4 Terminates the agent and the error handler.

18.2 Agent to email an expense report

This agent collects expense information from a list of documents the user has selected, totals the expenses, and sends the resulting report by email. The LotusScript code in this agent will also work for a scheduled agent that runs on the server. (For example, you might set it up to select all documents entered in the last month and schedule the agent to run on the first day of each month.)

First, create or open a test Discussion database, then edit the Main Topic form as follows:

1 Select Design|Forms and double-click on the Main Topic form.

2 Click below the Body field and select the Create|Field menu.

3 Name the field ExpenseAmount, type Number, and select the Currency option. Close the properties window.

4 Click to the left of the new field and type Expenses: as a prompt.

5 Save and close the Main Topic form.

Edit a few Main Topic documents and enter a currency value in the new field:

1 Select the Create|Agent menu item.

2 Under Name enter Expense Report.

3 Select the Shared Agent option.

4 Under the question When should this agent run? select the option Manually From Actions Menu.

5 Under the question Which document(s) should it act on? select the option Selected documents.

6 Under the question What should this agent do? select the Script option.

7 Select the Initialize event, and then enter the LotusScript code in listing 18.3.

Listing 18.3   Expense report agent

```
Dim doc As NotesDocument, newdoc As NotesDocument
Dim db As NotesDatabase
Dim session As New NotesSession
Dim collection As NotesDocumentCollection
```

Listing 18.3   Expense report agent (continued)

```
      Dim rtitem As NotesRichTextItem

      Set db = session.CurrentDatabase
1     Set collection = db.UnprocessedDocuments
      For i = 1 To collection.Count
          Set doc = collection.GetNthDocument(i)
2         total_expenses = total_expenses + doc.ExpenseAmount(0)
      Next

3     Set newdoc = New NotesDocument(db)
      Set rtitem = New NotesRichTextItem (newdoc, "Body")
      Call rtitem.AppendText("Expenses at   " + Format$(Now) + ": " + Format
4     (collection.Count) + " documents were selected, total expenses = $" +
      Format$(total_expenses))
      newdoc.Subject = "Expenses Report"
5     newdoc.SendTo = "Joe McGinn/Joe's Place"
      Call newdoc.Send (False)
```

Tip

For this kind of report, which is gathering information from several documents, it might be nice to include links to the documents that make up the report. You can do this using the NotesNewsletter class. The code in listing 18.4 shows how to implement this same agent with the results delivered in a newsletter that contains the document links.

Listing Notes:

1 Gets access to the collection of documents. This works whether the agent is working on selected documents or any other document selection criteria (e.g., as would be used in a scheduled agent).

2 Adds to the total expenses for each document in the collection.

3 Creates a new mail document.

4 Appends the total expenses information, along with the current date and time, to the mail document.

5 Addresses the mail document. (You'll have to change this to a valid email address for your Notes server.)

Listing 18.4   Expense report agent with NotesNewsletter

```
      Dim doc As NotesDocument, newdoc As NotesDocument
      Dim db As NotesDatabase
      Dim session As New NotesSession
      Dim collection As NotesDocumentCollection
      Dim item As NotesItem

      Set db = session.CurrentDatabase
```

Listing 18.4   Expense report agent with NotesNewsletter (continued)

```
    Set collection = db.UnprocessedDocuments
    For i = 1 To collection.Count
        Set doc = collection.GetNthDocument(i)
        total_expenses = total_expenses + doc.ExpenseAmount(0)
    Next
    Dim newsletter As NotesNewsletter
    Dim rtitem As Variant
1   Set newsletter = New NotesNewsletter( collection )
2   newsletter.DoSubject = True
3   newsletter.SubjectItemName = "Subject"
4   Set doc = newsletter.FormatMsgWithDoclinks( db )
5   doc.Form = "Memo"
    doc.Subject = "Expense Report"
6   Set rtitem = doc.GetFirstItem( "Body" )
    Call rtitem.AddNewLine(1)
    Call rtitem.AppendText("Total expenses = $" + Format$(total_expenses))
    Call rtitem.AddNewLine(1)
7   Call doc.Send( False, "Joe McGinn/Joe's Place" )
```

Listing Notes:

1 Sets the newsletter variable to a NotesDocumentCollection (In this example, the collection selected by the agent).

2 The DoSubject property tells the newsletter to include the text of document subject lines with the document links.

3 The SubjectItemName variable specifies the field name from which to get the subject text.

4 The FormatMsgWithDoclinks method creates the document links for all documents in the collection. The DoSubject and SubjectItemName properties must be set before calling FormatMsgWithDoclinks.

5 Specifies that the document is to be viewed with the Memo form when it arrives in a mail database.

6 Note that the FormatMsgWithDoclinks returns a document, which has all of the normal NotesDocument properties and methods. This line uses the GetFirstItem method to find the Body field on the document. (Normally, when creating a mail message, you have to create the Body field, but that is already done by the Format-MsgWithDoclinks method.)

7 Addresses and sends the email newsletter.

When you run this agent, it will send an email report that includes links to each of the documents in the report, as show in figure 18.1.

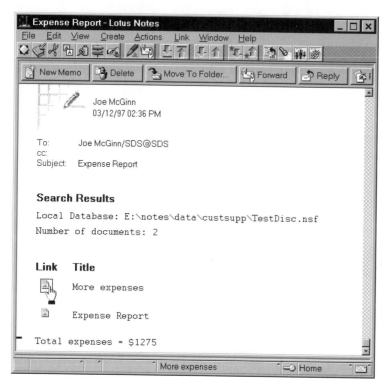

Figure 18.1   Newsletter report

18.3 Search and display multiple documents agent

In the section "Search and display a document" in chapter 13, I showed you how to write a search function that finds a document via LotusScript and then displays the document on the user interface. In this section, I'll show you how to write a searching function that takes advantage of the NotesNewsletter class to display multiple documents (i.e., a document collection) to the user. The technique presented here requires search result documents to be saved in a database, so it will be implemented in a database that is physically separate from the database you want to search.

First, create a test discussion database called TestDisc.nsf. Then create an empty database (i.e., not based on any template) called SearchDB.nsf in the same directory as TestDisc.nsf.

Before creating the search agent, you need to create a form in which to display the search results:

1 Select the Create|Design|Form menu to create a new form.

Tip For Notes 4.5 Users

For Notes 4.5 users there is a better solution that is easier to implement. See the section "Search and display multiple documents" in chapter 14.

2 Select the Design|Form Properties menu, and name the form Results. Close the properties window.

3 Use the Create|Field menu to create a field named `SearchFor`, type Text, Editable.

4 Type the text `Searching for:` as a prompt to the left of the SearchFor field. To be consistent with the Notes newsletter format, you should set the text properties for this text to the color light blue, size 10, style Bold.

5 Use the Create|Field menu to create a field named `Body`, type Rich Text, Editable.

6 Select the Create|Action menu. Under Title enter "`Close`", and select a button icon. Close the properties window and enter the following formula code for the action:

```
@PostedCommand([FileCloseWindow])
```

7 Click on the form so that the forms events show up in the programming pane, and then select the Queryclose event. Add the following line of LotusScript code to this event:

```
Call Source.DeleteDocument
```

This will prevent the search Results documents from being saved permanently.

8 Save and close the Results form.

Now you can create an agent that searches the TestDisc.nsf database for multiple documents:

1 Select the Create|Agent menu item.

2 Under Name enter `Search TestDisc Database Part 1`.

3 Select the Shared Agent option.

4 Under the question When should this agent run? select the option Manually From Actions Menu.

5 Under the question Which document(s) should it act on? select the option Run once (`@Commands` may be used).

6 Under the question What should this agent do? select the Script option.

7 Select the Initialize event, and then enter the LotusScript code in listing 18.5.

Listing 18.5   Display multiple documents

```
Dim session As New NotesSession
Dim workspace As New NotesUIWorkspace
Dim doc As NotesDocument
Dim db As NotesDatabase
Dim discussion_db As New NotesDatabase("","")
Dim collection As NotesDocumentCollection
Dim newsletter As NotesNewsletter
Dim text_to_find As String
Dim unid As String

text_to_find = Inputbox$("Enter the text you want to find:", "Find Docu-
ments")

Set db = session.CurrentDatabase
```
1
```
DB_Name = Left$(db.FilePath, Instr(1, db.FilePath, db.Filename, 1)-1) +
"TestDisc.NSF"
```
2
```
If ( Not (discussion_db.Open(db.Server, DB_Name))) Then
    Call session.SetEnvironmentVar("UNID","")
    Exit Sub
End If
```
3
```
Set collection = discussion_db.ftsearch(text_to_find, 0)
```
4
```
Set newsletter = New NotesNewsletter( collection )
newsletter.DoSubject = True
newsletter.SubjectItemName = "Subject"
```
5
```
Set doc = newsletter.FormatMsgWithDoclinks( db )
```
6
```
doc.Form = "Results"
doc.SearchFor = text_to_find
```
7
```
Call doc.Save(False,False)
unid = doc.UniversalID
```
8
```
Call session.SetEnvironmentVar("UNID",unid)
```
9
```
Call workspace.ViewRefresh
```

Listing Notes:

1   Constructs a text string that contains the file name TestDisc.nsf in the current subdirectory.

2   Opens the TestDisc.nsf database.

3   Conducts a full text search based on the text the user entered.

4   Creates a newsletter based on the collection of documents returned by the search.

5   Creates the document links to the documents in the collection.

6   Specifies the form in which to display the newsletter document.

7 Saves the Results document in the search database.

8 Stores the Universal ID of the results document into an environment variable so that it can be displayed by Part 2 of this agent.

9 Refreshes the current view so that the new search results document can be displayed.

Now you need to create the formula part of this agent, which will display the document on the user interface:

1 Select the Create|Agent menu item.

2 Under Name enter `Search TestDisc Database Part 2`.

3 Select the Shared Agent option.

4 Under the question When should this agent run? select the option Manually From Actions Menu.

5 Under the question Which document(s) should it act on? select the option Run once (`@Commands` may be used).

6 Under the question What should this agent do? select Formula.

7 In the programming pane enter the following line of code:

```
@Command([OpenDocument]; "0"; @Environment("UNID"))
```

As the last step in completing this function, now you can build a button that launches the search:

1 Select Design|Views, and double click on the (untitled) view.

2 Select the Design|View Properties menu and rename the view to (`$All`).

3 Select the Create|Action menu, and enter `Search TestDisc Database` as the Title.

4 Close the properties window, and in the programming pane select Simple Action(s).

5 Click on the Add Action button. Under Action select Run Agent, and under Agent select Search TestDisc Database Part 1. Press OK.

6 Click on the Add Action button a second time. Under Action select Run Agent, and under Agent select Search TestDisc Database Part 2. Press OK.

7 Save and close the view.

Now you can try running the search agent. Select the All Documents view and press the search action button. You will be prompted for search text, and the results of the search will be displayed as a document with links to all matching documents as shown in figure 18.2.

18.4 Search all databases in a subdirectory

One of the techniques that has been emphasized throughout this book is storing your multidatabase Notes applications in a subdirectory, to avoid filename conflicts (and to ensure that your programmed relations between databases always work). One of the apparent drawbacks in multidatabase applications is that the built-in Notes searching only works within a single database, which means it cannot search across your entire application. The Search Site template in Notes 4.5 alleviates this to some degree, but it is not that easy to set up (and, of course, it doesn't help at all for Notes 4.0 or 4.1 users).

In this section, I'll present a solution to this problem by creating a database with a LotusScript agent that searches all databases in the current subdirectory, and then presents the results of the search to the user. This database works with any filenames, so it can be placed in any subdirectory.

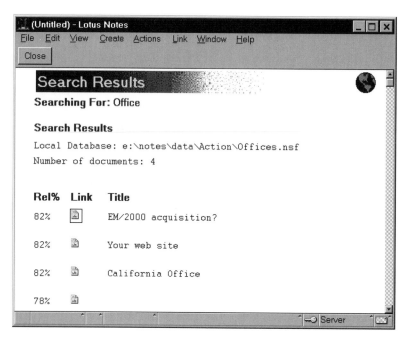

Figure 18.2 Multiple document search results

First, create an empty (i.e., not based on any template) database in a subdirectory that contains some Notes databases. Before creating the search agents, you need to create a form in which to display the search results:

1 Select the Create|Design|Form menu to create a new form.

2 Select the Design|Form Properties menu, and name the form Results. Close the properties window.

3 Use the Create|Field menu the create a field named SearchFor, type Text, Editable.

4 Type the text Searching for: as a prompt to the left of the SearchFor field. To be consistent with the Notes newsletter format, you should set the text properties for this text to the color light blue, size 10, style Bold.

5 Use the Create|Field menu to create a field named Body, type Rich Text, Editable.

6 Select the Create|Action menu. Under Title enter Close, and select a button icon. Close the properties window and enter the following formula code for the action:

```
@PostedCommand([FileCloseWindow])
```

7 Click on the form so that the forms events show up in the programming pane, and then select the Queryclose event. Add the following line of LotusScript code to this event:

```
Call Source.DeleteDocument
```

This will prevent the search Results documents from being saved permanently.

8 Save and close the Results form.

Now you can create the main agent that performs a full text search in all databases in the subdirectory:

1 Select the Create|Agent menu item.

2 Under Name enter Search Subdirectory Part 1.

3 Select the Shared Agent option.

4 Under the question When should this agent run? select the option Manually From Actions Menu.

Tip

If you completed the previous section in this chapter, you do not need to recreate the search database and Results form; you can simply add the agents in this section to the search database you've already created.

5 Under the question Which document(s) should it act on? select the option Run once (@Commands may be used).

6 Under the question What should this agent do? select the Script option.

7 Select the (Declarations) event and add the following lines of code to it:

```
Dim directory As NotesDbDirectory
Dim db_find As NotesDatabase
```

8 Enter the Get_SubDir_Filename function in listing 18.6. This function gets the names of Notes databases in a specific subdirectory.

9 Select the Initialize event, and then enter the LotusScript code in listing 18.7.

Listing 18.6   Search databases code—Get_SubDir_Filename function

```
1   Function Get_SubDir_Filename(Subdir As String, Find As String) As String
    Dim Filename As String
    If Find = "First" Then
        'find first db in current subdir
2       Set db_find = directory.GetFirstDatabase( DATABASE)
    Else
        'find next db in current subdir
3       Set db_find = directory.GetNextDatabase
    End If
4   If db_find Is Nothing Then
        Get_SubDir_Filename = ""
        Exit Function
    Else
5       Filename = db_find.FilePath
    End If
    'Make sure the database we've found is in the current subdir
6   Do While Left$(db_find.FilePath,Len(Subdir)) <> Subdir
        Set db_find = directory.GetNextDatabase
        If db_find Is Nothing Then
            Get_SubDir_Filename = ""
            Exit Function
        Else
            Filename = db_find.FilePath
        End If
    Loop
7   Get_SubDir_Filename = Filename
    End Function
```

Listing Notes:

1 This function accepts a subdirectory name and the commands `First` or `Next`. It assumes that a `NotesDbDirectory` variable is available and opened on the current server, and that a `db_find` NotesDatabase variable is available. When called with `First`, the function returns the filename of the first Notes database in the specified subdirectory. When called with `Next`, it returns the next filename, and returns the empty string when all the filenames in the subdirectory have been processed.

2 For the command `First`, sets the `db_find` database to the first database filename.

3 For the command `Next`, sets the `db_find` database to the next database filename.

4 Checks to see if the last filename has been retrieved, and returns the empty string value if it has.

5 Sets the `Filename` variable to the retrieved database filename.

6 Checks to make sure that the database filename retrieved is in the specified subdirectory. (That is, `NotesDbDirectory` returns the filenames of all files in the Notes DATA directory and all its subdirectories.)

7 Assigns the Filename string variable to the function name, so that the value is returned to the code that called this function.i

Listing 18.7   Search databases code—initialize event

```
      Dim session As New NotesSession
      Dim workspace As New NotesUIWorkspace
      Dim doc As NotesDocument
      Dim db As NotesDatabase
      Dim collection As NotesDocumentCollection
      Dim newdoc As NotesDocument
      Dim rtitem As NotesRichTextItem
      Dim text_to_find As String
      Dim unid As String, Notes_Directory As String
      Dim Subdir As String, Filename As String, DB_Name As String
      Dim j As Integer, db_number As Integer, total_matches As Integer

      text_to_find = Inputbox$("Enter the text you want to find:", "Find Docu-
      ments")

      Set db = session.CurrentDatabase
      If db.Server <> "" Then
1        Subdir = Left$(db.FilePath, Instr(1, db.FilePath, db.Filename, 1)-2)
      Else
2        Notes_Directory = session.GetEnvironmentString( "Directory", True )
         Subdir = Left$(db.FilePath, Instr(1, db.FilePath, db.Filename, 1)-2)
         Subdir = Right$(Subdir, Len(Subdir)-Len(Notes_Directory)-1)
```

Listing 18.7 Search databases code—initialize event (continued)

```
     End If
3    Set newdoc = New NotesDocument(db)
4    Set rtitem = New NotesRichTextItem (newdoc, "Body")
5    newdoc.Form = "Results"
6    newdoc.SearchFor = text_to_find + " in " + Left$(db.FilePath, Instr(1,
     db.FilePath, db.Filename, 1)-1)

     total_matches = 0
7    Set directory = New NotesDbDirectory( db.Server )
8    Filename = Get_SubDir_Filename(Subdir, "First")
9    Do While Filename <> ""
10      DB_Name = Left$(db.FilePath, Instr(1, db.FilePath, db.Filename, 1)-1) +
     db_Find.Filename
11      If Strcompare(DB_Name, db.FilePath, 1) <> 0 Then
12         Redim db_to_search(1) As NotesDatabase
13         Set db_to_search(0) = New NotesDatabase(db.Server, DB_Name)
14         If Not(db_to_search(0).IsOpen) Then
              Call db_to_search(0).Open("","")
           End If
15         On Error Resume Next
16         Set collection = db_to_search(0).ftsearch(text_to_find, 0)
           On Error Goto Error_Handler
           If collection.Count > 0 Then
17            Call rtitem.AppendText(db_to_search(0).Title + ":  found " +
     Format$(collection.Count) + " matches in " +  db_to_search(0).Filepath)
              Call rtitem.AddNewLine(1)
18            For j = 1 To collection.Count
                 Set doc = collection.GetNthDocument( j )
19               Call rtitem.AppendDocLink (doc, "")
20               If doc.HasItem("Subject") Then
                    Call rtitem.AppendText("  " + Trim$(doc.Subject(0)))
                 End If
     Next_Match:
21               total_matches = total_matches + 1
                 Call rtitem.AddNewLine(1)
              Next
22            Call rtitem.AddNewLine(1)
           End If
        End If
23      Filename = Get_SubDir_Filename(Subdir, "Next")
     Loop

24   If total_matches = 0 Then
        Call rtitem.AppendText("No matches for '" + text_to_find + "' found.")
     Else
        Call rtitem.AppendText(Format$(total_matches) + " matches for '" +
     text_to_find + "' found.")
     End If
```

Listing 18.7   Search databases code—initialize event (continued)

```
25 Call newdoc.Save(False,False)
   unid = newdoc.UniversalID
26 Call session.SetEnvironmentVar("UNID",unid)
27 Call workspace.ViewRefresh
   Exit Sub
   Error_Handler:
28 If Err = 4175 Then
       If doc.HasItem("Subject") Then
           Call rtitem.AppendText("Subject: " + Trim$(doc.Subject(0)))
       End If
       Call rtitem.AppendText(" (warning: " + db_to_search(0).Filename + " has
   no 'default view', doclink unavailable)")
       Resume Next_Match
   End If
   Messagebox "Error (" + Format$(Err) + ") on line number " + Format$(Erl())
   + ": " + Error$
   Resume Next
   Exit Sub
```

Listing Notes:

1 If running on a server, then db.FilePath has the format TESTDIR\SearchDB.nsf
   (where TESTDIR is the subdirectory under the Notes DATA directory). Therefore, we
   can determine the current subdirectory by simply removing the db.Filename por-
   tion of this string.

2 When running on a local hard drive, db.FilePath has the format
   C:\NOTES\DATA\TESTDIR\SearchDB.nsf. So, to determine the current subdirectory, we need to remove the Notes directory from the left side of the string, as well
   as removing the db.Filename from the right side.

3 Creates a new document in which to store the search results.

4 Creates a rich text item on the results document to store the document links to
   matching documents.

5 Specifies that the search results document should be displayed in the Results form.

6 Stores the text and subdirectory being searching into the SearchFor field, so that
   the user can see this information.

7 Creates a NotesDbDirectory variable on the current server.

8 Retrieves the filename of the first Notes database in the current subdirectory.

9 This Do loop looks at each NSF file in the subdirectory.

10 Constructs a full path name to the next Notes database to be opened.

11 Avoids searching in the `SearchDB.nsf` search database in which this agent is stored.

12 The `NotesDatabase` class does not contain a close method. But, here we must close the database so that we can open the next one in the current subdirectory. To get around this limitation, we store the database reference in an array (even though the array has only one element). This way, we can simulate a close event using the `REDIM` statement, which deletes the old array and reallocates storage for it. The result is that we can use a single `NotesDatabase` variable to access several different databases.

13 Opens the Notes database. Note that the `db_to_search` array of Notes documents must be referenced with the number `0`.

14 The `New NotesDatabase` method works differently on some versions of the Notes server and does not actually open the database. This code checks to see if the database is opened, and opens it manually if it is closed.

15 This `On Error` statement is needed because of a bug in the full text search method, which returns an error if you try to search a database that does not contain any documents.

16 Searches the opened database.

17 If matching documents were found, prints the database `Title`, filename, and the number of matches in this database.

18 This loop accesses each document in the NotesDocument collection returned by the full text search.

19 Appends a document link to the matching document.

20 If a Subject field is found, it is appended beside the document link. You could add more code here to display other fields. Just remember to do a `HasItem` check for each field so you don't generate an error.

21 Increments the total number of matches found so far.

22 At the end of each database an extra blank line is appended to make the results document look better.

23 Retrieves the next Notes database filename from the current subdirectory.

24 Appends the total number of matches found to the search results.

25 Saves the search results document.

26 Stores the Universal ID of the results document in an environment variable, so that it can be displayed by Part 2 of this agent.

27 Refreshes the current view so that the newly saved results document is available for viewing.

28 Error number 4175 (`Couldn't get default view ID for database`) is returned by the `AppendDocLink` method when this code is run in a database that does not have a default view. This behavior can also cause problems in mail-enabled databases, which often use `AppendDocLink`. As a general rule of thumb, you should always make sure every database has a default view. (In the list of views under Design|View, the default view is displayed with a * beside it.) To set a default view in a database:

- Open the database and select Design|Views.
- Double-click on any view. (The (`$All`) view is a good choice for the default view.)
- Select the Design|View Properties menu, and click on the Options tab.
- Select the option Default when database is first opened.

Now you can create the formula part of this agent, which will display the document on the user interface.

1 Select the Create|Agent menu item.

2 Under Name enter `Search Subdirectory Part 2`.

3 Select the Shared Agent option.

4 Under the question When should this agent run? select the option Manually From Actions Menu.

5 Under the question Which document(s) should it act on? select the option Run once (`@Commands` may be used).

6 Under the question What should this agent do? select Formula.

7 In the programming pane enter the following line of code:

```
@Command([OpenDocument]; "0"; @Environment("UNID"))
```

Last, you need to build a button that launches the subdirectory search:

1 Select Design|Views, and double click on the (untitled) view.

2 Select the Design|View Properties menu and rename the view to (`$All`).

3 Select the Create|Action menu, and enter `Search Subdirectory` as the Title.

4 Close the properties window, and in the programming pane select Simple Action(s).

5 Click on the Add Action button. Under Action select Run Agent, and under Agent select Search Subdirectory Part 1. Press OK.

6 Click on the Add Action… button a second time. Under Action select Run Agent, and under Agent select Search Subdirectory Part 2. Press OK.

7 Save and close the view.

Now try running the search agent. Select the All Documents view and press the Search Subdirectory button. You will be prompted for search text, and the results of the search will be displayed as a document with links to all matching documents, as shown in figure 18.3.

18.5 *Run saved queries on the server*

In the previous section, I presented a multidatabase search engine. Now we'll add a graphical interface for advanced searches, including an option to save searches and allow them to be run in the background by a scheduled agent on the server. The instructions here build

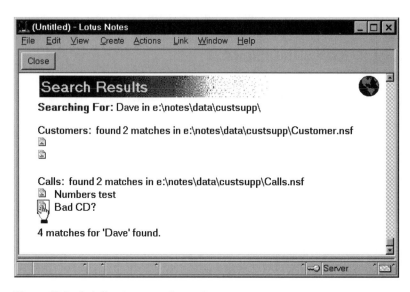

Figure 18.3 Subdirectory search results

upon the search database and Results form constructed in the previous section.

First, we'll create a form to use as a graphical interface to drive the search engine:

1 Open the search database, and select the Create|Design|Form menu.

2 Select the Design|Form Properties menu and name the form `Search SubDirectory`. Close the properties window.

3 Select the Create|Field menu. Name the field `SearchLogic`, type Keywords, Editable. On the keywords options tab select Radio Button, no frame, and 2 columns. Under keyword choices enter:
   - `Any`
   - `All`

   Enter "Any" as the default value for this field.

4 Use the Create|Field menu to create the following six fields on the form:
   - `SearchWord_1`, Text, Editable
   - `SearchWord_2`, Text, Editable
   - `SearchWord_3`, Text, Editable
   - `SearchWord_4`, Text, Editable
   - `SearchWord_5`, Text, Editable
   - `SearchWord_6`, Text, Editable

5 At the top of the form, create the following hidden fields:
   - `SearchName`, Text, Editable
   - `RunInBackground`, Text, Editable
   - `HowOften`, Text, Editable
   - `SaveOptions`, Text, Editable: Enter `"0"` (including the quotes) as the Default Value for this field.

   The `SaveOptions` field (with a value of `0`) prevents the normal Notes save document dialog from coming up when the form is closed. This makes the form act more like a dialog than a document; it is not saved unless users explicitly press the Save Search action button.

6 Create one more hidden field named `From`, type Authors, Computed when composed. Enter the following default value for this field:

Tip

The code in this section is all included in the `SearchDB.nsf` database on the *Inside LotusScript* CD. You can plug this database into any subdirectory where you want to search Notes databases. The only manual setup required is that you have to edit the Daily Searches and other scheduled agents to run on your server (i.e., open the agent, press the Schedule button and select your server under Run only on).

7 Select the Create|Action menu. Under Title enter `Save Search` and select a button icon.

8 Close the action properties window and enter the following formula:

```
@DialogBox("Save Search"; [AutoHorzFit]:[AutoVertFit]);
FIELD SaveOptions:="1";
@PostedCommand([FileSave])
```

The SaveOptions field needs to be set to `"1"`, or the document cannot be saved.

9 Double click on the *Edit Document action. Change the title to `_Edit Search`, and check the option Include action in button bar.

Then click on the hide/when tab and select the options Previewed for editing, Opened for editing, and Hide action if formula is true. Enter the following formula code:

```
@Name([CN];From)!=@Name([CN];@UserName)
```

10 Select the Create|Action menu. Under Title enter `Start Search` and select an appropriate button icon.

11 Close the action properties window and enter the formula code in listing 18.8.

12 Save and close the form.

Listing 18.8 Start search button formula

```
1  Logic:=@If(SearchLogic="Any";" | ";" & ");
2  Search_String:=SearchWord_1 + @If(SearchWord_2="";"";Logic + SearchWord_2)
   + @If(SearchWord_3="";"";Logic + SearchWord_3) +
   @If(SearchWord_4="";"";Logic + SearchWord_4) +
   @If(SearchWord_5="";"";Logic + SearchWord_5) +
   @If(SearchWord_6="";"";Logic + SearchWord_6);
3  @Environment("Text_To_Search";Search_String);
4  @If(Search_String="";@Prompt([OK];"Empty Search";"Type some words on the
   form before pressing the Start Search button.");@Do(
   @Command([ToolsRunMacro];"Search Subdirectory Part 1");
5  @Command([OpenView];"($All)");
   @Command([ToolsRunMacro];"Search Subdirectory Part 2")))
```

Listing Notes:

1 Puts the appropriate logical operator (i.e., & for and, | for or) into the `Logic` variable.

2 Constructs the string to search for, inserting the correct logical operator between each word.

3 Stores the search parameters into an environment variable. Later in this chapter, we'll modify the Search Subdirectory Part 1 agent to read this variable instead of getting its search string using the `Inputbox$` statement.

4 Checks to make sure the search string is not empty before starting the search. If it is empty, a warning message is displayed instead.

5 Switches to a view that contains the search results document. This is needed to prevent an error when the Part 2 agent tries to display the results document.

You must make a minor change to the Search Subdirectory Part 1 agent, so that it reads its search parameters from the environment variable created in the Search Subdirectory form:

1 Select Agents and double-click on the Search Subdirectory Part 1 agent.

2 Select the Initialize event.

3 Near the top of the agent, you'll find the following line of code:

```
text_to_find = Inputbox$("Enter the text you want to find:", "Find Documents")
```

4 Replace this line with the following code:

```
text_to_find = session.GetEnvironmentString("Text_To_Search", False)
```

5 Save and close the agent.

You can try running the search now by selecting the Create|Search SubDirectory menu. The user enters the search criteria in the form as shown in figure 18.4.

When the user presses the Start Search button, the search is executed, and the results are displayed on the Results form.

You still must to add a dialog box style form that is called when the user presses the Save Search button:

1 Select the Create|Design|Form menu.

Tip

You many want to add an action button to the All Documents view to begin a search. Use the following formula code to launch a search:

```
@Command([Compose];"Search Subdirectory")
```

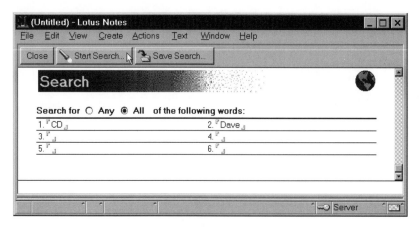

Figure 18.4 Subdirectory search form

2 Select the Create|Layout Region|New Layout Region menu.

3 Double-click on the layout region to open its properties, and select the 3D Style option. Close the properties window.

4 Use the Create|Field menu to add a field named SearchName, type Text, Editable.

5 Use Create|Field to add another field called RunInBackground. Set its type to Keywords, and in the Choices window enter the following text:

```
Run in background and send you Email reports | Run
```

The text to the left of the bar appears on the screen, the text to the right of it is what actually gets stored in the field. Click on the keyword options tab. Under Interface select Checkbox and under Frame select None. Select the option Refresh fields on keyword change.

6 Use Create|Field to add another field called HowOften. Set its type to Keywords, and in the Choices window enter the following text:

```
Once a day | Daily
First day of the week | Weekly
First day of the month | Monthly
```

Click on the hide/when tab. Select the option Hide paragraph if formula is true, and enter the following formula:

```
RunInBackground=""
```

This will cause the HowOften field to be hidden unless the option Run in background and send you email reports is selected.

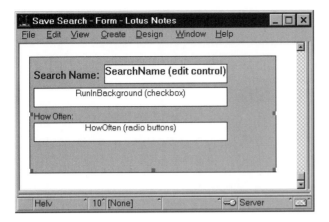

Figure 18.5   Save search form in design mode

7 Enter a text prompt for the `SearchName` and `HowOften` fields, so that the form looks like figure 18.5.

8 Save and close the form.

When the user clicks on the Save Search button, the form will be displayed as a modal dialog box as shown in figure 18.6.

You should modify the All Documents view so that it shows the names of saved searches:

1 Select Design|Views and double-click on the (`$All`) view.

2 Click on the # column, and in the programming pane select Formula and enter the following code:

```
@If(Form="Results";"Search Results";SearchName)
```

This will display the text `Search Results` for results documents; otherwise, it will display the saved search name.

3 Select Design|Column properties and enter `Search Name` as the column title.

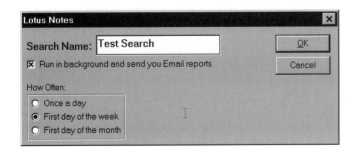

Figure 18.6   Running the save search form

4 Select the Create|Append New Column menu, and in the programming pane select formula. Enter the following code:

```
@Name([CN];From)
```

5 Save and close the view.

It's probably also a good idea to add a Your Searches view that shows only the searches authored by the current user.

1 Select the Create|View menu.

2 Name the view `Your Searches`. Select the options Shared and Personal on first use.

3 Press OK to save the new view.

4 Select Design|Views and double-click on the Your Searches view.

5 In the programming pane select formula, and enter the following selection formula:

```
SELECT (@Contains(From;@UserName))
```

6 Select the Design|View Properties menu and click on the propeller beanie tab. Under Discard Index select the option After each use.

7 Save and close the view.

If you try logging on as a different user and saving some searches, you will see that the Your Searches view shows only the searches you authored.

Last but not least, you need to add a scheduled agent that runs the searches on the server and sends the search results to the search's author via Notes email. This agent, which runs in the background on the server, is a bit different from the foreground agent Search Subdirectory Part 1. For a server agent, the server's hard drive appears as a local directory, which means we can do away with the extra function for extracting subdirectory filenames from the NotesDbDirectory class and use the simpler LotusScript `Dir$` function instead:

1 Select the Create|Agent menu item.

2 Under Name enter `Daily Searches`.

3 Select the Shared Agent option.

4 Under the question When should this agent run? select the option On Schedule Daily. Click on the Schedule button, and under Run only on, select the name of your Notes server.

Note: You may need to set permission to run scheduled agents on the server. In your Public Name and Address Book open the server document, and under Agent Restrictions make sure you have permission to run agents on the server.

5 Under the question Which document(s) should it act on? select the option All documents in database.

6 Under the question What should this agent do? select the Script option.

7 Select the Initialize event, and then enter the LotusScript code in listing 18.9.

Note: for detailed listing notes see listing 18.7. In listing 18.9, I provide only the listing notes for elements that are different from listing 18.7, since most of the code is the same.

Listing 18.9   Search databases scheduled agent

```
On Error Goto Error_Handler
Dim session As New NotesSession
Dim doc As NotesDocument, searchdoc As NotesDocument
Dim db As NotesDatabase
Dim collection As NotesDocumentCollection
Dim server_collection As NotesDocumentCollection
Dim newdoc As NotesDocument
Dim rtitem As NotesRichTextItem
Dim text_to_find As String, Logic As String
Dim Searchpath As String, Filename As String, DB_Name As String
Dim j As Integer, s As Integer, total_matches As Integer
Set db = session.CurrentDatabase
Set server_collection = db.Search( "RunInBackground="+Chr$(34)+"Run" +
Chr$(34) + "& HowOften="+Chr$(34)+"Daily" + Chr$(34), Nothing, 0)
For s = 1 To server_collection.Count
   Set searchdoc = server_collection.GetNthDocument( s )
   If searchdoc.SearchLogic(0) = "All" Then
      Logic = " & "
   Else
      Logic = " | "
   End If
   text_to_find = searchdoc.SearchWord_1(0)
   If searchdoc.SearchWord_2(0) <> "" Then text_to_find = text_to_find +
Logic + searchdoc.SearchWord_2(0)
   If searchdoc.SearchWord_3(0) <> "" Then text_to_find = text_to_find +
Logic + searchdoc.SearchWord_3(0)
   If searchdoc.SearchWord_4(0) <> "" Then text_to_find = text_to_find +
Logic + searchdoc.SearchWord_4(0)
   If searchdoc.SearchWord_5(0) <> "" Then text_to_find = text_to_find +
Logic + searchdoc.SearchWord_5(0)
   If searchdoc.SearchWord_6(0) <> "" Then text_to_find = text_to_find +
Logic + searchdoc.SearchWord_6(0)
```

The listing line markers are: 1 (Set server_collection), 2 (For s = 1), 3 (If searchdoc.SearchLogic), 4 (text_to_find = searchdoc.SearchWord_1(0))

Listing 18.9 Search databases scheduled agent (continued)

```
5    Searchpath = Left$(db.FilePath, Instr(1, db.FilePath, db.Filename, 1)-
     1) + "*.nsf"
6    Filename = Dir$(Searchpath)

7    Set newdoc = New NotesDocument(db)
     Set rtitem = New NotesRichTextItem (newdoc, "Body")
     newdoc.Form = "Memo"
     newdoc.Subject = "Searched for " + text_to_find + " in " +
     Left$(db.FilePath, Instr(1, db.FilePath, db.Filename, 1)-1)

     total_matches = 0
     Do While Filename <> ""
        If Strcompare(Filename, db.Filename, 1) <> 0 Then
           DB_Name = Left$(db.FilePath, Instr(1, db.FilePath, db.Filename,
     1)-1) + Filename
           Redim db_to_search(1) As NotesDatabse
           Set db_to_search(0) = New NotesDatabase(db.Server, DB_Name)
           If Not(db_to_search(0).IsOpen) Then
              Call db_to_search(0).Open("","")
           End If
           On Error Resume Next
           Set collection = db_to_search(0).ftsearch(text_to_find, 0)
           On Error Goto Error_Handler
           If collection.Count > 0 Then
              Call rtitem.AppendText(db_to_search(0).Title + ":  found " +
     Format$(collection.Count) + " matches in " +  db_to_search(0).Filepath)
              Call rtitem.AddNewLine(1)
              For j = 1 To collection.Count
                 Set doc = collection.GetNthDocument( j )
                 Call rtitem.AppendDocLink (doc, "")
                 If doc.HasItem("Subject") Then
                    Call rtitem.AppendText("  " + doc.Subject(0))
                 End If
     Next_Match:
                 total_matches = total_matches + 1
                 Call rtitem.AddNewLine(1)
              Next
              Call rtitem.AddNewLine(1)
           End If
        End If
8       Filename = Dir$()
     Loop

     If total_matches = 0 Then
        Call rtitem.AppendText("No matches for '" + text_to_find + "'
     found.")
     Else
```

Listing 18.9 Search databases scheduled agent (continued)

```
         Call rtitem.AppendText(Format$(total_matches) + " matches for '" +
    text_to_find + "' found.")
       End If
9      newdoc.SendTo = searchdoc.From
10     Call newdoc.Send (False)
     Next
     Exit Sub
     Error_Handler:
     If Err = 4175 Then
       If doc.HasItem("Subject") Then
         Call rtitem.AppendText("Subject: " + Trim$(doc.Subject(0)))
       End If
       Call rtitem.AppendText(" (warning: " + db_to_search(0).Filename + " has
    no 'default view', doclink unavailable)")
       Resume Next_Match
     End If
11   Call rtitem.AppendText( "Error (" + Format$(Err) + ") on line number " +
     Format$(Erl()) + ": " + Error$)
     newdoc.SendTo = searchdoc.From
     Call newdoc.Send (False)
     Exit Sub
```

Listing Notes:

1 Retrieves all saved searches where `RunInBackground` is set to `Run` and `HowOften` is set to `Daily`.

2 Goes through each saved search that is applicable for this agent.

3 Constructs the logical operator character depending on the value of the `SearchLogic` field.

4 Gets the text value for which to search. The subsequent lines add the other words (with the appropriate logical operator) if they are not empty.

5 Because this agent is run on the server, `db.FilePath` is set to `TESTDIR\SearchDB.nsf`, so we construct the search path by removing the filename and appending `*.nsf`. The result is `TESTDIR\*.nsf`.

6 The searchpath is passed to the `Dir$` function to retrieve the first NSF filename in the current subdirectory.

7 Creates the report document that will be emailed to the search author.

8 Calling `Dir$()` with no parameters returns the next NSF filename in the current subdirectory.

9 Addresses the email report to the author of the saved search document.

10 Sends the email report.

11 If an error occurs, the error message is sent as part of the emailed search results (we can't pop up a Messagebox since this agent is run on the background on the server).

Make two copies of the Daily Searches agent (i.e., by clicking on it and selecting the Edit|Copy and Edit|Paste menus). Name one of the copies `Weekly Searches`, the other one `Monthly Searches`. You only have to change one line of code in each agent. Near the top of the agent, you'll find the following line of code, which gets a document collection from the search database:

```
Set server_collection = db.Search( "RunInBackground="+Chr$(34)+"Run" +
Chr$(34) + "& HowOften="+Chr$(34)+"Daily" + Chr$(34), Nothing, 0)
```

In the weekly, agent change the word `Daily` to `Weekly`, and in the monthly agent change it to `Monthly`.

Under the question When should this agent run? select the options On Schedule Weekly for the weekly agent, and On Schedule Monthly for the monthly one.

Tip

You may want to initiate the search from a button within another database. (For example, you might want a Search Entire Application button on every database in your application.) Assuming you named the search database `SearchDB.NSF`, attach the following code to any button in a database in the same subdirectory as `SearchDB.NSF`. This code uses the current subdirectory and the current server to find the `SearchDB.NSF` database:

```
SubDir:=@LeftBack(@Subset(@DbName;-1);"\\");
DB_Name:=@If(SubDir="";"";SubDir+"\\") + "SearchDB.NSF";
@Command([Compose];@Subset(@DbName;1):DB_Name;"Search SubDirectory")
```

18.6 Summary

In this chapter you've learned some techniques for debugging server-based agents. I presented an agent that collates and emails a report. You've also implemented two powerful search agents—one that searches a database and presents the resulting document collection to the user, and another that searches all databases within a subdirectory.

Last, you've added a graphical user interface to the search database, and created an agent to run saved searches in the background.

C H A P T E R   1 9

Tips and tricks

This chapter contains some useful tips and techniques I've come up with while developing Notes applications. You will learn how to:

- Display any document using the formula open document command.

- Create response documents in the close event (i.e., if you want to automatically generate responses when certain documents are created).

- Implement data input validity checking in LotusScript.

- Access the Notes formula language via Dynamic Data Exchange (DDE)—a VB example is presented here.

- Store user-specific options in your databases.

- Create dynamic radio buttons and check boxes. (By *dynamic* I mean that the list of entries can be edited by the use.)

- Access Notes data via SQL.

- Manipulate rich text fonts and colors from LotusScript.

19.1 Formula display a document by universal ID

In chapter 13, you learned how to display a document in the current database by Universal ID, as shown in listing 19.1.

Listing 19.1   Display a document in the current database

```
1  @Command([OpenDocument]; "0"; Universal_ID)
```

Listing Notes:

1 Universal_ID must hold a unique document ID.

There are situations where you want to open a document in another database. For example, you can simulate a simple one to one database relation by storing the universal ID of a document in a text field on a form. Listing 19.2 shows how to display a Notes document, given a database name and a universal ID. This formula assumes that the current document has a RelatedDocument field that contains a Universal ID for a document in the Sales.NSF database. (For complete implementation details, including a button to set this field, see the section "One to many relations across databases" in chapter 16.

Listing 19.2   Display a document in another database

```
1  FIELD RelatedDocument:= RelatedDocument;
   SubDir:=@LeftBack(@Subset(@DbName;-1);"\\");
2  DB_Name:=@If(SubDir="";"";SubDir+"\\") + "Sales.NSF ";
3  @Command([FileOpenDatabase];@Subset(@DbName;1):DB_Name; "($ALL)");
4  @Command([OpenDocument]; "0"; RelatedDocument);
5  @Command([OpenView]);
6  @Command([FileCloseWindow])
```

Listing Notes:

1 Declares the `RelatedDocument` field as a variable, so that it can be accessed throughout the remainder of this agent.

2 Always use the safe method of referencing the database in the current directory. (See chapter 3 for a full explanation.)

3 Opens the Sales.NSF database to the All Documents view.

4 Opens the document specified in the `RelatedDocument` field.

5 Switches back to the `Sales.NSF` database view window.

6 Closes the view window. This leaves the related Sales document open on the screen, without the unwanted clutter of the Sales view screen. A single click on Close will return the user to the starting point.

19.2 Creating response documents in the close event

There are sometimes situations where you want to automatically generate certain response documents. For example, in a customer support application, you might want to generate a response document that allows your customer support staff to append comments to a previous conversation with a customer. You can easily accomplish this using the back end NotesDocument classes, in combination with the MakeResponse class as shown in listing 19.3. This code should be placed in a parent form's Queryclose event, so that it executes after the parent document has been saved. It assumes a response form named `Response` exists in the current database, and that this form has a text field named `Subject` on it.

Listing 19.3   Creating response documents

```
    Dim doc As NotesDocument
    Dim responsedoc As NotesDocument
    Dim db As NotesDatabase
    Dim session As New NotesSession
    Dim workspace As New NotesUIWorkspace
    Dim DB_Name As String
1   Set doc = source.Document
    Set db = session.CurrentDatabase
2   Set responsedoc = New NotesDocument (db)

    responsedoc.Form = "Response"

3   Call responsedoc.MakeResponse( doc )

4   responsedoc.Subject = "Subject for new response document."
5   Call responsedoc.Save(True,False)
6   Call workspace.ViewRefresh
```

Listing Notes:

1 Gets the current (parent) document. Optionally, you can search for the appropriate parent document (as shown in chapter 13) after prompting the user for some identifying information (i.e., its document number).

2 Creates a document.

3 Makes the new document a response document to the current parent document.

4 At this point, you can assign new values to fields on the response document.

5 Saves the response document.

6 Refreshes the current view, so that the new response document appears in the view.

Tip

If you want to automatically display the new response document after creating it, see listings 13.5 and 13.6.

19.3 Input validation in LotusScript

As you are probably aware, fields on your Notes forms have an Input Validation formula. You can use it to force a field to have a particular value or format. For example, if you want to require a value in a Subject field, you would use the following formula:

```
@If(Subject=""; @Failure("You must enter a value in this field.");@Sucess))
```

There can be advantages to writing this kind of code in LotusScript. For one, you can put the code anywhere you want, not just on the form save, as with input validation formulas. For example, by putting LotusScript validation code on a field's Exiting event, you can run the validation as soon as the user tries to exit the field, which can sometimes be more friendly than waiting until the save (i.e., especially on large forms with many fields). LotusScript also gives you complete control over the cursor focus; some validation errors cause the cursor to move to the offending field, while others (such as invalid date/time values) do not.

The most basic validation checking is specifying that a field requires a value, as shown in the formula example above. The following LotusScript code put into the Querysave event accomplishes the same thing:

```
If Source.FieldGetText("Subject") = "" Then
    Messagebox "You must enter a value in this
field."
    Call Source.Gotofield("Subject")
    Continue = False
    Exit Sub
End If
```

Tip

Entering valid date and time values is something that is difficult for many users. If you are using Notes 4.5 it's a good idea to use the new date/time popup editors. (See the section "Date and time popup fields" in chapter 14.) If you don't have Notes 4.5 it's a very good idea to initialize the field to a valid date/time (i.e., use @Now as the default value formula) so that the user at least has an example of a valid entry from which to work. If you absolutely must leave a date/time field blank, then put a sample date/time value in a Computed for Display field near the editable field as an example.

An equally common requirement is checking for the validity of date/time fields. The following code checks for valid date/times in a field called DateTime:

```
If Not Isdate(Source.FieldGetText("DateTime")) Then
    Messagebox Source.FieldGetText("DateTime")+ " is not a valid date, please
reedit it."
    Call Source.Gotofield("DateTime")
    Continue = False
    Exit Sub
End If
```

19.4 Adding carriage returns to fields

It seems to be a common Notes programming requirement to manipulate text fields programmatically, including adding carriage returns (i.e., the Enter key) to the data. This is reasonably easy to do in both formulas and LotusScript. In this section I'll demonstrate the techniques by implementing a button that allows you to append text with a carriage return to fields.

First, open or create a test Discussion database.

1 Select Design|Forms.

2 Double click on the Main Topic form to load it in edit mode.

3 Select the Create|Field menu, and name the field `TextComments`.

4 Select the Create|Hotspot|Button menu. Enter `Add Comment` ... as the button label.

5 In the formula pane enter the code from listing 19.4.

6 Save and close the form.

Listing 19.4   Formula code to add text and a carriage return

```
1  Text_Comment := @Prompt([OKCANCELEDIT]; "Add Comment";"Enter com-
   ment:";"");
2  @SetField("TextComments";TextComments + @Name([CN];@UserName) + " at " +
   @Text(@Now) + ": " + Text_Comment + @NewLine)
```

Listing Notes:

1 Prompts the user for the text to add.

2 Adds the user's name, the current date and time, the comments the user entered, and the carriage return character to the text field. The `@NewLine` function is used to represent a carriage return character in formulas.

You can accomplish the same functionality in LotusScript:

1 Select Design|Forms.

2 Double click on the Main Topic form to load it in edit mode.

3 Select the Create|Field menu, and name the field `TextCommentsLotusScript`.

4 Select the Create|Hotspot|Button menu. Enter `Add Comment` ... as the button label.

5 In the formula pane select Script, and then enter the code from listing 19.5.

6 Save and close the form.

Listing 19.5   LotusScript code to add text and a carriage return

```
Dim workspace As New NotesUIWorkspace
Dim session As New NotesSession
Dim uidoc As NotesUIDocument
Dim doc As Notesdocument
```

Listing 19.5   LotusScript code to add text and a carriage return (continued)

```
   Dim Text_Comment As String
1  Text_Comment = Inputbox$("Add Comment","Enter comment:")
   If Text_Comment ="" Then
      Exit Sub
   End If

2  Set uidoc = workspace.CurrentDocument
3  Call uidoc.FieldAppendText("TextCommentsLotusScript", session.CommonUser-
   Name + " at " + Now + ": " + Text_Comment + Chr(10))
```

Listing Notes:

1 Prompts the user for the text to add.

2 Gets a NotesUIDocument reference to the current document.

3 Appends the username, date, user entered text, and carriage return character. In LotusScript, `Chr(10)` represents the carriage return character.

Tip

In this section I've used ordinary text fields, but these techniques also work well on rich text fields.

19.5 Accessing Notes via DDE (Visual Basic example)

There is a little known but useful mechanism by which you can easily and conveniently control Lotus Notes from external programs, using DDE. DDE is not appropriate for large, complex communications, but it is simple and easy to use for certain tasks. For example, the code in listing 19.4 shows how to ask Notes to display a document requested by a program.

1 In Visual Basic, create a new project and open the default form.

2 Create a TextBox item on the form and name it `Text1`.

Set the LinkTimeout property to 30000 so that the DDE doesn't get a timeout error if it takes Notes a few seconds to open a database and document.

3 Create a CommandButton item on the form, and set its Caption property to Display Notes Document.

4 Double-click the button, and enter the code in listing 19.6.

Listing 19.6 Visual Basic code to run Notes formulas

```
     Text1.LinkMode = 0
1    Text1.LinkTopic = "Notes|Action"
2    Text1.LinkMode = 2
3    Temp$ = "9CE1DDC5FC70F9BC5222630D001FB596" ' A Universal ID
4    Text1.LinkExecute "@Command([FileOpenDatabase];" + Chr$(34) + Chr$(34) +
     ":" + Chr$(34) + "Sales.NSF" + Chr$(34) + ")"
5    Text1.LinkExecute "@Command([OpenDocument]; " + Chr$(34) + "0" + Chr$(34) +
     "; " + Chr$(34)  Temp$ + Chr$(34) + ");"
6    Text1.LinkExecute "@Command([OpenView])"
7    Text1.LinkExecute "@Command([FileCloseWindow])"
8    End
```

Listing Notes:

1 Sets the DDE conversation Application to `Notes` and the Topic to `Action`.

2 Establishes the DDE link with Notes. Notes must be running.

3 Sets `Temp$` to a known `Universal ID`.

4 Sends the first DDE execute command to Notes, which sends a one-line formula command to Notes, in this case, the open database command.

5 Sends the open document command to Notes using the `Universal ID` in `Temp$`.

Note: `Chr$(34)` is the double-quote character. The two `LinkExecute` commands in listing lines 4–5 evaluate to:

```
@Command([FileOpenDatabase];"":"Sales.NSF" )
@Command([OpenDocument]; "0"; "9CE1DDC5FC70F9BC5222630D001FB596");
```

6 Opens the Notes database view window.

7 Closes the view window, leaving the Notes document displayed.

8 Terminates the DDE connection.

You can use this technique from any Windows application or tool that supports programmed DDE.

19.6 Storing user specific options

A common requirement in any software program is the need to store user-specified options and preferences about how the application should run. You might want to store a list of predefined categories, for example, or a screen that allows users to turn certain application features on or off. Storing such a set of options and using them in Notes applications and forms is a three-step process:

1 Create a form to store application options and preferences.

2 Create a view that displays the preferences.

3 Create the LotusScript code or @DbLookup commands in the forms where you want to reference the preference settings.

For an example, we'll implement a feature, often requested for discussion databases, that allows users to store a personalized tagline that is copied into the Body field of new messages. Each user can specify his or her own tagline, and we'll add a default formula that pulls the current user's tagline from a preferences screen. (*Note:* In the next section, I'll show you how to create options that apply to the whole database, regardless of user.)

First, open or create a discussion database.

Tip for Notes 4.5 Users

If you have Notes 4.5, you should use the new profile document feature to more easily implement storing user options. For details on how to implement this tagline function using profile documents see the section "Using profile documents" in chapter 14.

1 Select Design|Forms and single click on the Main Topic form.

2 Select the Edit|Copy menu followed by the Edit|Paste menu.

3 Double-click on the Copy of Main Topic form to open it in design mode.

4 Select the Design|Form Properties menu and rename the form User Preferences. Close the properties window.

5 Delete the Categories field (and prompt) and delete the Body field. Click your mouse at the bottom of the form and select the Create|Field menu.

6 Name the field Tagline. Click on the Options tab and select the option Give this field default focus. Close the field properties window.

7 Click to the left of the Tagline field and type Enter Tagline: as a prompt for the field.

8 Click on the subject field, and enter the following formula in its default value event:

```
"Preferences for " + @Name([CN];From)
```

9 Save and close the User Preferences form.

Now you must create a view to display the preferences data:

1 Select the Create|View menu.

2 Name the view `User Preferences`

3 Select the Shared option check box.

4 Under selection conditions, select the Add Condition button.

5 Under Condition, select By Form Used, then click on the User Preferences form.

6 Select OK, and then select OK again on the Create View screen to create the new view.

7 Select Design|Views and double click on the User Preferences view.

8 Click on the By column and select Edit|Cut. Then click on the Date column and select Edit|Paste (i.e., so that the By column is the first column in the view).

9 Select Design|Column properties. (You should still be on the By column.) Click on the Sorting tab and deselect the option Secondary sort column. Close the properties window.

10 Select the Create|Append New Column menu.

11 In the programming pane click on Field, then select the Tagline field.

12 Select the Design|Column Properties menu and enter `Tagline` as the column Title. Close the properties window.

13 Click on the Subject column and delete it (i.e., select the Edit|Clear menu or press the Delete key).

14 Click on the Design|View Properties menu.

15 Select the propeller beanie tab, and under Discard Index, select the option after each use. This will ensure that the latest changes are always reflected in the view.

16 Save and close the view.

Last, you have to add the default value to the Body field in the Main Topic form.

1 Select Design|Forms and double click on the Main Topic form:

2 Click on the Body field, and enter the following formula as its default value:

```
temp:= @DbLookup("":"NoCache";"":"";"User Preferences";@Name([CN];From);3);
@If(@IsError(temp);"";temp)
```

This formula does a lookup in the `User Preferences` view using the current users name, (`@Name([CN];From)`), as the key. The number 3 is the column number of the Tagline field in the `User Preferences` view. Passing the result of the `@DbLookup` through the `@IsError` function prevents an error message from being displayed when no `User Preferences` document exists for the current user.

3 Save and close the Main Topic form.

Another important parameter used here is the `NoCache` option in the `@DbLookup` statements. This ensures that the most current data is always read from the `User Preferences` view.

Try out the new feature by selecting the Create|User Preferences menu, and enter a Tagline. Now when you create a new Main Topic document your Tagline is copied into the Body field as a default value. If you try logging on as a different user, you'll see each user can maintain his or her own Tagline.

Tip

You may want to copy the default value formula from step two to the Response form's Body field as well, so that Responses also include the Tagline.

Tip

You may want to edit the selection criteria for the All Documents view so that the User Preferences documents do not show up in this view:

1 Select Design|Views and double click on the `*($All)` view.
2 In the programming pane for the View Selection event, select the Formula option and enter the following formula:

```
SELECT (Form != "User Preferences")
```

3 Save and close the view.

19.7 Dynamic check boxes and radio buttons

Many users ask for Notes applications that have dynamic check boxes or radio buttons. By *dynamic* I mean that the user has the ability to modify the list of items in the check boxes. As an example, we'll add a user-editable check box list to a Discussion database to allow users to select a message priority. The check box list will apply to all users of the database. If you wanted each user to have his or her own list, you would organize this function as in the previous section. More commonly, however, users want a single "global" list of check box items for a database or an application, because the purpose of such lists is to ensure consistent user input.

First, open or create a discussion database. (You can use any Discussion database, including the one you created in the previous section.)

1 Select Design|Forms and single click on the Main Topic form.
2 Select the Edit|Copy menu followed by the Edit|Paste menu.

3 Double-click on the Copy of Main Topic form to open it in design mode.

4 Select the Design|Form Properties menu and rename the form `Database Prefer-ences`. Close the properties window.

5 Delete the Categories field (and prompt) and delete the Body field. Click your mouse at the bottom of the form and select the Create|Field menu.

6 Name the field `MessagePriorities`. Select the Allow multivalues option.

7 Click on the Options tab and select the option Give this field default focus. Close the field properties window.

8 Click to the left of the MessagePriorities field and type `Enter Message Priori-ties:` as a prompt for the field.

9 Save and close the Database Preferences form.

Now you need to create a view to display the preferences data. (This is also how an Editor accesses the database preferences for updates, through this view.)

1 Select the Create|View menu.

2 Name the view `User Preferences`

3 Select the Shared option check box.

4 Under selection conditions select the Add Condition button.

5 Under Condition select By Form Used, then click on the Database Preferences form.

6 Select OK, and then select OK again on the Create View screen to create the new view.

7 Select Design|Views and double-click on the Database Preferences view.

8 Delete the Topic and By columns.

9 Select the Create|Append New Column menu.

10 In the programming pane click on the Field option, then select the MessagePriori-ties field.

11 Select the Design|Column Properties menu and enter `Priorities` as the column Title. Close the properties window.

12 Click on the Design|View Properties menu.

13 Select the propeller beanie tab and under Discard Index select the option After each use. This will ensure that the latest changes are always reflected in the view.

14 Save and close the view.

Select the Create|Database Preferences menu, and enter `Low;Medium;High` into the MessagePriorities field, and save the new document. Now that you have created a Database Preferences document, you must go back into the form and remove it from the Create menu. This is because you only want one Database Preference document in the database; you don't want the user creating multiple ones. Because you are the author of the one Database Preferences document, only a user with Editor access to the database can edit these preferences (i.e., which is usually what users want as a security protection, so that Authors cannot change the database preferences).

1 Select Design|Forms and double-click on the Database Preferences form.

2 Select the Design|Form Properties menu.

3 Deselect the option Include in menu.

4 Close the properties window, and save and close the form.

Last, you have to add the priority check box field to the Main Topic form.

1 Select Design|Forms and double click on the Main Topic form.

2 Click to the right of the timeComposed field (it's above the Categories field), and press Enter to create a new blank line on the form.

3 Type the text `Priority:` as a prompt.

4 Select the Create|Field menu.

5 Enter `Priority` as the field Name.

6 Under Type select Keywords, and under Choices select the option Use formula for choices. In the formula window enter:

```
@DbColumn("":"NoCache";"":"";"Database Preferences";2)
```

This formula pulls in the values from the MessagePriorities column in the Database Preferences view. Because we specified the field as multivalued, each value in it becomes a separate item in the keyword field here.

7 Click on the keywords options tab (i.e., to the right of the Basics tab).

8 Under Interface select Radio Button, under Frame select None, and under Columns select 4. Close the field properties window.

9 Enter the following formula as the default value for the field:

```
"Medium"
```

10 Save and close the Main Topic form.

Tip

You may want to edit the selection criteria for the All Documents view so that the User Preferences documents do not show up in this view:

1   Select Design|Views and double click on the * ($All) view.

2   In the programming pane for the View Selection event, select the Formula option and enter the following formula:

```
SELECT (Form != "Database Preferences")
```

Note: If you have both User Preferences and Database Preferences documents in the same database, you can hide them both with the following view selection formula:

```
SELECT (Form != "User Preferences") & (Form != "Database Preferences")
```

3   Save and close the view.

Your users can now add check box items to the Main Topic form without programming, simply by editing the Database Preferences form. For example, they could add an Urgent category as shown in figure 19.1.

19.8 Notes SQL 2.0 (accessing Notes through ODBC)

In an example earlier in this chapter, I showed how you can use DDE to ask Notes to display a Notes document from VB. How do you get access to Notes Universal IDs in Visual Basic? The easiest way is to use NotesSQL 2.0, which is basically the 32-bit Notes ODBC driver. It's available on the Lotus Web site at `http://www.lotus.com/` (press Search, and search for NotesSQL). Once you've installed it, you can access Notes databases through the Visual Basic Jet database engine using ODBC. Views in Notes

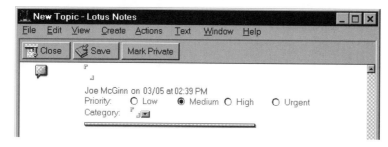

Figure 19.1   Main topic form with "urgent" category

become SQL tables to Visual Basic (or any other program that can access ODBC data sources). You define the column names in Notes, in the propeller hat tab in the column properties in a view.

You must create a view in Notes that shows the Universal ID, so that you can see it in Visual Basic. The only limitation in NotesSQL is that calculated columns are not supported; only columns that are actually stored on documents can be used. (This requirement is quite reasonable, by the way, because many SQL applications assume that the database engine can deliver a table of rows and columns very quickly, so application performance could suffer badly if NotesSQL supported calculated columns.) As a result, you cannot base the Universal ID column in your view on a formula (i.e., `@Text(@DocumentUniqueID)`). The Universal ID must be stored on the documents themselves:

1 First, on the form you want to show in the ODBC view, create a hidden text field named `Universal_ID`, type Text, Computed.

2 In the Value event for this field put the following formula:

```
@Text(@DocumentUniqueID)
```

3 Save and close the form.

4 Create or edit a view, and make a column based on the `Universal_ID` field.

5 Go into the column properties for each column in the view, and make sure the Name item on the propeller hat tab is set to something meaningful. These will be the column headers displayed in the ODBC table.

You can now access the view, including the critical Universal ID column, as an SQL table through the ODBC driver. When you are asked to supply an SQL statement by the ODBC application that you are using to access the Notes databases, use:

```
Select * From MyView
```

You can also use SQL query statements to retrieve just certain documents (or *records*, as they are referred to by relational SQL databases).

19.9 Creating Document links in a new document

There are often times when you want to create a document link while you are composing a document. For example, it's common to have a button in one database that composes a document in a different database. This kind of function is helpful to users who normally use only one database, but who occasionally have to post a message in another one. For example, you might have a button in a discussion database for marketing issues that allows a user to post an important message to a development database. Users usually want a document link from the new document back to the source document.

This isn't easy to implement, because the LotusScript classes for adding document links work only on back end documents, which means you can't use them on a new document that hasn't been saved yet. But it is possible to do so by combining a formula agent with a LotusScript agent. The formula agent uses the MakeDocLink command to put a Notes document link into the Windows copy buffer. The second agent uses the LotusScript NotesUIDocument classes to paste the doclink into a rich text field on the new document.

First, create two test discussion databases, one for marketing and one for development. Be sure to name the development one DevDisc.nsf. Then create the first agent.

1 Open the marketing discussion database, and select the Create|Agent menu.

2 Under name enter Copy To Development Part 1.

3 Under the question When should this agent run? select the option Manually From Agents List.

4 Under the question Which document(s) should it act on? select the option Run Once (@Commands may be used).

5 Under Run select Formula.

6 Enter the following formula code:

```
@Command([EditMakeDocLink])
```

This command creates a Notes document link to the current document, and places it in the operating system copy buffer.

7 Save and close the agent.

Now you'll create the LotusScript agent to compose a new document:

1 Select the Create|Agent menu.

2 Under name enter Copy To Development Part 2.

3 Under the question When should this agent run? select the option Manually From Agents List.

4 Under the question Which document(s) should it act on? select the option Run Once (@Commands may be used).

5 Under Run select Script, and under Event select Initialize.

6 Enter the code in listing 19.7, then save and close the new agent.

Listing 19.7   Copy to development database

```
Dim session As New NotesSession
Dim workspace As New NotesUIWorkspace
Dim uidocsource As NotesUIDocument
Dim uidoc As NotesUIDocument
Dim db As NotesDatabase
Dim doc As Notesdocument
Dim DB_Name As String
```

```
1   Set uidocsource = workspace.CurrentDocument
    Set doc = uidocsource.Document

    Set db = session.CurrentDatabase
2   DB_Name = Left$(db.FilePath, Instr(1, db.FilePath, db.Filename, 1)-1) +
    "DevDisc.NSF"

3   Set uidoc = workspace.ComposeDocument(db.Server, DB_Name, "Main Topic")

4   Call uidoc.Gotofield("Body")
5   Call uidoc.InsertText(doc.GetItemValue( "Body"))
6   Call uidoc.InsertText(Chr(10) + Chr(10) + "Source document: ")
7   Call uidoc.Paste

8   Call uidoc.FieldSetText("Subject", doc.Subject(0))

9   Call uidoc.Gotofield("Subject")
```

Listing Notes:

1 Gets the current document (i.e., the one in the marketing database) into a NotesU-IDocument variable. The following line converts it into a NotesDocument:

2 Constructs a filename variable to a database called DevDisc.NSF in the current subdirectory.

3 Composes the document in the development discussion database.

4 Moves the cursor to the Body field on the new document.

5 Inserts a copy of the text from the Body field on the original document in the marketing database.

6 Inserts two new lines and prompt text for the document link into the Body field of the new document.

7 Inserts the contents of the copy buffer into the `Body` field. The copy buffer contains the document link created in Part 1 of the agent—this is the only way to insert a Notes document link into a NotesUIDocument.

8 Inserts the contents of the marketing documents `Subject` field into the `Subject` field on the new document.

9 Moves the cursor to the `Subject` field (i.e., where the user expects it to be when the new form comes up).

Last, you need to create an action button on the Main Topic form to compose a new development document:

1 Select Design|Forms in the marketing database.

2 Double click on the Main Topic form.

3 Select the Create|Action menu.

4 Name the action `Copy to Development` ... .

5 Click on the hide-when tab and select the checkboxes Previewed for editing and Opened for editing. This will prevent the user from trying to use the action button on a document that has not yet been saved.

6 Close the action properties window and in the programming pane select Simple Actions.

7 Click on Add action.

8 Under action select Run Agent, and under agent select Copy To Development Part 1. Press Ok.

9 Click on Add action a second time.

10 Under action select Run Agent, and under agent select Copy To Development Part 2. Press Ok.

11 Save the Main Topic form.

Open a document in the marketing database and click on the Copy to Development ... action button. A new development discussion database document will be composed. It will contain the original Body and Subject text, as well as a document link back to the original marketing document, as shown in figure 19.2.

19.10 *Manipulating rich text fonts and colors*

A common complaint about LotusScript programming is that there are no methods for manipulating advanced properties of rich text fields, such as the colors and fonts of text. This makes it difficult to create attractive and richly formatted reports. Fortunately, there is a workaround for this limitation.

The solution is a two-step process. First, you copy the text to a rich text field that contains the text formatting properties (i.e., size, color, font) you want to apply to the text. The second step is to append the contents of that field to the destination rich text field. The result is that you can create mixed types of text in a single rich text field report.

First, you need to create a form that will contain several rich text fields, one for every format you want to use. Open or create a test Discussion database:

1 Select the Create|Design|Form menu.

2 Select the Design|Form Properties menu, and name the form `RichTextFormats`.

3 Select the Create|Field menu.

4 Name the field Red, type Rich Text.

5 Click on the text properties tab and under Text Color select the color red.

6 Close the field properties window.

7 Select the Red field and select the Edit|Copy menu.

8 Select the Edit|Paste menu twice.

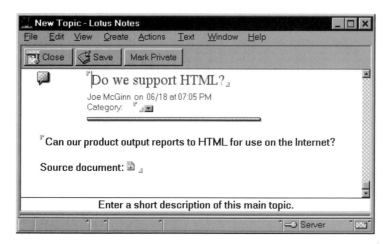

Figure 19.2   New document with a doclink

9 Go into the first copy and set the field name to Green, then set the text color to green. If you want, you can also set other text attributes such as size (e.g., I've made the green text very large so that it stands out).

10 Go into the second field copy and set the field name to BoldItalic. Select the Bold and Italic text properties for this field.

11 Save and close the RichTextFormats form.

Select the Create|RichTextFormats menu, and save and close the document (do not add any text to its fields). Now you can create an agent that will produce the formatted report:

1 Select the Create|Agent menu.

2 Under name enter Create Formatted Report.

3 Under the question When should this agent run? select the option Manually From Actions Menu.

4 Under the question Which document(s) should it act on? select the option Run Once (@Commands may be used).

5 Under Run select Script, and under Event select Initialize.

6 Enter the code in listing 19.8, then save and close the new agent.

Listing 19.8 Create formatted report

```
    Dim session As New NotesSession
    Dim workspace As New NotesUIWorkspace
    Dim collection As NotesDocumentCollection
1   Redim colordoc(1) As NotesDocument
    Dim newdoc As NotesDocument
    Dim db As NotesDatabase

    Set db = session.CurrentDatabase

2   Set collection = db.Search( "Form="+Chr$(34)+"RichTextFormats" + Chr$(34),
    Nothing, 0)
    Set colordoc(0) = collection.GetFirstDocument

    Dim reditem As Variant
3   Set reditem = colordoc(0).GetFirstItem("Red")
    Dim greenitem As Variant
    Set greenitem = colordoc(0).GetFirstItem("Green")
    Dim bolditalic As Variant
    Set bolditalic = colordoc(0).GetFirstItem("BoldItalic")

4   Set newdoc = New NotesDocument (db)
```

Listing 19.8   Create formatted report (continued)

```
      newdoc.Form = "Main Topic"
      newdoc.Subject = "Formatted report test"
      Call newdoc.Save(True,False)

      Dim reportitem As Variant
5     Call newdoc.CreateRichTextItem("Body")
      Set reportitem = newdoc.GetFirstItem("Body")

6     Call reportitem.AppendText("Body field default text")
      Call reportitem.AddNewLine(1)

7     Call reditem.AppendText("Some red text")
8     Call reportitem.AppendRTItem(reditem)
      Call reportitem.AddNewLine(1)

      Call bolditalic.AppendText("Some bold italics text")
      Call reportitem.AppendRTItem(bolditalic)
      Call reportitem.AddNewLine(1)

      Call greenitem.AppendText("Some green text")
      Call reportitem.AppendRTItem(greenitem)
      Call reportitem.AddNewLine(1)

9     Redim colordoc(1) As NotesDocument
10    Set colordoc(0) = collection.GetFirstDocument
11    Set greenitem = colordoc(0).GetFirstItem("Green")

12    Call greenitem.AppendText("DIFFERENT green Text")
      Call reportitem.AppendRTItem(greenitem)
      Call reportitem.AddNewLine(1)
13    Call reportitem.AppendText("More default text")

      Call newdoc.Save(False,True)

      Call workspace.ViewRefresh
```

Listing Notes:

1 The one tricky bit of this code is that we need a way of clearing used text values out of the items on the `colordoc` `RichTextFormats` document. The solution is to declare the document in an array and `Redim` it when we need to clear it out. See listing note 9 for more details.

2 Retrieves the `RichTextFormats` document.

3 Sets a variable to the Red rich text field on the `RichTextFormats` document.

4 Creates the new report document.

5 Creates a rich text field on the report document.

6 Use the `AppendText` method to add text with the Body field's default text attributes.

7 This is the first step of adding formatted text. First, the text is copied to the Red field on the `RichTextFormats` document, which cause the text to adopt that color.

8 This is the second step—using `AppendRTItem` to append the entire `Red` rich text field onto the end of the report. This is the key to formatting the text—when you add it using the `AppendRTItem` method the text retains its current formatting.

9 At this point, we've added some green text, and we want to add some more green text. But the original "some green text" value is still stored in the `greenitem` variable. The only way to clear it out is to reset the `colordoc` variable completely by using the `Redim` statement.

10 Because `colordoc` is effectively a new variable now, it has to be reinitialized.

11 The `greenitem` variable must also be reinitialized.

12 Now, when we copy `DIFFERENT green Text` to the `greenitem` variable we don't have to worry about the old text; it's been deleted.

13 At any time, you can always add more text using the report Body field's default properties.

When you run the agent (select the Actions|Create Formatted Report menu), it will create a document having colored text as shown in figure 19.3.

You may want to create a generic function to make it easier to format rich text, and to keep your code more readable. There is a minor difficulty. The trick of redimensioning an array variable to clear it out does not work if the variable is declared inside a local subroutine. The REDIM statement will execute but the variable is not cleared out. The `colordoc` NotesDocument array cannot be declared globally either, because REDIM only works inside a function or subroutine. The solution is to declare `colordoc` in your main subroutine, and pass a reference to `colordoc` to the generic text formatting function. A generic function to append rich text is shown in listing 19.9.

Listing 19.9   Append formatted text report function

```
    Sub Append_Formatted_Text (reportitem As Variant, format_type As
    String,
    text_to_append As String, colordoc() As NotesDocument)
    Dim item As Variant
1   Redim colordoc(1) As NotesDocument
```

Listing 19.9   Append formatted text report function

```
    Set colordoc(0) = format_collection.GetFirstDocument
2   Set item = colordoc(0).GetFirstItem(format_type)
    Call item.AppendText(text_to_append)
3   Call reportitem.AppendRTItem(item)
    End Sub
```

Listing Notes:

1 A pointer to `colordoc` is passed from the main function, and the variable is redimensioned here to clear out any previous values.

2 Sets an item variable to the specified format. The named format must be the name of a rich text field on the rich text formats document.

3 Appends the formatted rich text to the report you are generating.

As an example of using this function, the main code in Listing 19.10 will produce the same results you see in figure 19.3. You also need to put the following line of code in the (Declarations) event:

```
Dim format_collection As NotesDocumentCollection
```

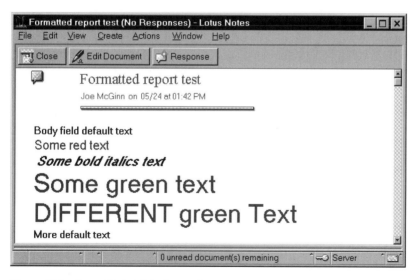

Figure 19.3   Formatted rich text report

Listing 19.10 Create formatted report

```
      Dim session As New NotesSession
      Dim workspace As New NotesUIWorkspace
1     Redim colordoc(1) As NotesDocument
      Dim newdoc As NotesDocument
      Dim db As NotesDatabase

      Set db = session.CurrentDatabase

2     Set format_collection = db.Search( "Form="+Chr$(34)+"RichTextFor-
      mats" +
      Chr$(34), Nothing, 0)
3     Set newdoc = New NotesDocument (db)
      newdoc.Form = "Main Topic"
      newdoc.Subject = "Formatted report test"
      Call newdoc.Save(True,False)

      Dim reportitem As Variant
      Call newdoc.CreateRichTextItem("Body")
      Set reportitem = newdoc.GetFirstItem("Body")

      Call reportitem.AppendText("Body field default text")
      Call reportitem.AddNewLine(1)
4     Append_Formatted_Text reportitem, "Red", "Some red text", colordoc
      Call reportitem.AddNewLine(1)

      Append_Formatted_Text reportitem, "BoldItalic", "Some bold italics
      text", colordoc
      Call reportitem.AddNewLine(1)

      Append_Formatted_Text reportitem, "Green", "Some green text", color-
      doc
      Call reportitem.AddNewLine(1)

      Append_Formatted_Text reportitem, "Green", "DIFFERENT green text",
      colordoc
      Call reportitem.AddNewLine(1)
      Call reportitem.AppendText("More default text")

      Call newdoc.Save(False,True)
      Call workspace.ViewRefresh
```

Listing Notes:

1 The `colordoc` array must still be initially declared in your main function.

2 The global `format_collection` NotesDocumentCollection points to the RichTextFormats document.

3 Creates a new report document.

4 Calls the generic function to add formatted text. The first parameter is the rich text item you want to add text to. The second parameter specifies the name of the rich text field on the RichTextFormats document that you want to use. The third parameter is the text to be added. The fourth and last parameter is a pointer to the `colordoc` NotesDocument array.

19.11 Summary

You have learned how to display a document in a different database, and how to automatically create response documents. We have covered how to save user-specific options for a database, and how to implement dynamic check boxes and radio buttons.

You also have learned how to access Notes via DDE with a Visual Basic example. We've covered how to access Notes data, including the useful universal IDs, as an ODBC data source. And last, you've learned how to set rich text fonts and colors from LotusScript.

C H A P T E R   2 0

The future of Lotus Notes

Lotus Notes 4.5 is an extremely powerful and flexible groupware and Internet development tool. In February 1997, International Data Corporation reported that the Notes install base doubled in 1996. A more recent report by Telecommunications Reports International (`http://brp.com/index.html`) confirmed that this explosive growth has continued in 1997, with the Notes install base reaching 13 million at the end of the second quarter. Nevertheless, as with all software, there is always room for improvement. In this chapter I'll make some of my own recommendations for improvements that would be helpful to programmers, and we'll take a look at what some of the Notes architects are saying about the next major releases of Notes. The topics covered in this chapter are:

- How you'll get improved programmatic access to the user interface, and how Java will be integrated with Notes to provide it.
- The Notes database format versus relational databases.
- Notes report generation and how it could be improved.

20.1 Notes user interface programming and Java

There are a few areas in which the Notes programming capabilities could be improved. The most obvious need is the general lack of access to the operating system's graphical user interface. There are a few user interface formula commands, and in chapter 13 I've showed you how to access them from LotusScript. But beyond that, the Notes programmer does not have nearly the control over the user interface that can be achieved in platform-specific tools like Visual Basic or C++.

One of the reasons for this is a good one, and related to a Notes strength. Notes is a multiplatform tool, available on all operating systems from Windows 3.x and Windows95/NT to OS/2, UNIX, and MacOS (and the Internet). It would have been an extreme programming challenge to include rich user interface classes in LotusScript that worked on all platforms. Doing so would have probably delayed the Notes 4 release by at least a year for a benefit that is useful only to some Notes applications (i.e., since the built-in Notes user interface is quite rich, so many applications don't need to go beyond that).

The solution for this problem today is much more attainable. Java is a high level language developed by Sun Microsystems that is available on all platforms, including the Web. And unlike LotusScript, Java does have complete access to the user interface. The solution is to add Java as a third programming language to Notes, and this is the direction Lotus is taking. Tim Halvorsen of Iris Associates (the Lotus-owned company that develops Notes) has this to say about Java integration:

> "… to provide a huge increase in programmability headroom, we will shortly allow execution of Java applets in the Notes Client application. This will allow you, via Java, to implement your own windows and dialogs that interface with the user in the appropriate way for your application."

This is exactly what Notes programmers need to have full control over the user interface. According to Bob Balaban (also of Iris), Java functionality will be provided in two phases this year. Phase One (Notes 4.6) will include Java functionality that is the equivalent of the current LotusScript (except for user interface access, which won't be provided in Java until Phase Two):

> "Using this Phase One deliverable, you can write Java applications that make use of all the back end objects to which you currently have access via LotusScript. You will also be able to import these Java apps into a Notes database as agents. Everything that can be currently performed with LotusScript agents (scheduled execution, appropriate access control, etc.) will be available using Java."

Phase Two will arrive with Notes 5.0 (which is expected to be released in the first quarter of 1998):

> "… [in Phase Two] you can write Java applets stored on a Domino server. Those applets can leverage the tremendous power of the Notes back end classes to create, store, retrieve and otherwise manipulate data in Notes databases. These applets can be linked into HTML pages, downloaded to any Web browser, and launched there. This technology at last brings true client/server programmability to the Web, and also highlights Java's usefulness. An applet written in Java on any Web server will run in any browser on any other kind of computer."

Halvorsen has said that Iris will continue to enhance the LotusScript user interface classes as well, so that programmers who need basic access to the user interface from LotusScript can do so more conveniently (i.e., without resorting to some of the workarounds presented in this book).

In addition to Java integration, another area of user interface improvement will be the integration of HTML formatting into the Notes client. This will enable richer applications, and will also make programming and authoring of Web sites and applications easier. You'll be able to view HTML formatting directly in the Notes client; you won't have to go out to a Web browser as much during development. Again, quoting Halvorsen:

> "In addition, we will continue to enhance our document formatting to ensure that the best features of HTML are also available in the Notes client. For example, we

demonstrated at the Lotusphere General Session 'tables within tables' (recursive tables) that will soon be available in the Notes client, directly as an outgrowth of our desire to blend the two different formatting feature sets."

There is one final area of user interface improvement needed in Notes—component integration. Component-based programming has proved to be the most powerful and efficient way of improving a program's interface. For example, if you need advanced charting functions in a Visual Basic or C++ program, you do not have to implement it from scratch. You just buy the ActiveX component and plug it into your application.

Notes does have some limited ActiveX integration, in the form of a customized set of ActiveX components available for Notes. You cannot use off-the-shelf ActiveX components, however, which really eliminates the major benefit of components in the first place. And second, since Notes is a multiplatform tool, it is of limited utility to have a component standard that is only available on one operating system (i.e., Windows95). Importantly, one of the newest platforms supported by Notes is the World Wide Web, which is itself available on all operating systems. It is therefore very important to have a component solution that is available on all operating systems.

The solution is Java Beans, a cross platform component standard. Java Beans provides all the capabilities of ActiveX, but in a multiplatform format like Notes. (For more information on Java Beans technology, see `http://www.sun.com/java/` on the Sub Web site). According to a Lotus press release on 6 November 1996, Java Beans will be available on both the Notes client and server in Notes 5.0:

> "At the Domino Web Developers' Conference … Lotus Development Corp. today announced a series of initiatives to open and extend the world's leading groupware application development platform for intranets, Lotus Domino, through Java, the leading application development language for the World Wide Web. These initiatives will range from enabling the execution of Java applets in Domino 4.7, to full support of Java in Lotus APIs and Java Beans in Domino 5.0 servers and Notes 5.0 clients."

The result of all this will be an incredibly powerful software development tool. As Balaban puts it:

> "Because of its wide acceptance and platform portability, we are convinced that the combination of the Notes Object Interface (for basic application building power) with a Java programming interface (for portability and ease of implementation) will yield amazing power and benefit for our developer community."

20.2 The Notes database format

The Notes database format is both a great strength and weakness of Notes. An object-oriented data store, it is ideally suited for document management and workflow, groupware, and Internet programming. The database template format provides an extremely useful and powerful way of distributing and updating source code and programs electronically. And of course, the database replication capability provides multiuser and remote user access unmatched by any other PC software.

There are some limitations, however, that are clear to anyone who's used relational databases. Relational database have none of the benefits described above, but they do have a few important capabilities that would be very valuable in Notes:

- Referential integrity and disaster recovery
- Record locking
- The ability to handle very large volumes of data

Complete, declarative referential integrity ensures that related data are always consistent. An important part of this is transaction processing. Transaction processing allows you to group a series of databases changes together in one transaction. Once you've completed the group of edits or changes, you can choose to either commit (i.e., save) the changes or execute a rollback command, which returns the database to the state it was in before any of your changes. Transaction processing also allows better disaster recovery. If a server crashes, for example, in the middle of a transaction, it can automatically rollback the changes when it starts up again.

Complete referential integrity and disaster recovery is probably not a practically achievable goal for a wide area network database like Notes. But some parts of it—a limited transaction processing capability, for example—may be possible. Or perhaps what is needed is a tighter integration of Notes and relational database engines at the server level, in a way that is relatively transparent to programmers and users.

Record locking is another very valuable feature available in relational databases. It is available in a limited form in Notes (see the "Record locking" section of chapter 17). But it would be nice to have it in a more reliable, proactive format, such as a Locked property of a NotesDocument that programmers could set and read to explicitly determine whether a Notes document is being updated by another user.

Last, Lotus needs to continue to increase the volume of data that can reasonably be handled in a Notes database. It is not practical to store more than 100,000 documents in a Notes database, and many databases become unwieldy and slow with only 20,000 to 30,000 documents. This is not an easy challenge to meet, because Notes has to do a lot more processing of each document than a relational databases does for a record. But as

Notes becomes more and more popular for storing enterprise-wide data, this is an area that needs improvement.

20.3 Notes report generation

Once of the biggest complaints from Notes users is the lack of an integrated report writer. Notes Reporter is available as an add-on product, but it needs to be beefed up to compete with best-of-breed reporters available for other databases such as Microsoft Access (for example, the ability to display a header field on each page when detail fields run over multiple pages). It is theoretically possible to access Notes data through ODBC to use it with Microsoft Access or other third-party report writers, but in practice this is too difficult and unreliable for nontechnical end users.

Notes Reporter needs to be improved, and it should also be integrated into the core Notes product so that application developers can develop predefined reports as part of their application. A high level user interface report wizard (again, as available in the excellent Microsoft Access reporter) is also needed to allow nontechnical users to develop complex reports.

20.4 Summary

In this chapter we've looked at the future of Lotus Notes. You've learned about the exciting new user interface improvements that Lotus has promised, Java integration in Notes 4.6 and multiplatform Java Beans component integration in Notes 5.0.

I've discussed some of the strengths and weaknesses of the Notes database format. Last, we've looked at the need for an improved integrated Notes report writer.

Now that you've finished this book, you are well equipped to respond to the challenges and opportunities of Notes software development. With the promise of complete Java support in Notes 5.0, the future looks to hold even more possibilities.

PART 5

Appendices

appendix A

References

This appendix includes a list of Internet World Wide Web references and a list of known Notes user groups.

Internet references

Lotus Development Corporation:

- Home Page:

`http://www.lotus.com/`

- Domino Applications and Templates:

`http://www.net.lotus.com/action4/homepage.nsf?OpenDatabase`

- Lotus Domino Site (Domino discussion database, Domino product information, library of Domino Web site links):

`http://domino.lotus.com/`

Iris Associates:

Iris Associates is the Lotus-owned developer of the Lotus Notes products.

- Home Page:

`http://www.iris.com/`

- Iris Domino Site (Domino discussions, technical information, download complete Domino/Notes 4.5, download incremental upgrades):

`http://www.notes.net/welcome.nsf`

Other useful links:

- Notes Frequently Asked Questions (FAQ):

`http://metro.turnpike.net/kyee/NotesFAQ.html`

- Notes Programmer's FAQ:

`http://www.keysolutions.com/NotesFAQ/programmingtips.html`

- European Lotus Notes Home Page (this page contains hundreds of links to Notes related sites):

`http://www.infohiway.com/LotusNotes/`

- Complete Hypertext Markup Language (HTML) specification:

`http://www.w3.org/pub/WWW/MarkUp/html-spec/html-spec.html`

Web browsers:

If you need to download a Web browser, you can find them at the following locations:

- Netscape Navigator:

`http://live.netscape.com/cgi-bin/123.cgi`

- Microsoft Internet Explorer:

`http://www.microsoft.com/ie/download/`

User groups

The following is a list of Notes user groups. For current contact and other information, go to the following Web site and select User Groups:

`http://www.infohiway.com/LotusNotes/`

Notes user groups in the USA

- *ACGNJ*   New Jersey Lotus Notes User Group (Iselin, NJ)
- *ALNUG*   Atlanta Lotus Notes User Group
- Connecticut Notes Special Interest Group (Danbury, CT)
- *DANUG*   Detroit Area Network User Group (Southfield, MI)
- Kansas City Lotus Notes User's Group (Kansas City, MO)
- *LNUGC*   Lotus Notes Users Group of the Carolinas (Greenville, SC)
- *NCLNUG*   Charlotte Lotus Notes User Group (Charlotte, NC)
- *NEFNUG*   North East Florida Notes User Group (Jacksonville, FL)
- *SFNUG*   South Florida Notes User Group (Ft. Lauderdale, FL)
- *PUG*   Pacific Users Group (San Jose, CA)

European Notes user groups

- *INI*   The User Group (London, UK)
- Lotus User Group (UK) & Lotus Notes Forum (Windsor, UK)
- *DNUG*   Deutsche Notes User Group (Jena, Holland)

appendix B

LotusScript and formula user interface reference

This appendix is a reference guide to the LotusScript user interface classes and handy user interface formula functions. If you need access to a formula interface command from LotusScript, see the instructions in chapter 13.

LotusScript user interface classes

This section lists the Notes user interface classes and their methods. Optional parameters are enclosed in square brackets. All LotusScript user interface commands are accessed through the NotesUIWorkspace class.

Compose a document

ComposeDocument ([Server], [Database file name], Form name) creates a new document using the form you specify.
Example:

```
Dim workspace As New NotesUIWorkspace
Dim uidoc as NotesUIDocument
Set uidoc = workspace.ComposeDocument( "", "", "Main Topic" )
```

Edit a document

EditDocument (Editmode) opens the current document in the specified edit mode (True for edit mode; otherwise specify False).

Example:

```
Dim workspace As New NotesUIWorkspace
Dim uidoc as NotesUIDocument
Set uidoc = workspace.EditDocument( True )
```

Edit a specific document (Notes 4.5 only)

EditDocument (Editmode, NotesDocument) opens the specified document.

Example:

```
Dim workspace As New NotesUIWorkspace
Dim doc as NotesDocument
'... set value of doc ...
Set uidoc = workspace.EditDocument( True, doc )
```

Open a database

OpenDatabase (Server name, File name, [View name], [View key]) opens a database on the Notes user interface.

Example:

```
Dim workspace As New NotesUIWorkspace
Call workspace.OpenDatabase ( "", "Discussion.nsf", "By Category")
```

Refresh the current view

ViewRefresh refreshes the current view to reflect the latest changes to the database.

Example:

```
Dim workspace As New NotesUIWorkspace
Call workspace.ViewRefresh
```

Edit a profile document (Notes 4.5 Only)

EditProfile (Profile form name, User name) displays the specified profile document in edit mode.

Example:

```
Dim workspace As New NotesUIWorkspace
Dim session As New NotesSession
Call workspace.EditProfile ("User Options", session.UserName)
```

Formula user interface commands

This section is a reference to the most common and useful formula user interface commands.

By far, the two most useful commands are @Prompt and @Picklist. These commands have several different formats that make them very flexible for getting user input. The other command we'll look at in this appendix is @Command, which has a number of useful interface variations.

The @Prompt command

@Prompt is used to display a message, or to get input from the user in a number of different formats:

- `@Prompt([Ok]; "Window Title"; "A sample message")` displays a message box with the specified window title and text.

- `@Prompt([YesNo]; "Window Title"; "Please select Yes or No")` displays a yes/no question box. If the user selects Yes, the return value is `1` (one, or the constant True); if they select no, `0` (zero) is returned.

- `@Prompt([YesNoCancel]; "Window Title"; "Please select Yes, No or Cancel")` displays a yes/no question box with a Cancel button. If the user selects Cancel the return value is `-1` (minus one).

- `@Prompt([OkCancelEdit]; "Window Title"; "Prompt please enter a value below:"; "Default Value")`—displays a text editing window with the specified default value, and returns the value the user enters.

- `@Prompt([OkCancelList]; "Window Title-Select Color"; "Prompt- select your favorite color:"; "Purple"; "Red" : "Blue" : "Green" : "Purple")` displays a menu of the list items and returns the item the user selects (see figure B.1). The default selection (in this case `Purple`) is specified before the list.

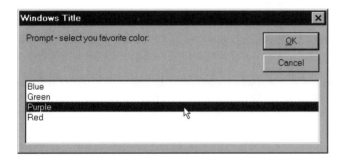

Figure B.1   List selection

- `@Prompt([OkCancelCombo]; "Window Title-Select Color"; "Prompt- select your favorite color:"; "Purple"; "Red" : "Blue" : "Green" : "Purple")` is the same as `OkCancelList`, except the list is displayed as a drop down list (see figure B.2).

- `@Prompt([OkCancelEditCombo]; "Window Title-Select Color"; "Prompt- select your favorite color:"; "Purple"; "Red" : "Blue" : "Green" : "Purple")` is the same as `OkCancelCombo`, except the user has the option of entering any text value as well as selecting from a drop down menu.

- `@Prompt([OkCancelListMult]; "Window Title—Select Color"; "Prompt- select your favorite color:"; "Purple"; "Red" : "Blue" : "Green" :`

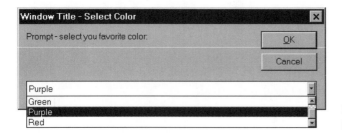

Figure B.2   Drop down
selection

"Purple") is the same as OkCancelList, except the user can select more than one
item from the list (see figure B.3). The return value is a list of items.

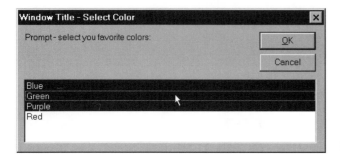

Figure B.3   Multilist selection

- @Prompt([PASSWORD]; "Enter Password"; "Please enter your password:")
  displays a text editing window, but the text entered is not displayed on the screen
  (see figure B.4). Note that a warning message is displayed so the user does not con-
  fuse this window with a built-in Notes password dialog.

Figure B.4   Password screen

The @Picklist command

`@Picklist` is an extremely useful command that allows you to display a view in a menu and let the user select documents from the view. For example, the following command displays a view in the Contacts.NSF database on the current server (i.e., the current server is specified by `@Subset(@DbName;1)`). The contacts selected are returned as a list of items from the specified column of the view—in this case column 1, a hidden column that contains the documents' Universal IDs (see figure B.5).

```
Choice:=@PickList([Custom];@Subset(@DbName;1):DB_Name; "Contacts";"Select A
Contact";"Select the related contact.";1);
```

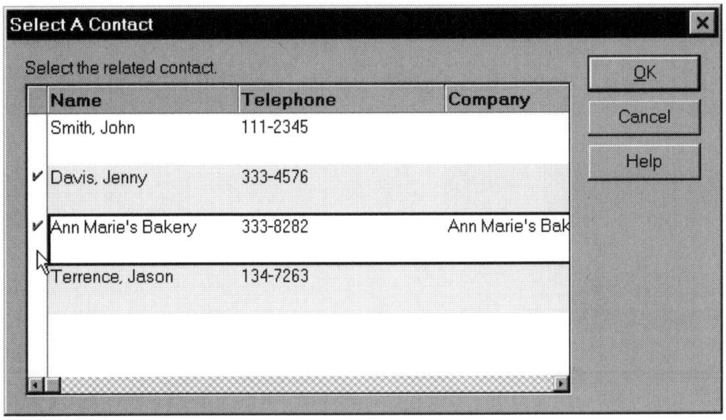

Figure B.5 Picklist from a view

The user can select a single item by clicking anywhere in the menu, or he or she can select multiple items by clicking in the check-mark column on the left. Notes 4.5 has a new feature that allows you to display a complete line of the view by pausing your mouse cursor over any entry (see figure B.6).

@Picklist has one other format that is used to display a selection list of names from all available Name and Address Books. You simply specify the `[Name]` parameter as

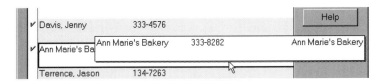

Figure B.6 Picklist view item preview

If you want to force the result to be just a single item, use the following line of code to extract the first item from the user's response:

```
Single_Choice:=@Subset(Choice;1);
```

follows, and the names are displayed in a user selection menu (similar to the mail addressing dialog), as shown in figure B.7.

```
@Picklist([Name])
```

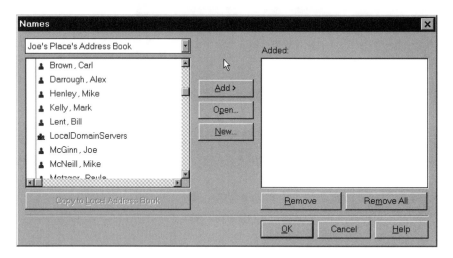

Figure B.7   Picklist names

With this option, you can also specify the [Single] parameter as follows, to force the user to select only one name from the list.

```
@Picklist([Name]:[Single])
```

The @Command function

The @Command function features a wide variety of options that are useful for user interface programming. The following are the most common ones, presented in order of importance:

- `@Command([FileOpenDatabase];@Subset(@DbName;1):"Con-tacts.NSF";"People")` opens the People view in the Contacts.NSF database on the current server.

- `@Command([OpenDocument]; "0"; DocumentUNID)` opens the specified document. (The document must exist and be visible in the current view.)

- `@Command(EditDocument])` puts the current document into edit mode.

- `@Command([Compose]; "Main Topic")` composes a Main Topic document in the current form.

- `@Command([OpenView])` goes to the view window.

- `@Command([OpenView]; "By Category")` opens the `By Category` view.

- `@Command([OpenNavigator]; "Main Navigator")` opens the `Main Navigator`.

- `@Command([FileCloseWindow])` closes the current window.

- `@Command([EditMakeDocLink])` creates a link to the current document in the clipboard.

- `@Command([EditGotoField]; "FieldName")` moves the cursor to the specified field.

- `@Command([Paste])` pastes the clipboard into the current field.

- `@Command([FilePrintSetup])` displays the print dialog. (A database must be open to a document or view.)

- `@Command([RefreshHideFormulas])` forces a refresh of hide formulas on the current form.

- `@Command([ToolsRunMacro]; "Agent Name")` runs the specified agent.

- `@Command([UserIDSwitch])` displays the window to let the user switch Notes user IDs.

Other user interface commands

- `@PostedCommand` takes the same parameters as `@Command`, but the `@PostedCommand` function is not run until after the rest of the formula is run.

- `@SetField("Fieldname"; "Value")` sets the `Fieldname` field to the specified value.

- `@DialogBox('Form name")` allows you to edit fields from the current document in a dialog box via the specified form. For example, the following command displays a form called `Edit Date` in a dialog box. The `Edit Date` form consists of a single layout region with fields on it. If the fields on the form have the same names as fields on the current document, the values the user enters are automatically copied to the current document when the user presses OK.

```
@DialogBox("Edit Date"; [AutoHorzFit] : [AutoVertFit])
```

Figure B.8 "Edit Date" Dialog box

This command displays the dialog box shown in figure B.8. The `[AutoHorzFit] : [AutoVert-Fit]` parameters scale the dialog box automatically to fit the size of the layout region.

appendix C

The Inside LotusScript CDROM

CDROM contents

The *Inside LotusScript* CDROM contains the following databases, files, and programs.

- Databases:
  - CodeList.NSF: This Notes database contains all LotusScript and Formula code listings from the book.
  - Agents.NSF: All the agents from this book—ready to be cut-and-pasted into your applications.
  - Figures.NSF: Contains all the book's graphics images and screen captures in color.
  - SearchDB.NSF: A compete search engine (from chapter 18) that searches all databases in a subdirectory. It can be plugged into any Notes application without modifications.
  - DocNums.NSF: The back end database needed to implement LotusScript code for sequential document numbering.
  - Chap15.NSF: A LotusScript list processing library (requires Notes version 4.5).
- Supplemental graphics files:
  - LAYOUT.PCX and WORLD.PCX are used in chapter 6 in the tutorial.
  - USA.PCX and CANADA.PCX are used in chapter 9.
  - SPLITTER.PCX and VIEWNAV.PCX are used in chapter 11.
  Note: PCX files are convenient for Windows users to load into Windows Paint. These files are also included in the Figures.NSF database under the appendix C section so that they can be accessed by non-Windows users.
- Windows Setup.EXE program. This program can be used to install the CD contents to your hard-drive. It works for Windows 3.1, Windows95, and Windows NT.
- All the files that are installed by the Setup program are also included uncompressed on the CD, so that they can be accessed by non-Windows platforms. The files are in the \IL_FILES directory on the CD-ROM.
- LNSpade is a new shareware utility that helps you debug and maintain Notes applications and databases. It includes features like listing all fields that don't contain a help entry, finding all references to fields, searching all LotusScript code within a database, etc. LNSpade is currently only available for Windows platforms (Windows 3.1, Windows95, and Windows NT).
  You can use the trial version of LNSpade included on the CD for thirty days. Readers of *Inside LotusScript* can purchase LNSpade for the special price of $125 (USA currency), 50% off the regular price of the product.

Installation for Windows users

Run the Setup.exe program from the root directory of the CDROM, and follow the instructions on the screen. The Setup program will allow you to select the drive and directory to which you want to install, and it will build icons on your Windows desktop for accessing the CDROM contents.

If you are not using Windows, use your operating system file copy command to copy all files from the CDROM \IL_FILES directory to your hard drive.

Installing LNSpade

Run the Setup.exe program from the \LNSpade directory on the CDROM, and follow the instructions on the screen. You can select a drive and directory. The Setup program will automatically install the correct files for your operating system (i.e., 16-bit Windows or 32-bit), and set up the needed PATH variables in your AUTOEXEC.BAT. You can also select the drive and directory to which you want install LNSpade.

Using LNSpade is easy. You select a Notes database using the Notes|Select Database menu. Then you use the Notes menu to run a variety of reports on the database. For example, you can select the Notes|List LotusScript Locations menu to find out which objects (i.e., forms, views, agents, script libraries, views, etc.) in the database contain LotusScript code. When running a report, you can define the scope of your search, as shown in figure C.1.

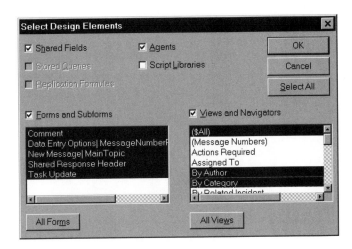

Figure C.1   LNSpade Search dialog box

You can use LNSpade to run many kinds of searches and reports, including:

- List locations of all LotusScript code.
- List locations of all formula code.
- List all fields that don't have field help.
- Dump all field help to a text file (i.e., for spell checking).
- Search for specific strings in all LotusScript code.

glossary

Access Control List (ACL)   An Access Control List is a Notes security system that specifies a list of users and the permissions they have for a database. You can see the ACL for any database by clicking on it and selecting File|Database|Access Control (or by clicking the right mouse button and selecting Access Control).

Action Bar   An action bar is a user interface element introduced in Notes 4.0. It allows you to attach a context-sensitive set of action buttons to the top of any form or view, as seen in figure G.1. The buttons often change depending on the user's context. For example, when the Edit Document action in figure G.1 is selected, the document enters edit mode. The buttons often change depending on the user's context—for example, when the Edit Document action in figure G.1 is selected, the Edit Document button is replaced with Close and Save buttons.

Back End Documents   Notes documents stored on the disk, and accessed programmatically (i.e., from LotusScript or @functions, as opposed to being edited graphically by the user).

Client/Server   Notes is a client/server program. This means that there are two different parts to the program. The Notes server runs on a centralized multiuser computer that is shared among several Notes users. The server centralizes Notes administration and other tasks, such as replicating databases, maintaining database designs, and so on. The Notes

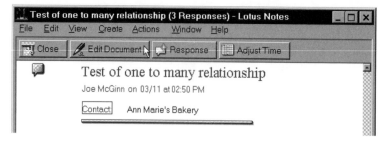

Figure G.1 A form action bar

client runs on desktop computers, and can work in cooperation with the server (e.g., accessing a database that is stored on the server) or independently, unconnected to any server (e.g., a laptop computer accessing databases on the local hard drive).

Database   A Notes database contains both end user data (i.e., documents) and all the forms, views, programming code, and other application design elements of a Notes application. A Notes application consists of one of more databases.

Document   An item of data in a Notes database is called a document. Documents contain fields of end user data. (That is, documents are the equivalent of records in other database systems.)

Domino   Domino is the Notes Internet server. It allows Notes applications and databases to be run on the World Wide Web with a regular Web browser (i.e., Netscape Navigator or Microsoft Internet Explorer). If you have Notes 4.5 or higher, the Domino server is included as part of your Notes server.

Form   A form is the user interface for viewing and editing a Notes document. Like most modern database programs, Notes includes an interactive form designer that allows you to create forms easily.

Front End Documents   Notes documents being accessed graphically via the Notes user interface are referred to as front end documents. The LotusScript classes that correspond to them (e.g., NotesUIDocument) are called front end classes.

Internet   The Internet is a public communications network based on standard protocols (TCP/IP, HTTP, HTML, etc.). Internet Service Providers (ISPs) that allow you to connect your computer to the Internet with a local phone call are available in almost all areas. Domino allows Notes applications to be run over the Internet.

Internet Explorer   Internet Explorer is the name of Microsoft's Web browser for accessing data over the Internet. See *World Wide Web.*

Intranet   An intranet is a private network based on the same standards as the Internet. An intranet is often used by corporations which want to build or use solutions based on Internet-standard protocols and technology, but which also need the security of using a private network.

Name and Address Book (NAB)   The Name and Address Book is a database of Notes users and other contacts. You normally have access to at least two NABs—your organization's public NAB on your Notes server, and your private NAB on your own workstation.

Netscape Navigator   This is Netscape's Web browser for accessing data over the Internet. See *World Wide Web*.

Server   The Notes Server runs on a centralized computer and is usually shared by many Notes users. See Client/Server.

Subform   A subform has all the properties and capabilities of standard forms, plus the ability to be embedded in other forms. For example, if you have fields or code that are common to many different forms, you can centralize the common elements by putting them on a subform and embedding the subform into the other forms.

Template   A template is a special kind of database that acts as a master copy of the source code for Notes databases. Databases are usually based on a template; the template can then be changed to automatically update the code and design elements of all databases derived from that template. This allows for powerful and flexible electronic updating of applications not available in any other PC database.

Relational Database Management System (RDBMS)   Relational databases are a system of databases designed to maintain referential integrity across large volumes of related data. They also have transaction processing and disaster recovery mechanisms that make them well suited for "mission critical" applications like point-of-sale systems, airline reservation systems, etc. Examples of RDBMSs include Oracle, DB/2, and SQL Server.

Replication   Database replication is the most powerful and unique feature of Lotus Notes. It allows Notes data and programs to be distributed over any geographic area, including support for multiple servers and remote (e.g., laptop) users. Replication is a two-way transfer of data and program design items that keeps all Notes databases synchronized, even if a computer is only intermittently connected to a Notes server. Remote users can enter Notes data "off line" and replicate changes when it is convenient to be connected to the network (either with a normal network connection or over a phone line and modem).

SmartIcon SmartIcons are series of buttons on the top of the Notes screen that allow you to carry out common Notes commands. You can customize the display of Smart-Icons using the File|Tools|SmartIcon menu. By pausing your mouse over a SmartIcon, you can display a help item that describes its function (see figure G.2).

Figure G.2   SmartIcon with help displayed

Structured Query Language (SQL) Structured Query Language is the standard query language of relational databases. SQL can be used on Notes data by accessing the data as tables through ODBC. (See the section "NotesSQL 2.0—accessing Notes through ODBC" in chapter 19.)

Universal ID Every Notes document is automatically assigned a Universal ID that is guaranteed to be unique. It is often used to create links to Notes documents from other documents or databases.

View A view is a list of Notes documents, as shown in figure G.3. Views can be used to search Notes databases and access documents.

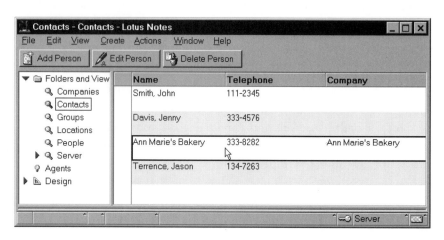

Figure G.3   A Notes view

World Wide Web   The World Wide Web (WWW) is a user friendly graphical interface for accessing Internet data. It is accessed through a Web browser (i.e. Netscape Navigator or Microsoft Internet Explorer) as shown in figure G.4. Notes databases and applications can be accessed through a Web browser, although this does put some constraints on what features the application can utilize. (See the section "Web client versus full Notes client" in chapter 8.)

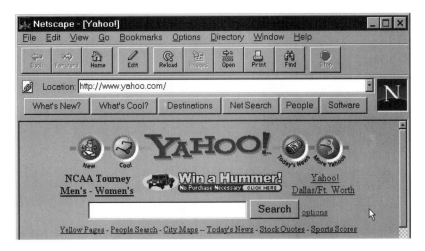

Figure G.4   Netscape Navigator Web browser

Workspace   The Notes workspace is comprised of the user-customizable pages of tabs displayed when Notes first starts, as shown in figure G.5. The user can name and add tabs, and add Notes database icons to any tab.

Figure G.5   The Notes workspace

index

Guide to the CD

Inside LotusScript includes a CDROM with many valuable utilities for the Notes programmer:

- All formula and LotusScript code listings are included on the CD in the CodeList.NSF database.
- All the book's agents in Notes agent format, ready to be copied-and-pasted into your applications, in the Agents.NSF database.
- Full color versions of all screen captures and images are in Figures.NSF.
- LNSpade, a new shareware utility that helps you debug and maintain Notes applications and databases. It allows you to list all fields that don't contain a help entry, find all references to fields, and search all LotusScript code within a database. LNSpade is currently only available for Windows platforms (Windows 3.1, Windows95, and Windows NT). You can use the trial version of LNSpade included on the CD for thirty days. Readers of *Inside LotusScript* can purchase LNSpade for the special price of $125 US, 50% off the regular price.

You can access these files directly from the CD, or you can install them onto your hard drive. See appendix C—The *Inside LotusScript* CDROM for instructions on installing the CDROM.

Purchase of this book entitles you to free online author support. For details see page xx.